DANTE TH

An understanding of Dante the theologian as distinct from Dante the poet has been neglected in an appreciation of Dante's work as a whole. That is the starting point of this vital new book. In giving theology fresh centrality, the author argues that theologians themselves should find, when they turn to Dante Alighieri, a compelling resource: whether they do so as historians of fourteenth-century Christian thought, or as interpreters of the religious issues of our own times. Expertly guiding his readers through the structure and content of the *Commedia*, Denys Turner reveals – in pacy and muscular prose – how Dante's aim for his masterpiece is to effect what it signifies. It is this quasi-sacramental character that renders it above all a theological treatise – whose meaning is intelligible only through poetry. Dante, as Turner has it, "knows that both poetry and theology are necessary to the essential task and that each without the other is deficient."

Denys Turner is Horace Tracy Pitkin Professor Emeritus of Historical Theology at Yale University. His widely acclaimed books include *The Darkness of God* (Cambridge University Press, 1995, which famously separated medieval mystical thought from contemporary ideas of experiential spirituality), *Julian of Norwich, Theologian* (Yale University Press, 2013), and *Thomas Aquinas* (Yale University Press, 2014). This new book is a loosely related companion to the latter titles, completing a trilogy.

Advance Praise for *Dante the Theologian*

"*Dante the Theologian* is a significant, brilliant, and illuminating contribution to theological reflection on Dante's *Commedia*. As such, it can both build on and help strengthen further the growing body of scholarly reflection on the theological dimensions of Dante's work. It presents an unusually compelling combination of depth of content and accessibility of style while offering new insights into Dante's poetry. Its central argument is that a theological analysis that ignores the poetic prevents us from recognizing both the uniqueness of Dante's theological voice and the contribution this can make even today to our theological thinking. Among the most significant contributions of the book are its splendidly incisive highlighting of the theological nature of Dante's poetry as poetry, and its marvellously fruitful treatment of the question of the relationship between fiction and truth. In both respects, Denys Turner's book is a powerful and novel contribution to key debates concerning Dante's work and its theological implications."

Vittorio Montemaggi, Reader in Religion, Literature
and the Arts, King's College London, author of
Reading Dante's Commedia *As Theology: Divinity Realized
in Human Encounter*

"This is a superb book, and will be very welcome. It's written with energy, and a sense of excitement and fun – all qualities which are often lacking in books on Dante. It brings a series of fresh and very strong lines of argument, many of which will open up new avenues for research on and discussion of its subject. There are all sorts of important new readings: on Dante's place among the vernacular theologians; on the nature of Purgatory (and the nature of the *Commedia* as a Purgatorial poem); on the nature of 'conversion' in the Earthly Paradise; on the 'mysticism' of the Paradiso; and on poetry, and the failure of poetry, as fundamental to the theological enterprise. There are wonderful insights throughout. The idea of the whole *Comedy* as Purgatorial, for instance, is absolutely brilliant as a way of understanding Inferno – it's Hell, but we travel through it as Purgatorial pilgrims. Other highlights include the account of the different contemplative models – Pseudo-Denys, Bernard,

Bonaventure – in relation to the Paradiso, and the emphasis on the poetic and linguistic workings of Inferno as a way to help understand what is happening in the Paradiso. For a single, relatively short, book to do all this is quite something. The tone of the book is also highly engaging. The author is encouraging us to let go of certain preconceptions about medieval theology, in order to develop a better understanding of Dante, and it takes this sort of personal voice – one which is in dialogue both with Dante and with medieval theology – to do this effectively."

Matthew Treherne, Professor of Italian Literature, University of Leeds, author of *Dante's* Commedia *and the Liturgical Imagination*

DANTE THE THEOLOGIAN

Denys Turner
Yale University

Shaftesbury Road, Cambridge CB2 8EA, United Kingdom

One Liberty Plaza, 20th Floor, New York, NY 10006, USA

477 Williamstown Road, Port Melbourne, VIC 3207, Australia

314–321, 3rd Floor, Plot 3, Splendor Forum, Jasola District Centre, New Delhi – 110025, India

103 Penang Road, #05–06/07, Visioncrest Commercial, Singapore 238467

Cambridge University Press is part of Cambridge University Press & Assessment, a department of the University of Cambridge.

We share the University's mission to contribute to society through the pursuit of education, learning and research at the highest international levels of excellence.

www.cambridge.org
Information on this title: www.cambridge.org/9781009168694

DOI: 10.1017/9781009168687

© Denys Turner 2022

This publication is in copyright. Subject to statutory exception and to the provisions of relevant collective licensing agreements, no reproduction of any part may take place without the written permission of Cambridge University Press & Assessment.

First published 2022
First paperback edition 2025

A catalogue record for this publication is available from the British Library

ISBN 978-1-009-16870-0 Hardback
ISBN 978-1-009-16869-4 Paperback

Cambridge University Press & Assessment has no responsibility for the persistence or accuracy of URLs for external or third-party internet websites referred to in this publication and does not guarantee that any content on such websites is, or will remain, accurate or appropriate.

For Robin Kirkpatrick, Vittorio Montemaggi, and Matthew Treherne
In gratitude

How short mere speaking falls, how faint against my own idea / And this idea, compared / To what I saw ... well, "little" hardly squares.
Paradiso 33.121–123

CONTENTS

Preface *page* xi
Acknowledgments xvi

1 Theology and Poetry 1

Part I Hell

2 Hell: Dante and Aquinas 41
3 *Inferno* as Anti-narrative 79

Part II Purgatory

4 Purgatory and Purgation 117
5 Hope, Memory, and the Earthly Paradise 159

Part III Paradise

6 Paradise and *Paideia* 201
7 Paradise and the End of Poetry 243

Select Bibliography 290
Index 295

PREFACE

I wrote this little work with the purpose of helping in some way to bring Dante's *Comedy* to the attention of a readership whose principal interests are in, or else derive from, the theologies of the Middle Ages. Those who approve of this priority but wish for a more thorough working through of Dante's theology than I offer here would be well advised to consult the work of properly qualified Dantisti, in particular, of course, Vittorio Montemaggi's *Reading Dante's* Commedia *as Theology*, and Alison Cornish's forthcoming *Believing in Dante*. In the meantime, I won't mind if those with less theological and more historical interests in mind want to read my little foray into the theological Dante, though they will find much missing that they might have hoped for by way of the assessment of the material circumstances of Dante's writing, especially political ones, and of how such matters bear on his poem and its theology. Some historians are but historians, just as some theologians seem to find it impossible to break out of a narrowly defined theological role, and both can sometimes be a little overbearing methodologically. All the same, I concede that the historians would be justified in regretting in this work the absence of reflection on Dante's political and personal fourteenth-century context, finding in it an odd, even perverse, lacuna. But they shouldn't complain, not to me. There is, without doubt, no end of books that perhaps I should have written about Dante, but I haven't written them. I offer herein no comprehensive tour of the *Comedy*, no more, in fact, than some moments of reflection on places here and there in his *Comedy* that shed light on Dante's theological agendas when they do so with very particular force and clarity. I expect that many learned Dante scholars, were they to read this work, would want to say that there is a lot more to the *Comedy* than that. Of course, there is more to it than that. But it is *at least* that.

For the principal purpose I have had in mind is to make good an odder omission than my neglect of the material historical context, which is the neglect of a theological Dante by so many students of medieval theology who seem to suppose that he isn't properly speaking a theologian at all but that he is, rather, a poet who may have had some incidental theological axes to grind, at most adding some value within a minor theological tributary such as the religion with literature course though otherwise contributing nothing of theological significance to what can be extracted from more formally dedicated mainstream theological sources in the medieval schools.

In that judgment, such theologians join in an unholy alliance with those literary historians in whose assessment the *Comedy* turns out to be poetry rather than theology. It is that "rather than" that would have got in the way of my even attempting to write what follows had I felt compelled to pay attention to such modern academic scruples about the divisions of intellectual labor. My purpose has been to offer a reading of Dante's *Comedy* as the work of a writer who knows of a poet's need to write theology just as he understands why, for the theologian, poetry is what you ought to find yourself having to do at least in the end; for Dante knows both that poetry and theology are necessary to the essential task and that each without the other is deficient.

The impetus to write about Dante the theologian therefore arose from the need to do something more than adding one more work to the sources for medieval theology, and rather to call for a more wholesale revision of what counts as theology in the Middle Ages that comes into view once Dante is included in the mix. Decades ago, Caroline Walker Bynum led the fray and showed how to do that job for medieval women. She and many another since have shown how we have had to shift the model away from the dominance of an academic style and method. Within what Bernard McGinn calls the "flowering of mysticism" in the thirteenth and fourteenth centuries, the women leap in one bound out of the obscurity of the merely pious into the clear light of the theological, and in that one stroke the distinction between the one and the other is more or less done away with.

Dante's is a similar case. Does it matter that Thomas Aquinas would not have thought of Dante as a theologian? Does it matter that even Dante himself didn't seem to think of himself as a theologian? After all, he has Aquinas with other representative theologians in his heavenly Circle of the Sun and not one poet is to be found therein, all the poets being either in Hell or at least with substantial purgatorial work still to do. But if it makes no difference to Dante it makes a good deal of difference to us, to theologians – to me, who is neither poet nor theologian – that, as we have had to rethink the scope and methods of theology in light of the difference made by the inclusion of medieval women, so must we once more rethink theology's nature in light of the proposition that Dante-poeta is in virtue of his poetic self also Dante-theologus, as Hollander says. This has a result that is more than incidental to theologians today, in that our conception of the theologian in the Middle Ages must now accommodate by equal right in the same school Mechtild of Magdeburg's *Flowing Light of the Godhead*, Thomas Aquinas's *Summa theologiae*, and Dante's *Comedy*, all three of them instances of the one *sacra doctrina*, "holy teaching," even though they do it by way of very different writing strategies. Such is the proposition the thought of which caused me to make the case on behalf of the poet Dante's theological credentials, the case, that is, for the difference it makes as to how to conceive of theology when Dante's *poetry* is seen to belong centrally to it as a defining element. When you do this, in one stroke you make the case conversely for the difference it makes in how you read the *Comedy* when you think through his poetry as, perforce, theological.

In setting out to do this, I have therefore resisted the temptation to read Dante as theologian on the terms of a narrower model that fits but the likes of Aquinas, Giles of Rome, Duns Scotus, or even the often less methodologically dialectical Bonaventure. My point is not that Dante fits the same theological model as did the male university professor – though he was perfectly capable of doing so when he wanted to, if for the most part he had no such inclination – but that he transforms the model by expanding it in such a way as to place the work of the schoolmen too in a different light, a light contributing its distinctive hue within a more polychrome theological variety. There is much more to be said about this than I argue for in this book. I have been more concerned to show the need for it than actually to do it, and for me the need arose because, as it is with the women theologians of his time, so it is with Dante: once you include him within the model of theology as practiced in the Middle Ages you have to expand that model – not by making a marginal concession to a further minority subclass but wholesale, thereby changing the view of all included in it. Hence, when the model changes it is not just that Dante gets into the mix alongside the women; Aquinas and Scotus change too because of Dante's poetry – and all, including not only them in their time but we also in ours, are as a result much the better for it.

ACKNOWLEDGMENTS

I am not a scholar of Italian history or literature, and in this work on the theology of Dante's *Comedy* I have relied with more enthusiasm than knowledge of my own on the translations of others, sometimes on that of the late Jean Hollander together with the interpretative work of Robert Hollander, whose notes to his wife's translation are meticulous and informative, but more especially on Robin Kirkpatrick's work in both capacities. I am as much attracted by Kirkpatrick's translations' raw, demotic directness – one might read his rendering of *Inferno* canto 33 to see this – as by almost the opposite strength in matching that directness with a sensitivity to the technical complexity of Dante's syntax in intelligible and elegant English. It is a combination the achievement of which must be the greatest challenge set for all Dante translation.

Much that there is to admire in the translations both of Jean Hollander and of Robin Kirkpatrick is down to their both being fine poets themselves, and as I put together some thoughts of my own on the theology of Dante's *Comedy* it became clear to me that, while Dante has much to offer the theologians on their terms, they have more to gain theologically from Dante on his terms as a poet. It is in Kirkpatrick's readings of the *Comedy* that poetic instincts combine with an acute sensitivity to and erudition in the theological literatures of Europe in the late Middle Ages, and it is from what I have learned from him that I hope I have derived something to pass on from Dante not only to us fellow, under-laboring historians of medieval theology but also to the systematic theologians in their first-order theological tasks. For, when writing this short work, I entertained the hope that I might persuade especially the latter of how much there is to be gained from the incorporation of the *Comedy* into the company of the key sources of their constructive theologies.

I have been indebted in a different way but no less deeply to Vittorio Montemaggi's work. He read a version of this book in draft and saved me from making some straightforward mistakes both of fact and of interpretation. Our association goes back more than two decades, beginning in Cambridge, where I learned more from him as doctoral student than he ever learned from me as professor – which, as university academics will know, is the usual way of things with the supervision of the best doctoral candidates. It was from Vittorio that I first learned to read the *Comedy* as a work governed by an essentially ethical intent, bearing upon the transformation of persons, above all, of course, of Dante himself, in ways that matter theologically today. Vittorio has always called for a reading of Dante primarily as a fourteenth-century poet, because only when you do so is it possible to grasp how he has managed to speak to us across the ages, and how he resonates in one way or another with our times – that is, unless some limiting academic scruple about the divisions of intellectual labor draws us into the fray to prevent it.

I owe a third debt to Matthew Treherne, who, like Vittorio, read my draft manuscript closely and made important suggestions, some of which retrieved me from errors that I would have made for want of his advice, and others that made for improvements even when wholly in line with what I inexpertly had had in mind to say. Just as Vittorio had served to make the case for Dante's essentially moral purpose, so Matthew has insisted on another, complementary, emphasis upon the liturgical resonances of Dante's thought, imagery, and poetry, a priority that, when added to those of Robin and Vittorio, served to convince me of the essentially theological identity of the *Comedy*.

Others have helped in ways that have been of critical importance even though I am now often unable to identify exactly at what point in the process of writing this book their influence was most crucially formative. Nate Gadiano, formerly an undergraduate major in Italian at Princeton University, offered discussions online and in person on how to read the *Comedy* and made detailed comments on earlier drafts of this book. He persuaded me of the importance of Boccaccio's understanding of Dante as theologian, and though he was unable to dissuade me of my universalist inclinations whether in the reading of Dante on Hell or simply as a matter of theological truth, he did succeed in keeping me on my toes on that and several other matters, as a reader will be able to observe from several footnote references.

I am grateful to Professor Peter Howard, the director of the Australian Catholic University's Institute of Religion and Critical Inquiry (IRCI). Most chapters of this book were once lectures presented to a Zoom seminar organized by Peter, the first three in June 2020 chaired by Rachel Davies and Lexi Eikelboom, and another three in March 2022 chaired by Rachel and Jonathan Teubner, all research fellows at IRCI. By and large, I have let these lectures stand in style and shape as they were when I delivered them, with some moderate expansion sometimes directly prompted by exchanges at those Australian seminars.

It is good to be back with Alex Wright, the commissioning editor at Cambridge University Press. We worked together more than twenty years ago and have kept in touch since, though I had strayed into other editorial arms in the meantime. His enthusiasm for the general notion of reading Dante at once as poet and as theologian kept me at it when at times it all seemed too much for me and beyond my capacity to complete successfully.

Finally, as ever, I am grateful in many more ways to my wife Courtney than to any other person. We endlessly discuss general issues of the sort that Dante's *Comedy* raises and as often Dante's text and his thought in detail. This little book has been much inspired by Courtney's work on the early fifteenth-century Christine de Pisan, from whose take on Dante's sense of literature's moral purpose derives her criticism of the poets, especially of Jean de Meung's contribution to the *Roman de la Rose*, who proposed happily to sacrifice the moral in the name of the literary. What is more, Courtney has read every line with the critical eye and ear of a historian, novelist, and poet, and with the love of a wife. It was on her account that this work has been for me a labor of love.

I am not a properly trained theologian – the only course I ever took in theology was at the age of thirteen, and it is the only examination I have ever failed; those familiar with the depths of innumeracy to which I spontaneously plunge may be surprised to note that in those same examinations I did marginally better as a mathematician than as a theologian. Worse still, I am no poet. But, if it is as Courtney suggests and Dante's lesson is that only poets get to Paradise, then, for those whose prosaic minds are, like mine, sadly lacking in poetic sensibilities, purgatory as Dante imagines it will be as Kirkpatrick says it is for us all, the place where we will joyfully make good that deficiency and, in the end, all become the poet-theologians that, from the very first we were made to become.

I

Theology and Poetry

~

Dante, Theologian by Way of Poetry

Bluntly, I say that Dante's *Comedy* is a work of theology. It is many other things besides – political, ethical, psychological – and it is a personal story of conversion, an apology for a life. In genre, of course it is a poet's work, an apology for poetry, and, putting both together, it is a poet's *apologia pro vita sua*. But it is a theologian's work too, and not just in content. Indeed, it would be unhelpful from the outset to suppose that Dante the poet and Dante the theologian are properly distinguished as between a poetic vehicle and a theological passenger incidentally taking a ride on it, just as it would be a mistake, indeed the same mistake, to think of it as a theological work that is incidentally written in vernacular verse. For the poet and the theologian are one undivided Dante, and, whether it is theology as poetry or poetry as theology, Dante wrote the *Comedy* out of the one compulsion, that is, simply for truth's sake – for truth's sake you write theology because there is something that needs saying that calls for it, and you write poetry because that is the only way truthfully to say it.[1] Therein is in Dante a general guide to all good theological practice, one that is

---

[1] See Vittorio Montemaggi and Matthew Treherne, eds., *Dante's Commedia: Theology As Poetry*, Notre Dame, IN: University of Notre Dame Press, 2010, for wide-ranging discussions of issues of Dante, the theologian and poet.

relevant to this day: Do only such theology as you have discovered out of intellectual need you have to do, there being a lot more theology done than anyone needs doing. And when you do what is needed theologically, in no time at all it turns out that poetry is the one thing necessary to saying it and at that same time the only thing sufficient to the task.

Out of the conviction that theologians need Dante for reasons that Dante-poet understands and has shown, I have called this little book *Dante the Theologian*. It is an attempt to explain why theologians should allow Dante into their conversation as a compelling voice, and why their failure to do so has left them bereft, whether as historians of fourteenth-century Christian theology or as theologians addressing agendas of our own times.

You might of course deny both propositions – some do – and say that in the end there is no specifically theological agenda that needs Dante and then deny that he has any compelling poetic need to do theology, and that, questions of belief or disbelief suspended, you might as well just stick to the poetry and be done with it. For, like music, dance, and having a pint with your friends, poetry is its own justification and need not be done for some further purpose. But if, short of a rather gaunt skepticism of this kind, you do anything at all for an end, then an intellectual obligation to do some theology imposes itself. For, though in a life there is a multiplicity of penultimate ends the study of which is the business of other disciplines, one end leading to another and subordinate to it, still, if there is to be any conclusive obituary, a judgment on a life taken as a whole – and you might say that there isn't one, and that all life is simply left hanging unjudged unless, if noticed at all, by the local newspaper's obituary columns – then there are only two possible verdicts that are truly final and survive when death has done for everything else, and they are, as Dante describes them, Hell and Heaven. And let us note here for the first time but not for the last that Dante's Purgatory is not a condition undecided between Hell and Heaven, for Purgatory waits attendance only at Heaven's gates for those whose death has left requirements of the *ars moriendi* unmet. That is not to underrate Purgatory. Far from it: for Purgatory is where Dante-writer and we his readers ourselves really are, learning how to die well. It is our common moral mise-en-scène, and purgatory is its practice. It is from there that reader and writer have come when they meet in the *Comedy*. Purgatory is more than a place in the *Comedy*'s scheme: In so many ways, the purgatorial *is* the *Comedy*'s scheme.

We should start, though, with Dante's being a theologian, for of this even the professional theologians are in need of some persuasion. There is nothing outlandish in proposing Dante's theological standing, neither is anything implied exclusive of other ways of reading the *Comedy*. The notion that the theological is exclusive of something else, indeed of anything else, is a deep error caused by the intellectual divisions of labor that dominate today's academic practices. It is a mistake that some theologians themselves seem all too ready to make as they yearn for a private space cut out for themselves alone – whether within the academic curriculum or within the wider culture – where they can play to their own rules without interference from others. Dante himself was not so narrow. You do theology when not doing it amounts to an evasion of core, common, intellectual responsibilities, and we read Dante amiss if as readers we neglect his sense of what those responsibilities are. We should admit Dante to the theological schools for reasons analogous to those that in recent decades caused some of us to recognize the case for the theological credentials of the fourteenth-century English writer Julian of Norwich, who, like Dante, was not taken seriously by academic theologians because, like Dante when writing the *Comedy*, she didn't write academically as the schoolmen of her times customarily did.

As recently as forty years ago it was still unusual to think of Julian as a theologian with as good a claim to that title in the Middle Ages as have either the university men – a Thomas Aquinas, a Duns Scotus – or the monk theologians – a Gregory the Great or a Bernard of Clairvaux – for in those days other softer and weaker taxonomical terms were reserved for women writers – "spiritual" or "mystical" came to mind, those weasel words that have commonly been thought more accurately to describe Julian's style so as to entail, without too openly saying it, that her work did not pass muster as theological.[2] Thereby in one stroke the notions of the theological, of the mystical, and of women as writers were misconstrued. As to Julian, in more recent decades it has come to seem right to resist those descriptions of her writing as typically misrepresenting the hard theological core of her thought, implicitly taking for granted misleading caricatures both of the

---

[2] And you might correspondingly want to restore some true theological meaning to the word "spiritual" as Bernard McGinn does to the word "mystical" in his *Foundations of Mysticism: Origins to the Fifth Century*, New York: Crossroads, 1991, appendix 1, section 1, pp. 266–291, and as I tried to do in my *Darkness of God: Negativity in Christian Mysticism*, Cambridge: Cambridge University Press, 1995, and again in Chapters 6 and 7 in this present book.

kind of writing that a medieval woman might be expected to be good at and of a corresponding antitype of what the men were good at, the men typically doing something that the women typically didn't do because, not being university trained, the women were at best amateurish theologically and not up to doing the real thing.[3]

This mentality produced a caricature of Julian's work. She was challenged by a tough theological call, being given sixteen "showings" and only very general indications as to how she was supposed to understand them – no more than that in some way they were all given to her by love and for love's sake. Start there, she was told; after that it was left for her to work it out for herself, which meant that she would have to find some way of squaring the revelations of love with her primary experience of evil, and, more precisely, of sin, as a constant which she was not prepared to leave to the theologians to explain away, as if you could solve the problem simply by showing that there is a formal consistency between God's omnipotent goodness and the world's evil. She allows that, at the very least, you can demonstrate rational grounds, if not for full consistency, at least for resisting claims to their formal inconsistency. But even consistency doesn't explain why God would do it all that way in the first place, since she sees that God could have created a world of rational free human agents who never consented to sin. So why did God *not* do so?

---

[3] There are exceptions: for myself, I am indebted to the late Grace Jantzen's *Julian of Norwich: Mystic and Theologian*, Mahwah, NJ: Paulist Press, 2000; to Denise Baker's *Julian of Norwich's Showings: From Vision to Book*, Princeton, NJ: Princeton University Press, 1990, and to Fritz Bauerschmidt's *Julian of Norwich and the Mystical Body of Politics*, Notre Dame, IN: University of Notre Dame Press, 1999.

She wants to know what the story is that makes some sort of sense of God's having allowed the quantity and viciousness of sin that all can observe in our world. In that way, Julian's worry about sin seems to ring truer to our sense of its predicament today than does, for example, that of Thomas Aquinas; and, for sure, she seemed to have little time for Augustine's take on the matter.

If, granted that much, you tried to identify aspects of her *Revelation of Love* in virtue of which Julian would stand out as male or female, then you might guess from some relatively incidental features of the *Revelation*'s style, imagery, and vocabulary that a woman wrote it. It also seemed that nothing much of the work's substantive *theological* importance could be put down exclusively to her gender, but, if so, even less could be put down to her generally falling in with the men's way of doing it. If there was a typically women's way of writing theologically in fourteenth-century England, then we are stuck with Julian as the one and only exemplar of it, for in that century she is the first and only woman known to be writing about anything at all in the English vernacular. Let us therefore just say that she was in practice a writer who seemed to do what she wanted as and when she pleased and not fall in with any exclusive stereotype; and *then* you can say that it is precisely the freedom from stereotype that, in the fourteenth century, is womanly about her style; for it is the men who create the stereotypes and seem compelled to stick with them. Other than that, it becomes a sort of useful tautology: We know that she writes as a woman does in fourteenth-century England because she is the only woman writing in English that we know of in that century.

Whatever the general explanations, the fact is very obvious in her case: When she wanted she wrote in a dialectical style as skillfully as any man of her time – she wrote of "substance" and "sensuality" as technical terms of theology,[4] with a mastery of how to distinguish them, of which the apostle Paul,[5] or Thomas Aquinas, would have fully approved.[6] They, especially St. Paul, might even have been quite surprised by her account of the complexity and nuance of it all. But on other occasions, when other styles served to get across something else, she wrote quite differently – as when she told of her own prayer-life in ways autobiographical that have no place within the dialectical styles of the fourteenth-century university man in the conduct of a disputed question.[7] She shows herself to be in control not only of either style at will but also of both ways at once, as when she speaks of her "holy mother, Jesus," as "he" who saves us, getting across a sense of how both gender ascriptions succeed and fail together. Thus she was able to say in a terse oxymoronic phrase what other theologians could sometimes explain about theological language and gender only at tediously

---

[4] See Julian of Norwich, *A Revelation of Love* [Long Text], in *The Writings of Julian of Norwich*, ed. Nicholas Watson and Jaqueline Jenkins, University Park: Pennsylvania State University Press, 2006, chapter 57, pp. 303–307.

[5] Romans 8:5–9.

[6] Thomas Aquinas, *Commentary on Romans*, chapter 8, lecture 1, 596–599, where he reads St. Paul's distinction between *sarx* and *pneuma* not as that between body and soul, but as between a person spiritually dead and a person spiritually alive. See Saint Thomas Aquinas, *Commentary on St Paul to the Romans*, trans. F. R. Larcher OP, eds. J. Mortensen and E. Alarcón, Lander: Aquinas Institute for the Study of Sacred Scripture, 2012.

[7] Julian of Norwich, *A Revelation of Love* [Long Text], chapters 40–42.

pedantic length.⁸ In all this, there seemed to be reason to write of her just as a theologian, so that by getting the word "theology" to embrace Julian's writing you bring good news to theologians generally, Aquinas and Scotus included.⁹ By such means you would situate the university men and their like where they are best understood, not as defining the field of theology as such with the hard stuff of dialectics to the exclusion of the merely pious but as offering but one theological subclass, the academic, within the much expanded range of theological possibilities that Julian's work in its own way represented. For all that she is neither professor nor abbot, she may not be cast out of the circles of the theologians into the outer darkness where women are best staying at home in theological frustration, there to weep and gnash the teeth of mere pious devotion.

It seemed best, then, to allay scrupulous taxonomical anxieties in respect of medieval theological writing and say in a more informal spirit that Bernard of Clairvaux is a "monastic theologian" simply because he was a monk and wrote like one meditatively or, as an abbot, instructively to fellow monks; then Thomas Aquinas falls into place as a "school theologian" simply

---

[8] Ibid., chapter 59, where she says, "And Jesus is our true mother by nature, at our first creation, and he is our true mother in grace."

[9] Nor is there any need unsubtly to stereotype the "academic" style with a view to devising a cheap term of contrast. The medieval university did not "academicize" the theological otherwise than to make of it the foundation of a taught training course for the acquisition of preaching and pastoral skills in the Church. There are no full-time tenured university academic theologians in the Middle Ages. A full-time tenured and purely academic profession of theology is an invention of modernity.

because he was a university master and taught with problem-based theological agendas in mind appropriate for the training of urban preachers. That done, you can place Julian in a room of her own as an "anchoritic theologian," meaning in general that she wrote theologically in ways that exhibited the concerns of a woman theologian who was an anchoress, *ana chora*, without *any* restricted community, whether of learning or of piety, whether monastic or academic, working out her relationship with the wider worlds of theological reflection on her own terms and in her own way as an independent thinker, and that it was her addressing this open, unspecified life-world of what she called her "even Christens" that accounted for the distinctively exploratory character of her thought. After all, you do have to think differently about theology when, unlike Thomas Aquinas and the schoolmen, you are writing for anyone at all who might be persuaded to take an interest. But in all events, it seemed as if we have only to loosen the grip of the monks and of the university men on the title and we could be happy to call Julian a theologian and otherwise stop fussing about exclusive methodological dogmas.

In a parallel case, there is the question whether there is a sense, and if so what, in which Dante may be regarded as a theologian doing a theologian's day job – as distinct, that is, from his espousing incidentally some theological opinions while pursuing other principal purposes, above all those of the poets. There is of course a subfield of Dantean scholarship devoted to finding traces in his thought of Aquinas's influence or of Bonaventure's, and it is often illuminating, as is Griffin Oleynick's essay on

Bonaventure and the influence of the Spiritual Franciscans on Dante's theology;[10] but it is far from being the case that it is on the strength of such source criticism alone that there is justification for granting Dante the standing of a proper theologian. Were the question of Dante's credentials as theologian answerable only by reference to such sources of influence upon him as Aquinas or Bonaventure, then one would have to conclude that Dante is only incidentally a theological writer at best, and not in any way essentially so. It is perhaps because some Dante scholars have regarded the question of Dante's theological credentials to be well posed in those terms that there are critical literatures today which seem able blithely to ignore his own theological standing as incidental, in that way being very easily reassured when confining themselves to literary considerations of allegory only.

Therefore, as it was with Julian, so it is with Dante, and it seems better to begin without prejudging the theological character of the *Comedy* on any terms other than those discernible as operating immanently within his own work and then allow Dante the poet-theologian to set out on his own terms what counts for theology and what doesn't. Even then, though, one is easily misled by the criteria of theological standing that Dante himself seems to have had in mind when in cantos 10–14 of *Paradiso* he assembled a representative cohort of theologians on terms that, wherever he, the poet, would have

---

[10] See Griffin Oleynick's Dante's *Franciscan Way*, New Haven, CT: Yale University Press, 2014. For a wider engagement with the intellectual currents of his day, see Etienne Gilson's *Dante and Philosophy*, trans. David Moore, London: Sheed and Ward, 1949.

hoped to find himself in Paradise *post mortem*, it would not have been in their company – and that in spite of the fact that the theologians in Dante's Paradise are a generously mixed lot. There in Paradise are, unsurprisingly, the Parisian theological masters Aquinas and Bonaventure, though neither had been formally canonized in Dante's lifetime; then, very surprisingly, they are joined by Aquinas's neo-Averroist philosophical opponent in Paris, Siger of Brabant, who never will be canonized. All three were, at least for a time, university men. But they are far from exhausting the variety of possible theological styles that Dante has in mind, for together with them are Gratian the canon lawyer, the venerable Bede historian and scriptural commentator, Albert the Great, a theological commentator, but distinctive in being also an empirical scientist of sorts, happier perhaps in his laboratory in Cologne than in the theological lecture theatre in Paris, and elevated above all of them is Solomon, that biblical peer of wisdom, human and divine. All these in the Sphere of the Sun, representing philosophers, scientists, historians, lawyers, and wise rulers, are chosen to represent the range of exploratory methods available to the Christian theologian in the medieval West, within which Aquinas is placed as just one. It is a selection that Dante the author makes, as Sinclair says, precisely so as to introduce the pilgrim to that diversity of theological styles.[11]

It might seem that on his own account of his work – even especially on those terms – that methodological diversity

[11] John D. Sinclair, *The Divine Comedy of Dante Alighieri, Volume 3: Paradiso*, New York: Oxford University Press, 1961, p. 159.

appears not to make room generous enough for Dante the poet in their theological company, for all Dante's poets find their place in Hell or in Purgatory, and none yet in Paradise. That fact should not dismay the poets. On the contrary, as Courtney Palmbush commented, for Dante poetry is the universal language of Paradise, so that if you are to find yourself there then it must be that in one way or another you have recovered a poet's soul and have learned how to do it. And true enough, how else but in poetry could you speak when, face to face with God, you are reduced to baby talk, Dante's own standard for good theological writing,[12] like the "bah, bah, bah" of the prophet Jeremiah?[13]

It is not as such that Dante's poets do not make it into his theological company, though it is no more than sixty years ago, when I first stepped foot into a university, that most scholars were of a mind as to who in the Middle Ages counted as a theologian and who did not, based on criteria that were far more constrained even than any of Dante's. There were some few exceptions, Etienne Gilson for the philosophers and Kenelm Foster for the Dantisti being among the best known.[14] But by and large, in those days it took heavy scholarly labor by the Benedictine Jean Leclerc to find a place even for the fully Latinate monks in a theological subclass.[15] Roughly, we thought in

---

[12] *Inferno* 32.1–9. [13] Jeremiah 1:6.
[14] See, for example, Foster's "Dante and Eros," *Downside Review*, 84 (1966), pp. 262–279, and "The Two Dante's," in *The Two Dante's and Other Studies*, London: Darton, Longman and Todd, 1977.
[15] Jean Leclerq, *The Love of Learning and the Desire for God: A Study of Monastic Culture*, trans. Catherine Misrahi, New York: Fordham University Press, 1974.

those days that none but a Latin-competent university man counted. As a result, in our academic Circle of the Sun in 1962 there was no Jan van Ruusbroec, Flemish mystic and on that account not considered a theologian[16] no women, and so not the visionary Hildegard of Bingen, not my Middle English Julian of Norwich, not her contemporary Italian Catherine of Siena, and for sure no poets even in Dante's own time, and therefore not the Dutch author of lyric poetry Hadewijch of Brabant, not Mechtild of Hackeborn the Thuringian musician and narrator of visions, not Meister Eckhart the Dominican vernacular preacher, and certainly not the Old French Marguerite Porete, deemed heretical in Paris and in 1310 executed by the Parisian Inquisitor for her pains.[17] All of these, like Dante, wrote in their respective vernaculars, the reputations of many of them flourishing, whether in their lifetimes or soon after their deaths,[18] in the few years between 1300 and Dante's own death in 1321. Setting out

---

[16] With good reason did Rik van Nieuenhoven take me to task for having said in my *Darkness of God* that Ruusbroec was a mystic but no theologian; see his *Jan van Ruusbroec, Mystical Theologian of the Trinity*, Notre Dame, IN: University of Notre Dame Press, 2003. It is just in criticism of that narrowly scholastic view of the medieval theologian that would have the likes of Ruusbroec cast out from their company that, twenty-six years later, in this work, I make up for a silly statement in 1995.

[17] But not always elsewhere: Her *Mirouer des ames simples* circulated quite freely in translation in Italy after her death and was given a Middle English translation by the Carthusian Richard Methley in the late fourteenth century when the text was transcribed without attribution to Marguerite herself. It was even published in a modernized version in London in the 1920s attributed to an "anonymous Carthusian of the fourteenth century," together with the *nihil obstat* of the Roman Catholic Archbishop of Westminster.

[18] As in the case of Mechtild, who died in 1299. She was widely read in the early fourteenth century.

as now we do in a more inclusive spirit that will naturally embrace a theological crew this motley, and no longer with a univocal definition of theology that confines the class of theologians to the likes of Aquinas, Bonaventure, Henry of Ghent, Duns Scotus, or Giles of Rome, we are better placed to inquire with an open mind whether Dante is truly a theological writer even in medieval terms, never mind in the revisionary terms of our times.

And it is because this multiplicity of styles cannot be herded into a univocal theological pen that to make the claim on the common name of theology for all of them calls for a spirit of an analogical pluralism, which can be safely permissive of variety without lapsing into mere equivocation. For conceding that they do not share a common essence, we can, loosely following Wittgenstein, allow that they do share between them certain "resemblances," in the way that all sorts of features, physical, linguistic, temperamental, are shared within a biological family, some between brothers and sisters, others between cousins and their aunts, reckoned by dozens – some having the same nose, others chins or eyes alike, some of the one sharing some of the other, their likenesses forming a sort of map, a network, of shared family facial features, though no one feature is common to all as the requirement of their belonging together.[19] And it was the point of Wittgenstein's critique of a mentality that is made uneasy by anything looser than univocal conformity, and the point of his case for a contrasting metaphor of how to assemble kinds by way of such "family

---

[19] *Philosophical Investigations*, trans. G. E. M. Anscombe, Peter M. S. Hacker, and Joachim Schulte, Oxford: Blackwell, 2006, sections 66–69.

resemblances," that in the same spirit in which families organize ways of agreeing, necessarily in consequence they organize distinctive ways of disagreeing, even of characteristic agreements to differ, as distinct from their being simply heterogeneously at cross-purposes, as when speaking from within different frames of reference that do not intersect at all.

It is in this sort of way that Dante's work can be thought of as belonging within the family of theologians though he is no Thomas Aquinas or Bonaventure except when he chooses to be. There would be no good gained by excluding him from that company on the ground of some univocal definition of the theologian, even were it one of his own devising. Rather, we must allow him into the theological company because the failure, or refusal, to think of theology in terms comprehensive enough to include the *Comedy* diminishes both theology and poetry for want of Dante's defining presence in the mix. And, having allowed him into that company, why not take the one step further that comes to mind as a result? Why not turn the tables entirely on those Parisian university men and ask, concerning them, why it would be in any way wrong to say that the terms on which Dante's work may be considered theological have an analogical openness such that Aquinas and Bonaventure must be required to allow him into the theological fold else it is *they* who fail to meet the case? The reason why it might still today seem too paradoxical to do so almost certainly has to do with the triumph, less perhaps in their times and more in ours, of university divisions of labor over all other considerations in defining what do and what do not count as appropriately academic forms of study.

But it is worth giving thought to the shift that would be experienced in one's understanding of medieval theology were one to say, as Aquinas does, that theology is indeed a *scientia*, a word hard to define at the best of times but that whatever its meaning it is one more fully exhibited by Dante's *Comedy* than by that other subclass which is the *Summa theologiae*, and then rejoice at the sight of the fresh theological landscape that thereupon comes into focus.

The proposal is a little extravagant, but it is not absurd. For the sense in which you would then think of the theological is that represented in the original and distinctive inner energy of the *Comedy* as a whole, in its overriding *telos*, which drives Dante personally toward dramatic conversions of desire and of intellect in respect of both his poetic self and his theological self, each as necessary to the other. The conception of theology as a *scientia* that Dante inherits – it fits with the requirements of a *sacra doctrina*, a "holy teaching," set out in the first question of Aquinas's *Summa theologiae*[20] – calls for a distinct and self-critical method of inquiry, for the specification of distinct sources of its own in the Scriptures and traditions of the Church, and for the exploration of such in light of what he calls its "formal object," that is to say, its understanding of all that substance *sub ratione Dei*, as truths revealed to us by God. There is a reason, deriving from a peculiarly eccentric Anglophone habit that restricts the notion of the "scientific" to the empirical methods of the natural sciences, why it seems so implausible to speak of what Dante sets out to do in the *Comedy* as a "scientific"

---

[20] *Summa theologiae*, Ia q1 aa 2 and 7.

inquiry; but, short of the vacuously circular proposition that only physics and the like are scientific on criteria of scientificity so designed that only they turn out to be obedient to them, there is every reason to think in Dante's terms of the *Comedy* as meeting the theological conditions of a *scientia*, a systematic, evidence-based, discipline, because therein Dante sets out a consistent and comprehensive set of truths, a coherent story the telling of which amounts to a call to the conversion of intellect and will made by the summons of an ultimate love: in short, that the *Comedy* is a work of *intellectus* in just that sense.

So understood, the general character of Dante's theological pursuit is in the whole tendency of the *Comedy*, and it is akin to the understanding of theology that Augustine and Aquinas share, who, though in many ways differing, have in common the proposition that the ground of all human truth is to be found ultimately in its source in the divine mind. It would be in a spirit nearer to Aquinas's apophatic inclinations than to Augustine's to say that the energy of the theological must in the end, if not before, yield to the poetic, for poetry is what you find yourself *having* to do when confronted by the inexpressible, and that the true measure of the inexpressible is when even poetry, or as Dante himself calls it, *alta fantasia*, isn't enough and has to bow to the imperatives of the same love that moves the sun and the other stars.[21] For when even poetry has to give up the ghost, then we know that we have truly met with the unknowable and that it's not just that we have thrown in the towel for want of intellectual stamina. Now *that* would be a very surprising notion

[21] *Paradiso* 33.145.

of the "scientific." But it is a notion with which Dante himself was quite familiar, and it is all there in the first question of Aquinas's *Summa theologiae*.

More specifically, indeed in more specifically personal terms, the theologian Dante strives to be by way of his writing the *Comedy* is just that which in a sequence of cantos at the end of *Purgatorio* Beatrice demands that he become – and, even more to the point, when she insists that theology is what she herself *in persona* represents, that is, a conformity to Christ, in whom alone among human beings is the true and complete knowledge of God. In those cantos at the end of his journey through Hell's depths to the summit of Mount Purgatory, Dante was at no point but a tourist: Going through Hell he was indeed going through hell. Likewise, in Purgatory he was far from merely observing the penance of its inhabitants,[22] for at every stage he is forced to endure a real purgation himself. And there, in having endured the ascetical disciplines of Purgatory, Dante finally spells out in full the further processes of radical conversion demanded of him as the condition of his writing the *Comedy* – not just the narrative following thereafter that tells of his entry into Paradise, but also, and more to the point, of his becoming able to compose the fiction that is the whole peregrination of the *Comedy*, and so of *Inferno* and *Purgatorio* too. Now, he tells us, he had already gone through these *as person* as the condition of his being able to write of them *as fiction*, even if it is in the medium of his fiction that he goes through that personal conversion. It is in this way that the question is addressed whether Dante "really"

[22] See Chapter 4.

traveled through Hell, Purgatory, and into Paradise, or did so only fictionally: to which the answer must be that the question, put that way, itself falsifies. *Of course* he really traveled through them and did so entirely by way of a poetic fiction. Or is it that we are supposed to think two bad thoughts in conjunction, first that all fiction is, as Plato thought, *but* a distracting fantasy and in consequence that truth-values can't apply to it?[23]

In this way, Dante's narrative of his journey loops back upon itself so as to tell of the total conversion of person that Beatrice demanded of him as the condition of his being able to write the *Comedy*. Hence, the theology that Dante strives to do by means of the *Comedy* is none other than that which Beatrice teaches him to do by means that at times are so relentless and harsh that he is reduced to tears of shame and humiliation as the price of his getting there. In Purgatory he has discovered the cost of his newly discovered authorship to be no less than the price of his transformation as person. In that sense the journey that the *Comedy* records is not only undertaken at the instigation of the Virgin Mary, Lucy, and Beatrice, as we know from the second canto of *Inferno*;[24] it is above all the work in which Dante became able to write about Beatrice only because of the profound transformation of his life that Beatrice's active intervention has brought about. It is, then, not only *from* Beatrice's telling him that Dante learns what theology is; it is *in* Beatrice herself, in her role in his conversion to theology, that he comes to understand theology's true

---

[23] See Robin Kirkpatrick, *Dante: The Divine Comedy*, Cambridge: Cambridge University Press, 2004, p. 1.

[24] *Inferno* 2.52–126.

telos. For Dante, Beatrice *is* theology personified, and as she converts Dante to a properly constructed theology, so it is by her means that he regains the poetic voice that in his earlier *Vita nuova* he tells us he had lost.[25] The same conversion does for life, for theology, and for poetry inseparably. In short, it is in those final cantos of *Purgatorio* that Dante-narrator and Dante-narrated, Dante-theologian and Dante-poet, become inseparably, because indistinguishably, one. At that point, you know that you must read the narrative not only forward from there to Paradise but also backward to Hell, and that even if the journey's chronological order begins in Hell the theological order must begin from Purgatory. Throughout the *Comedy*, Dante is a purgatorial writer: Indeed, you could say that for Dante writing is in general a purgatorial act and that *Inferno* describes nothing except as understood from that standpoint. For Dante cannot survive the experience of Hell unscathed except as one whose presence there is purgatorial and not infernal, just as *Paradiso* describes something it was possible for him to bear witness to only given the purgatory that the second cantica has put Dante through. For what makes possible the experience of either is also what it takes to describe them. Each cantica disappears into its successor until when *alta fantasia* finally fails even Paradise disappears into the vision of Christ in the Trinity. It is then that we come to see that all of it, from the first canto of *Inferno* to the last canto of *Paradiso*, was at every moment moved by that same love that moves the sun and the other stars.

[25] *La vita nuova*, ed. and trans. Mark Musa, Bloomington: Indiana University Press, 1973, p. 86.

Poetry by Way of Theology

So much, for the time being, as to the Dante for whom the pressures innate to the theological draw him inevitably into poetry. When we turn to the Dante who has the poet's need to write theology, first thoughts turn to the matter of the vernacular, for Dante, the poet's preferred idiom. Here, it is important to get some distinctions clear that are not immediately obvious, bearing in mind only some statements in his earlier work on vernacular poetry, the *De vulgari eloquentia*. Immediately one notes the irony of an essay written in formal scholastic Latin devoted to the promotion of the vernacular as the best idiom for lyric poetry. And he is emphatic in what he says about that – I will have to give the Latin first, for the translation is problematic – as between the merits of the *gramatica* and the *eloquentia vulgaris*, he says, *melior est vulgaris*.[26] It's deceptively difficult to translate the phrase, but at a first attempt he means that, for the composition of the lyric, the comparatively easygoing and open-textured character of everyday speech, the *eloquentia vulgaris* – or, as he puts it in the *Comedy*, *la lingua che chiami mamma o babbo* (the speech you learned on your mother's breast where you first learned to cry "Mummy" and "Daddy")[27] – is preferable to the tight, overdetermined disciplines of those technical, philosophical, or theological, but in any case, essentially adult, discourses that he calls the *gramatica*.

Dante's account of vernacularity in *De vulgari eloquentia* is, of course, restricted to the special case of the lyric,

---

[26] *De vulgari eloquentia*, ed. and trans. Steven Botterill, Cambridge: Cambridge University Press, 1.4, p. 2.
[27] *Inferno* 32.9.

and it advocates a correspondingly restricted case for the need of a vernacular idiom and of the poetic gains made by its employment. When Dante turns to the composition of that towering epic that is the *Comedy*, he makes it clear that every style is needed, the high style and the simple, the academic and the lyrical, the adult and the childlike. He needs every resource that the vernacular Italian of his day makes available, and when he needs more than what the vernacular of his day provides, he invents the more that he needs.[28] What is at stake, therefore, in this explicit and conscious turn to the vernacular in Dante, and in early fourteenth-century theology generally, is therefore much more than a simple matter of translation, for to speak of a "vernacular theology" in fourteenth-century Europe is not at all as if to refer to Latin theology translated in another tongue. For that reason, better as a way of characterizing the literary modes of the non-Latin theological writers of Dante's times is Alastair Minnis's word "demotic."[29] "Vernacular" doesn't really capture the *theological* significance of this turn away from the technical prose of the university man, for insofar as it stands in contrast with Latin it obscures the fact that in the Middle Ages there exist both a truly demotic Latinity and a grammatical vernacular.

---

[28] I am grateful to Matthew Treherne for alerting me to the importance of the distinction between the more restricted understanding of vernacularity in *De vulgari eloquentia* and the more expansive understanding of it in the *Comedy*. See his *Dante's Comedy and the Liturgical Imagination*, Oxford: Peter Lang, 2020.

[29] Alastair Minnis, *Translations of Authority in Medieval English Literature: Valuing the Vernacular*, Cambridge: Cambridge University Press, 2009; Alastair Minnis, *From Eden to Eternity, Creations of Paradise in the Later Middle Ages*, Philadelphia: University of Pennsylvania Press, 2016.

As to the first, in Dante's Italy, as everywhere else in the European fourteenth century, ancient phrases from the Latin of the liturgy, as distinct from the more recent Latin of the schools, strategically linking up canto after canto across the pages of *Purgatorio*, are plainly demotic. Throughout *Purgatorio* there are twenty-one quotations in a Latin familiar to everyday Christians at regular worship, in the way for them that it was for me in my youth, when phrases familiar from the Latin of the Psalms and the daily common of the Mass still come to my memory as a kind of ritual chant, for I got to know the *sounds* well enough, if not their sense: "Dominus vobiscum," the priest would say after an initial sign of the Cross and an invocation of the Trinity; I, an acolyte, would respond "et cum spiritu tuo"; "introibo ad altare Dei," he would go on, and I would answer "ad Deum qui laetificat iuventutem meum," quoting the Vulgate of Psalm 43. Those phrases of the common of the Mass and others of the Beatitudes were the *eloquentia vulgaris* of regular worship, in Dante's day, as 637 years later also in mine, learned not long after leaving mother's breast – no matter that most people whether in 1310 or, like myself in 1947 when I was five years old, could translate not one word of it, though we found plenty of meaning in the act of saying it all. Just as obviously, Beatrice's academic lecture in *Paradiso* 2 on the dark spots on the moon's apparent surface is written in a *gramatica* as technical as anything to be found in Duns Scotus's *Reportata Parisiensia*, no matter that it is a lecture delivered in Dante's native Italian. The distinction is not so simple, a matter only, or even at all, of that between Latin as *gramatica* and Italian as *eloquentia vulgaris*.

Preferable is an account of *gramatica* as technical discourse in any language, not necessarily in Latin, and of an *eloquentia vulgaris* as the everyday demotic in any language, including possibly Latin. And we can start with an account of the demotic relevant to Dante in Oliver Davies's way of describing the language of Meister Eckhart's German sermons as "quasi-poetic" just insofar as it is a language that "foregrounds the signifier" itself,[30] and therefore conveys not just, as in a technical discourse, the *res significata*, the meaning signified, but more, and principally, the material features of the act of signifying itself that govern its *modus significandi*. And this "foregrounding" of the signifier connects the demotic with the poetic in that whereas the *gramatica* in Dante's sense is technical discourse in which the distinctive physical properties of the language itself disappear into the pure transparency of meanings conveyed – as in the technical schoolman's Latin of the *Summa Theologiae* – in the poetic it is the signifiers themselves that step forward into prominence, displaying in all their aural immediacy the physical properties of rhyme and rhythm, of assonance and syncopation, of pacing fast and slow, all of which are there not somehow in a manner incidentally decorative but with their own substantive work to do, for they are a sort of music in contrapuntal interaction with formal semantic meanings. Truly this is an *eloquentia vulgaris*. It does something deeply mysterious, but it is exactly what

---

[30] See Oliver Davies, *Meister Eckhart: Mystical Theologian*, London: SPCK, 1991, p. 180, where he speaks of the "foregrounding of language, as bearer of meaning, rather than meaning itself – a phenomenon which is usually judged to be a prime characteristic of poetic texts."

we learn to do and to deliver when we first learn to speak. All poetry is thus at least a *double* fugue, of sound and of sense, each reading the other in constant interplay, a paradigm case being the Welsh rhyming and rhythmic shapes and sounds, the *cynganedd* (as the Welsh call it) adapted into English poetry by Gerard Manley Hopkins as what he called "consonant-chime."[31]

At one time I thought it worth trying out the idea that the hard work done specifically by such material features of the language being thus "foregrounded" shares in a certain way that characteristically done by the sacramental, in the sense in which in the twelfth century Peter Lombard, summarizing a broad Augustinian consensus, had understood the generic meaning of that term,[32] in that the sacramental is embodied in speech acts that both signify and enact, say something and do something, and more properly still, in that *as* they signify *so* they enact – *efficiunt* quod *figurant*, he had said. For the doing is in the saying and the thing done says it all. You can best see this performative character of speech acts, how the saying and the doing play off one another, when the two elements are both present but fall apart from one another within the same utterance. For Judas betrays Jesus when he greets him with a kiss, the greeting of friends, so that what the kiss *says* by way of a gesture of friendship is subverted by what it *does* in thereby enacting betrayal: indeed, more

---

[31] Letter to Robert Bridges, November 26, 1882, in *A Hopkins Reader*, selected and ed. John Pick, Oxford: Oxford University Press, 1953, p. 138.

[32] Peter Lombard, *Sententiae* IV, d. 1, c. 4, a. 2, 233; see also, Hugh of St Victor, *De sacramentis Christianae Fidei*, 1.9.2 (*Patrologia Latina* 176:317d–318b).

betrayals than one. For it's not just Jesus who is thereby betrayed, but as much the language of greeting itself. And that is why Jesus's response to Judas is freighted at once with terrible sadness and fierce indignation: "Judas, do you betray the Son of Man with (of all things) a kiss!" he exclaims, protesting at the cynical mendacity of it.[33]

Judas disengages the saying from the doing, setting them at odds, what the act says being contradicted by what the saying enacts. By contrast, what we need in the sacramental is a three-way connection between the poetic and the performative, mediated by the demotic, of which a limit case is in that "for this is my body" of the Mass, the *hoc est enim corpus meum*. Those words uttered by the celebrant must be the most demotic Latin sentence ever written, for centuries said on behalf of billions in the Western Church, who may not have understood the Latin but bowed their heads in awe at what the words, thus uttered, *did*. You need all three together – the poetic, the performative, and the demotic – if you are to grasp what Dante is up to in the *Comedy*. Perhaps we can see this with clarity if we do some further counter-intuitive muddling with the apparently obvious. Thomas Aquinas's Eucharistic poetry, composed for the feast of Corpus Christi, may be in rhyming scannable verse *about* the Eucharistic act. But for all that they rhyme and scan consistently, the verses of his hymn *Pange lingua* could be straight out of a conciliar decree or a papal encyclical – or, for that matter, the *Summa theologiae*. This is not because they are in Latin. It is because though with wonderful theological precision they say plenty, they do nothing. Formally they may be verse, and are neatly done, just as you would

---

[33] Luke 22:48.

expect of Aquinas. In fact, though, they are pure, if rhyming, *gramatica*, also just as you would expect of him.

All this is but to say that Dante is a poet and that Aquinas is not, though it is to add that there is at least a certain analogy between Dante's poetic and Aquinas's sacramental. For they share the exploitation of the performative character of their respective speech acts. But there is also difference. For whereas Aquinas's hymn *Verbum supernum prodiens* merely reflects in verse on the nature of the performative, Dante performs. That's where the poetry is. And it is somewhere here in that consideration of the quasi-sacramental and performative nature of poetry that the space opens up to a gulf between Dante the poet, his poetic self being embedded in his vernacular communities, political and ecclesial, and the Ulysses of *Inferno* canto 26, that pretentiously individualistic seeker after knowledge and virtue in a world "sanza gente," in a universe emptied of human beings. Ulysses is poetry's Judas.[34] Ulysses represents for Dante a more seductively tempting perversion of his poetic vocation than even Francesca and Paolo do when earlier, in *Inferno* 5, they represent the conception of romantic love of which, as we will see, it is Beatrice's task in *Purgatorio* finally to relieve Dante. In both cases, though, whether Francesca's or Ulysses', Dante feels vulnerable to Hell's critique, for he knows that in his past poetic self he also has sailed too close for comfort to the winds of Ulysses' Promethean individualism, his poetry too close to the mythical hero's unanchored rhetoric, his poetic passion too close to Francesca's conception of romantic love, the thought of which at the end of *Inferno* 5 causes him to

[34] *Inferno* 26.117.

panic and faint in alarm at how its sheer beauty had in the past seduced him into his own poetic betrayal of Beatrice. Ulysses and that past Dante had ripped up poetry and love from their roots in a well-ordered community upon which their respective performative efficacies are conditional. Dante's *Comedy* is at once the journey described and the journey taken, the journey back into a truthful poetic.

Later we will see how ironic that inversion is in consideration of Ulysses' amoral, individualistic adventurism, which trades upon conditions that are secured only by the compliance of others with the demands of good community.[35] Ulysses is a moral parasite, traitor to what in his treachery he must assume. In *Inferno* 26, then, Dante is still engaged in the search that preoccupied him in *De vulgari eloquentia*, and in the *Comedy* he urgently needed to highlight the contrast between that poetic ambition that will stay with him into *Paradise* itself and that which has Ulysses eternally in Hell. His earlier more limited search in *De vulgari eloquentia* was for the community whose common speech was a vernacular fit specifically for the purposes of an Italian lyric and he could find none, for the Italian vernacular, he says, wanders about Italy in search of the community in which to be grounded, and there is none to be found.[36] Now, in the *Comedy*, his search is more general and for an *eloquentia vulgaris*, a demotic fit for a theological epic, a language, that is, of humanity as such; and correspondingly, of the community that could be the bearer of that demotic.

Though it will need qualification, it is worthwhile pursuing a little further the thought that there is an analogy,

---

[35] In Chapter 3.
[36] *De vulgari eloquentia*, I: xvi, n. 4, ed. and trans. Botterill, p. 39.

at least partial, between the character of the sacramental and the *poiesis* of Dante's epic. And to take one step further on the way to clarity about the nature of the speech acts that define Dante's work in those terms, it seems profitable to give thought to the seminal statement of Charles Singleton that, taking the *Comedy* as a whole, "the fiction ... is that it is not a fiction,"[37] a statement that is as revealingly misconceived as it is possible to be. It is, as one might put it, wrong with *perfect* exactness. Why this is so is evident if we ask what distinguishes Singleton's supposed Dantean pretence that the *Comedy* is no fiction from that parallel but limit case of the priest's saying those words of consecration in the canon of the mass, "*hoc est enim corpus meum.*" At face value the priest's words uttered are grammatically in the form of an *oratio obliqua*, for they are the priest's recollecting Luke's Gospel's report of the words of Jesus at that last supper – which fact is the reason why some say that the Eucharistic words are but a memorial, an imitative invocation of the historical record, a history play. But within the ritual of the Mass, they are uttered as *oratio recta*, for the priest is standing in for Christ's saying the words and thus it is he, the priest, who, by uttering them, makes the words to be true; and if his doing so is but instrumental within the economy of divine grace, still it is by means of *his* utterance of them that the thing is done. Therefore, one asks which is correct: To say that the priest is not pretending to be Christ but only reporting his words? Or that it is just by means of his pretending that Christ is made to be truly present? Historically the

---

[37] Charles Singleton, "The Irreducible Dove," *Comparative Literature*, 9 (1957), p. 129.

difference is significant, for the first is Protestant, typically Zwinglian, the second is Catholic, typically Thomist.

Naturally it is not the first, the Zwinglian option, not if you are the Dante obedient to the doctrinal requirements of the orthodox sacramental theology of his day. For when the priest utters those words he does so not as an individual but *as* priest, that is, on behalf of the Church, which acts in obedience to Christ's command. Nor are the words to be heard as if in quotation marks, as they would be heard were the priest merely reporting Jesus to have said them. For he utters them *in persona Christi*, and so it is that what otherwise would be impossible is true, namely that the priest's uttering those words on behalf of the Church truly effects as instrumental cause what they signify. And if this causality is but instrumental, it is still true that it is by his saying them that the deed is done: He is not pretending at all. The ax truly cuts though it is I who wield it; and in the same way the priest's uttering the words instrumentally and as subordinate to the divine agency truly does it. So here there is a fiction but no pretending: it is the priest, standing in for Christ, whose utterance makes to be true what the words signify, makes them do what they say. Here there is a fiction that is, as one might say, a true faction.

Given this, what are we to say about Singleton's account of Dante's authorship of the *Comedy*? Is it that though Dante's standing vis-à-vis the narrative truth of his *Comedy* is that of the priest, Dante's fiction but imitates the priestly act and cannot have the same *ontological* value as it, whose sacramental fiction brings about the fact? In a way it is. What is in any case certain is that it cannot be in the same sacramental sense that Dante's epic "effects what it signifies." For the Eucharistic signification is a unique case among performatives, it is what the Church alone does and alone can do. Even if it is true that in *some* way Dante's epic "does what it says," that in some way his ritual act of "saying" pulls off the doing, the *poiesis* achieving the *praxis*, the question remains whether, if it is not sacramental, what the *Comedy* effects is no more than what poetry always effects, simply as poetry; or does Dante claim more for the *Comedy's* efficacy, something more than the rhetorical efficacy of the poet, something closer to the sacramental efficacy of the priest? Is it in that sacramental sense that Dante's *Comedy* is a performative act, a *poiesis*?

The answer to that question in the end must be that the analogy between them does succeed, but only with careful qualifications. Dante's is a poetic praxis, the *Comedy's* speech acts do effect what they signify in its own way, that is, by rhetorical force; but the work's "efficacy" is not strictly sacramental, because if the poetic act by itself – that is to say, in its own reality as poetry – belongs within a sacramental act, and within it may realize a certain sacramental force, it does not do so in its own right as poetry. For the poet's performativity is not in itself an act of the ecclesial community in its specific agency, as the words of the liturgy are. The *Comedy* is *Dante's* authorial act, the priest's action is the Church's.[38] Therefore, even if there is some sort of sacramental shape to Dante's self-understanding as poet, a shape that derives from poetry's generic character

---

[38] In saying this I am keeping matters relatively simple. There is more to be said about the relationship between Dante's poetics and ecclesial practice, and some of what else matters in this connection is beautifully set out in Matthew Treherne's important work on Dante's poetics and liturgical practice, see *Dante's* Commedia *and the Liturgical Imagination*, London: Peter Lang, 2020.

as performative, Dante-poet is not, *qua* poet, priest. What is it, then, if it is not to cast Dante as a priestly poet, to say that he is a *poeta-theologus*, a poet-theologian?

For an answer I think that we must turn to the vexed question of what Dante is saying about the *Comedy*, and what is he claiming for himself as its author, when he says in his *Epistle to Can Grande della Scala* – assuming it is his, and if so, written when he is well into the composition of the *Comedy*, – that his poem is to be interpreted according to the theologian's understanding of allegory and not, as he had once said in his *Convivio*, merely according to the allegory of the poets.[39]

First, though, let us not be too quick to set the two allegories in principle at odds. Where today theologians claim to be sharp and clear as to what has the authority of inspired canonical Scripture and what is merely secondary commentary on it, medieval writers, and especially reflective theologians in the fourteenth century, can allow the categories endlessly to seep into one another. Indeed, they positively encourage the seepage.[40] Two hundred

---

[39] See John Frecerro's discussion of Dante's two allegories in "Allegory and Autobiography," in *Cambridge Companion to Dante*, ed. Rachel Jacoff, Cambridge: Cambridge University Press, 2007, especially pp. 169–176.

[40] Though there are in Dante's time reactions to this medieval practice, as in Nicholas of Lyra's account of the primacy of the literal sense: For Lyra it was essential to distinguish and then keep well apart, the literal and spiritual senses of Scripture. Along with Aquinas he holds that theology may be founded only upon the literal sense of Scripture, but their case for this proposition makes no sense, or at least entirely distorts what they had in mind, if one fails to see that for them, literary tropes, broadly "metaphor," are parts of Scripture's *literal* meaning. See my *Eros and Allegory*, Cistercian Publications: Kalamazoo, 1995, for translations of Aquinas's *Quaestio de quolibet* VII, q6 a2, and from Nicholas of Lyra's *First Prologue to the Postilla Litteralis on Sacred Scripture*.

years after Dante, the Protestant reform will stem the seepage and construct dykes and ditches designed to stem the easy flow between text and interpretation, and even in Dante's own time Nicholas of Lyra, and, thirty-five years before Dante, Aquinas, had insisted upon sharp theological demarcations between literal and allegorical senses of Scripture, as also in general between the allegory of the theologians and the allegory of the poets.

Still, for Aquinas, not all distinctions are disjunctions. As to the distinction itself he is indeed quite firm: The literal sense of Scripture is "all that can genuinely be got from the meaning of the words themselves,"[41] and he is far from denying that Scripture itself is littered with every form of literary trope (he rather lazily calls it all "metaphor") as part of Scripture's way into the literal *historia* of salvation, salvation's *res gestae*. For Aquinas, it is those *res*, facts, events, of salvation history, not the words that record them, that provide the literal ground of theological allegory, or have moral bearing on a personal life, or make gesture to an eschatological, mystical, sense of creation as a whole – those so-called allegorical, tropological, and anagogical, senses of Scripture. All three, he says, are grounded in Scripture's literal sense.

And having said all that, Aquinas explains why the distinction between the literal and the allegorical senses of Scripture matters: Don't confuse the literary devices of the poets that generate complex, overlapping, associative, meanings, with the significance that the Holy Spirit inscribes in the events of salvation history.[42] All the same,

---

[41] See Turner, *Eros and Allegory*, p. 348.
[42] *Summa theologiae*, 1a q1 a9 *corp*.

if it is necessary not to confuse the allegory of the poets with the allegory of Scripture, that distinction, Aquinas says, by no means rules out the allegory of the poets having a scriptural role. On the contrary, he is insistent that the literal sense of Scripture is frequently, or, as in the case of the *Psalms* almost entirely, constructed out of literary trope, the literal out of the poetic, which is much what Nicholas of Lyra, Dante's contemporary, said about the *Song of Songs* too: Literally it is salvation history, he said, by way of poetry.[43] So, for Aquinas and Nicholas, in such cases the allegory of the poets is part of the theologically literal sense of Scripture, so that Scripture itself contains fiction not needing to pretend that it is not a fiction and for all that, he says, containing the *literal* truth.

In such ways within the Church's own reception of the Scriptures of which it is also the author – Scriptures that are at once authoritatively regulative for the Church and written by it – the categories do begin to seep into one another, text into hermeneutic, trope into literalness, and in both cases in reverse directions too, in the manner that most medieval theological writers of his times took quite for granted as proper and desirable, and not just in the case of scriptural texts. If in search of a sense, then, in which Dante's *Comedy* can, even on Aquinas's account, be read according to the theologians' four senses of Scripture one should think of that early twelfth-century creation, the *Glossa Ordinaria*, that written-out page of Scripture, the *sacra pagina*, visibly setting between the lines of the inspired text an interpreter's

---

[43] See Turner, *Eros and Allegory*, pp. 394–396.

interlinear gloss and surrounding it with the marginal gloss containing whole traditions of interpretation, and so presenting to the eye Scripture received and absorbed over a thousand years or so by the communities whose writings they are, writings that are reciprocally regulative of the communities which wrote them. Scripture is the whole complex interaction of text, the community interpreting it, and the community for which it is interpreted, the Church, *thus far*,[44] the *Sacra Pagina*. And the manuscript pages look like what in truth they are hermeneutically, scriptural text interleaved and surrounded by its centuries of reception, writing that is read, Scripture proclaimed, Scripture as historical ecclesial practice of the teaching community at prayer, witnessing to salvation history. In the medieval world in which Dante writes his *Comedy* the inside and the outside of Scripture leach into one another through a thin and porous skin – for the very distinction between literal and allegorical is itself authorized by the Scriptures it exists to interpret, as in the famous passage in *Galatians* 4:22–27, where St. Paul instructs his audience to read the fates respectively of Hagar and Sarah as a second-order allegory of the first-order allegorical text of Scripture itself. This hermeneutic is not thought of as *added* to Scripture: It is there *in* what is written.

---

[44] See the early printed texts that include the twelfth-century collections of biblical glosses, interlinear and marginal, together with, at the bottom of the page, the literal interpretations done by Nicholas of Lyra in the early fourteenth century. Such, in Dante's time, is the *sacra pagina*, "holy writ," a visual layout displaying a record of thirteen hundred years of the Church's practices of scriptural writing and reading.

So now what has happened to Singleton's "fiction?" Have we not turned the tables on at least the anti-realist versions of his formula? Is it not truer to say that Dante's fiction is that his narrative is *but* a fiction, and that by means of a poetic epic and *as if* in a literal narrative he gives us what could be got at in its theological truth by no other means, or by no other means as well, in the same way that by means of seven openly sexy poems the *Song of Songs* offers the best way into the truth of the love affair between Israel and Yahweh – that is, by way of its erotic *allegory* of making love truly to *make* it? In the same way the Dante of the *Can Grande* epistle knows he has no other way into the literal truth at the heart of the *Comedy*'s narrative than by means of the allegory of the poets, and that in its being precisely *as such* theological allegory his poem is to be read as a para-scriptural text, accessing Scripture's literal truth. And might it not be that Dante realized that his poetic strategy was forced upon him by a necessity that is truly theological? Could it not be the case that there are some theological truths he knew can be got at *only* by way of a poetic narrative fiction, thereby to get at those "facts" to which poetry alone can give expression? If that is how Dante thinks, would it not be better to say that for him the fiction of the *Comedy* is that it *is* a fiction, for of course the journey he describes is theologically impossible, but in its description is contained a profound theological truth? And why should we be surprised to find Dante thinking that a poetic fiction is sometimes the only way into a theological truth, since from Origen in the third century all the way through to Dante's own day theologians almost invariably knew that such are the necessary devices of their scriptural authors, especially of the biblical poets? For what else are those 150 Psalms doing centrally in the biblical canon?

In such a thought-world one can begin to see just how theologically judicious, and lacking in theologically self-important pretentiousness, was Dante's conception of his *Comedy* as bearing the hermeneutical weight of *theological* allegory: Its truth is scriptural, a truth got at by means of a fiction which, precisely as fiction, gets to the fact. And then, if we read it that way, we no longer need in Aquinas's name to demote the theological standing of poetry as such, as some of his more confused *soi-disant* followers and opponents alike suppose him have done, and so to have depreciated the theological deployment of the distinctively literary apparatus of allegory. For if we follow the logic of this argument that literary trope is a compositional device of the theologically literal sense of the *Comedy*, then of course metaphor and literary allegory and the rest do belong to it as literary text, but as trope required by the theologically allegorical intent of the *Comedy*, bearing its *literal* meaning. Thereby Scripture itself, read within and by the community whose Scriptures they are, retains some of the core meaning of the sacramental, effecting in its own way what it signifies, in the sort of way in which for the partners in a marriage rite to have *said* before the community "I do" *is* to have done it.

Distinctions, then, matter. But not all distinctions are dichotomies, excluding one another – not for Dante. The fact is that in Dante's time the very notion of literal meaning was passing through a phase of development, and he knew exactly what that development was and what he was doing with it. In short, Dante perceived the need to be a poet in order adequately to meet the demands of the theologian that, as author of the *Comedy*, he claimed to be, claiming, not exactly for himself personally but for his poem, a place within the historically continuous scriptural practices of the Church, and in consequence claiming for it the right to be read according to the appropriate hermeneutic, the allegory of the theologians.

If in response to the pressures of the sixteenth-century reforms the two senses of allegory fall apart into opposition, as do the two senses of the literal, if indeed allegory in the theologian's sense falls entirely away, leaving a regnant literary allegory unchallenged and a contrasting notion of the literal truth of Scripture scarcely defined at all, that is no good reason for a neglect of the theologian's allegory in the reading of Dante. There is no better reason for wielding the allegory of the theologians as a stick with which to beat down the allegory of the poets as of little or no theological concern. For Dante's poetic allegory is a literary device crucial in the *Comedy*'s foundation in a literal reading of Scripture. And if that is at the heart of Dante's intent, then it is reason enough to claim Dante for the theologians precisely insofar as he is a poet-theologian who boldly plays the two allegories in and out of one another, each interpreting the other.[45] Truth is not wisely said always to be better than fiction, for sometimes fiction is the only way into the truth. And very often it is the best way of all.

---

[45] A "poelogian" as my friend in the Yale Divinity School, Ashley Makar, put it.

PART I
HELL

2

Hell

Dante and Aquinas

∼

Dante's Choice

The first canto of *Inferno* opens not with Dante's entry into Hell but with a prologue, telling how midway in his life's course he became lost on a hillside, there to be harassed by three wild beasts, a leopard, a lion, and a she-wolf. They represent some three vices or other, though which Dante doesn't say – perhaps they are lust, pride, and avarice, as John Sinclair, Robin Kirkpatrick, and Allen Mandelbaum all propose, following an older tradition; or fraud, violence, and incontinence, as Mark Musa and others have it.[1] Whichever vices they represent, Dante is in terror of them, and it is as one who is tempted by the thought that if you can't beat them then there is nothing for it but to join them, that he encounters Virgil, who had been called upon by Beatrice to help him. Beatrice in turn had been sent by St. Lucy at the instance of the Virgin Mary – the roll call reads a little like an author's acknowledgment of debts owed to teachers and colleagues in the field – and on their recommendation Dante claims Virgil as his model and mentor, appointed to lead him out of the dark wood into Hell.

---

[1] See Robert Hollander, *Inferno*, New York: Anchor Books, 2000, pp. 16–17, where he summarizes the range of interpretations of these beasts from early readings to the latest.

That is, if Dante so chooses. One way or another, choose he must, though at first sight the options put to him seem to be strange, uninviting, even paradoxical: If he does not wish to submit to the power of those vices, he may not slip past them either, for he must go with Virgil through the infernal world they create as the only way to overcome them in himself. Either way, whether as to his eternal fate, or in taking the one path that will lead him out and beyond it, there is no alternative to the next step's being into Hell. Nor may he make a quick trip of it, a sampler, just to get a taste of what it is like, for he will have to travel throughout its whole extent and hear in painful detail the insiders' stories of every vice and every kind of punishment endured eternally by every kind of sinner known to Dante, thereby discovering the traces of them that there are in himself.

Why Must Dante Enter Hell?

We should pause for a moment here and not rush headlong into the narrative of the journey that follows without first noting that, if what you want in reading the *Comedy* is existential excitement, this is where you will get it. Knowing what Dante will in fact choose to do is our reader's privilege, and we know which he will choose from the fact that he is in a position to tell the story of his experience in Hell in a way possible only to one not condemned for all eternity to remain there. But Dante reports that at the time, when everything was still at stake, when the options were down to all or nothing, to comedy or farce, he did not know which he would do.[2]

---

[2] Farce, not tragedy. There is no tragedy in Hell. It is a place of absurdity.

Why Must Dante Enter Hell?

It is a truly existential moment, a moment of choice, not, indeed *whether* to enter the gates of Hell, for as to that he was given no choice, but whether he will do so simply conceding to the inertia of his sinfulness, to sin's gravitational weight that would have him there willy-nilly, or whether by choice to go there as required by a journey of redemption. At this point the question is whether the outcome is to be the story's end there and then in the farce that is Hell's eternity, or the story's beginning inaugurating a comedy that is truly divine. The question before Dante is whether or not he is prepared to meet the conditions that writing the *Comedy* demand of him? They are a burden that is overwhelmingly unappealing, terrifying.

It is with reluctance that Dante in the event chooses to take the path through Hell. It was not a foregone conclusion that he would do so. It will turn out that to have chosen to travel through Hell had been no backward step, that, on the contrary, his choosing to do so was the first step forward for a self who is lost, and he will come to see that it was a necessary step if ever he was to find himself. But for Dante that was not so obvious. And, being the first of several such critical moments that punctuate the *Comedy*'s journey right to the very end, this one is in a way the most existential, most fundamental, choice of all. For whereas the later crises recorded in the final cantos respectively of *Purgatorio* and *Paradiso* call upon Dante to look back upon and reassess the meaning of the journey that had got him there, this crisis at the beginning of *Inferno* concerns whether there is to be any journey at all. Here at the outset, the choice Dante faces is threatening, dark, and dangerous, not least because, unlike those later crises that, however radical, are the culminations of a preceding journey and are intelligible in their light, here the choice is, as it were, *ex nihilo*, altogether lacking in antecedent reassurances. No comfortable, compromised, and halfway settlements are on offer; either way it's going to be Hell, and, taking the *Comedy* as a whole, that grim statement of the options, the poem's *status quaestionis*, sets the scene at once theologically and personally. Without that emphatic and stark challenge his epic has no defining agenda, and it becomes a limp 14,000 lines of solution without the problem they solve, no more than the traveler's tale of a voyeuristic theological tourist.

It might seem surprising that escape from the grip of the vices is possible only by passing through the one place where they have made their home and seem to rule unchallenged. Dante, at any rate, is disconcerted. He asks why he must take that dark route rather than simply take note of Hell's horrors and steer clear, for he is intimidated by the prospect of entering it, and, frightened that it will be too much for him, he adds, "am I in spirit strong enough | for you to trust me on this arduous road?"[3] And then he panics entirely: "But *me*? Why me? Who says I can?" he exclaims to Virgil, "I fear this may be lunacy."[4] He has in fact no option because it is not as if, faced with this choice, he stands on neutral territory, the options concerning which way to move being of equal standing. He is *already* in Hell and the options are to do nothing, or at best to seek

---

[3] *Inferno* 2.11–12.   [4] *Inferno* 2.31–33.

a compromise and stay there perhaps on acceptable terms, or else to pass through Hell and leave in search of an entirely new world beyond its limits. Given this choice he knows that he would far rather he hadn't to embark upon so arduous a journey at all, and he asks why should he not just leave Hell altogether behind, leave Hell altogether out of it? He doesn't see why he may not do so, there being, he supposes, agenda enough for him midway in life's journey in the confession of his own sins. May he not bypass Hell's world of sin by way of repentance of his own relatively minor contribution to that world, thus taking the direct route through to a personal Purgatory? And if not, why not? he asks. You may guess that he longs for the further and less demanding options that bad faith would provide him with. Would they not do instead?

The question, then, for Dante the author, as for his reader, is why may he not bypass Hell entirely? Why does he need to write an *Inferno* at all? The answer Dante gets to that easier first question is a firm no. Virgil accuses Dante of cowardice in not facing the fact that there is no alternative to his going through Hell – Dante's is an "ignominious dread," Virgil says.[5] He may not be let away with so little as the acknowledgment of his sinfulness, even a superficially honest one, for his guilt is far greater, deeper, than as yet he knows. The significance of Dante's being lost in that dark wood is that it is his very selfhood, his personal identity, that is lost, not just the inadequacy of his life's performance thus far. For not yet confronted is, as John Donne calls it, "the sinne where I begunne/Which

[5] *Inferno* 2.45.

was my sin, though it were done before."[6] If he is to enter into his own guilty self he must enter the Hell to which that self truly belongs, he must pass through its world, its seemingly natural habitat. Moreover, his guilt is more far-reaching than he knows, and he may not settle accounts on his own terms because in any case what is at stake is no private affair; the guilt he bears is the guilt he shares with every member of the human race.

Later, we will need to give more thought to the matter of how exactly Dante understands the nature and effects of the Fall, of Adam's sin, on human moral responsibility thereafter, especially in the light of cantos 16 and 17 of *Purgatorio*. For there, in the mouth of Marco Lombardo Dante appears to say that it is not some general corruption of human nature but bad government that is the cause of the world's having gone astray.[7] If we can put that particular question to one side until Chapter 5, what we must say here is that whether we read Dante as understanding sin as having caused a catastrophic collapse of human nature as such, or primarily to be a condition brought about by some in the exercise of corrupt

---

[6] John Donne, "A Hymne to God the Father," in *Before the Door of God: An Anthology of Devotional Poetry*, ed. Jay Hopler and Kimberly Johnson, New Haven, CT: Yale University Press, 2013, pp. 139–140. A theologically ill-informed footnote adds in explanation that Donne is referring to "The doctrine of Original Sin," which "holds that human nature is inherently, hereditarily sinful as a consequence of the Fall of Adam and Eve." Well, then, if original sin is inherited then just for that reason it is not "inherent." See Chapter 5 on why this mistake is so damagingly wrong as to Donne and quite as foreign to Dante's understanding of the doctrine of the Fall.

[7] The question of how to interpret Dante's understanding of sin's universal and/or original character in light of *Purgatorio* cantos 16–17 was put to me by Matthew Treherne. See the discussion in Chapter 5.

misuses of power, either way it is essential to the meaning of *Inferno*'s first canto that the full weight of Dante's own sins' evil does not lie in his private acts alone. Indeed, we will see later that, whichever explanation of the presence of evil and sin in the world seems to be his, either way personal guilt for actual sin is but the lesser of Dante's worries, for the responsibility that he sees himself as bearing has a concrete, practical weight that goes beyond the worst that he personally has ever done or could ever do.

Aristotle had said that we are individually only partially responsible for our states of character, for we bear the weight of biology, family, bad culture, and indeed bad politics upon our persons before ever we are imputable individual agents.[8] For Aristotle this is not, or need not be, a deterministic and depersonalized understanding of guilt, nor is it a denial of free will to say, as Dante appears to do, that going beyond even that impersonal weight borne by the interaction of individual free choices with the pressure upon choice exerted by inherited moral burdens – always a complex mix – our sinful responsibility has a universal character that is borne by all, though *none* of us are the cause of it, for it is in some way inherited. For Dante knows what Aristotle and every Greek or Roman philosopher or poet, including Virgil himself, didn't know, that we bear the weight of sin in the darkest places within us prior to any choice, prior to any burden of culture or history, for we are implicated in that world-historical condition of sinfulness that John's Gospel calls "the sin of the *world*," the sin that makes actual historical worlds of sin for itself. This is the sin that

---

[8] *Nicomachean Ethics*, 1114b 21–25.

Augustine thought of as "original" not, indeed, because it is arbitrarily imputed to us by some divine decree, but because it is embedded in us all as a general condition of fallenness, affecting us prior to any sin that we do. We will see that indeed Dante is less than happy with that Augustinian notion of the catastrophic fallen condition as having been caused "originally" by Adam's sin; nonetheless, Dante does seem to think that human free will, and so the exercise of human choice, is in some way *antecedently* – that is, by way of a prior cause – limited, borne down upon by a general condition. It was this general condition that medieval theologians sometimes called the *languor naturae*, the general impersonal moral deadweight that sucks us down, causing us all equally to be wallowing in sin's mud, leaving aside the different degrees to which we knowingly walk ourselves deeper into it. And it is Dante's sense of this *languor* that threatens him in *Inferno*'s first canto, leaving aside any particular theological account of it its origin and cause.

Leaving that question of sin's origin aside for the time being – sin's character of having been "done before," of its being in *some* way prior to the free choice of the will – the mud, ancient or contemporary, does indeed stick. It is for this reason that, if Dante is to confront and come to terms with his own moral failures, then he is going to have to do so by entering into sin's own world, into the place where sin is at home, the place where, on account of the world's sinfulness, he has come habitually to belong, there to undertake a journey of encounter with sin's own self-created regime and with the community of sin of which upon birth he became a citizen. That is the reason why the *only* route to somewhere better than Hell is through Hell. There is no other route into Purgatory.

Sin's World

One way or another, then, Dante's Hell is at least the representation of vice as somehow systematically embedded in the ways of the world, in the world as regime and as politics, and the voices of Francesca da Rimini,[9] popes Boniface VIII and Nicholas III,[10] Ulysses,[11] Bertran de Born,[12] Ugolino,[13] and all the others speak of their vices in that regime's vulgar patois, in the tediously repetitive language of sin, wherein each of them has but one song of their own and none can do anything except endlessly sing it, obsessively, like a trashy melody that you can't ever get out of your head. It is true that *Inferno* is the description of a place of punishment, of pain inflicted for sins, a place regulated by a penal code listing the punishments that fit the crimes. But the more powerful point of the *contrapasso* that attaches appropriate schemes of punishment to different species of sin is that your condition in Hell conforms exactly to the shape and form of your own desires,[14] of those desires of yours acting upon which got you there in the first place. In that sense you make your own Hell for yourself. Therefore, the narrative of *Inferno* tells the inside story of the self-inflicted punishment that *is* the sin, sin being its own punishment. As Herbert McCabe once said, whatever pain an individual's sin may cause to others, it cannot do to others

---

[9] *Inferno* 5. [10] *Inferno* 19. [12] *Inferno* 28. [11] *Inferno* 26.
[13] *Inferno* 33. [14] See *Inferno* 3.124.

the harm it does to the sinner – it is that self-harm that makes it sinful[15] – and Hell is the place for each sinner of that specific self-harm that is theirs, the place where the implications of choosing it spin out in the specific shape of an endless life so defined. And Dante must go through Hell in the company of the damned because, in the form and shape and extent of his own life's sins, that is where he too, thus far provisionally, belongs.

Hell, then, is a place Dante is in; but he can visit it because Hell is also a place in Dante. Hell is both the social form of Dante's sinful interiority and the interiorized form of Hell's social world, and they map on to one another exactly. And you do not visit that Hell in yourself for the purposes of polite chat. It is horrible. Hence Beatrice's initiative in calling upon Dante voluntarily to go through Hell in Virgil's company places upon him the demand that he does so as a first step in a journey of self-knowledge, a journey that was bound to be hellish on the way. Had Dante refused to take that journey with Virgil *through* Hell that would have been to choose to stay there forever. For as the judgment of his life stood at that point, Hell was the destination entailed. And it is in the fact that he has a choice between a willing journey through Hell in the meantime and final surrender to the teeth and claws of the mountain's vicious beasts that a truth fundamental

---

[15] This is why utilitarianism gets the evil of sin the wrong way round. For Dante, the evil you can wrongly do to others is in the act itself by which you do it. Naturally, it has consequences for others, for that goes along with the evil you do. It may even be your intention to harm others, but the true evil of *sin* lies in the abuse of a responsibility, and that is yours.

to the understanding of the *Comedy* in its character of a journey is made clear.

Dante's Journey through Hell Is His Purgatory

The truth is that because Dante's journey through Hell is a matter of open choice it is a journey that is for him purgatorial and not infernal. When, in *Inferno* 3, Charon, Hell's gatekeeper, recognizes Dante as a person not yet dead, he tells Dante that he may not make the journey down the river Styx from the same shore as do the damned.[16] What for Hell's condemned inhabitants is a place of eternal torment is for Dante a first salvific step forward, because for all the pull that Hell exerts upon him to stay, he has chosen to pass through it as a first penitential step. It is that difference that enables Dante to take that journey through Hell unscathed by the horror of hopelessness that afflicts those eternally condemned there, so as thereby to experience its pains not as unending punishment but as a life-transforming penitential experience. He must enter the gates of Hell *without* abandoning hope, or else there is no way out of it.[17] That being so, Dante's narrative of a journey through Hell and beyond is told from the standpoint of his arrival at that further end, in the way that Augustine in his *Confessions* told the story of his journey of discovery of God from the standpoint of his having arrived at its goal.[18] Naturally, the story must be told in its time-bound narrative sequence, the journey through Hell naturally preceding that through Purgatory; but

---

[16] *Inferno* 3.127–129.   [17] *Inferno* 3.1–9.   [18] See Chapter 4.

it is thus told from the standpoint of Dante's conversion, achieved at Beatrice's instance in the last cantos of *Purgatorio*. Therefore, chronologically, the journey takes its course from that initial decision to follow Virgil through Hell. Theologically, it must start from Purgatory, which makes his journey through Hell a wholly different matter, principally because he has a story to tell unlike those condemned to Hell forever who have no true story at all, just the unchanging repetition of regrets. Infernal time allows no possibility of true narrative but only that endless sameness, time present and time future having no reality of their own, being present only as locked into time past. Dante, therefore, has a story to tell because, and only because, his entry into Hell is *not* without hope.

But, if that is so, we are compelled to ask whether this journey that is so imaginatively described in some of the finest, most vivid, poetry ever written, is theologically possible. Literary interpreters have their reasons for distinguishing between one Dante, the early fourteenth-century Florentine poet-narrator in exile, the author of the tale that tells of his being on a journey through Hell and Purgatory to Paradise, and a second Dante, Dante the pilgrim narrated, the actor internal to the story told. That the distinction has its purposes is shown by the fact that, while there are a few directly autobiographical references in the *Comedy*, two seem especially significant, the first, when Beatrice, addressing Dante directly gives him his poetic mission to "write down what you see when you go back"[19] and the second

---

[19] *Purgatorio* 32.103–105.

in *Purgatorio* 30.57 when, as rarely, he calls himself by his name, "Dante," and then very dramatically and as it were redemptively. Nonetheless, no purpose is well served if, in making the distinction between self-as-author and self-as-authored, the more fundamental issue is neglected, namely that in the text itself it is clear that the Dante narrated and the Dante narrator must be the same not only in reference, one and the same individual Dante, but also one and the same in signification, that of Dante on a journey through all the possibilities of human choice and so in a place of judgment. Logically prior to the poem's being *about* the journey told by the poet Dante it *is* the journey Dante takes by way of the poem he composes. That is to say, the poetic narrative is how Dante lives the thing it describes.

Aquinas had made a general distinction between speculative and practical knowledge in that the causal relations between knowledge and fact are respectively reversed: Speculative knowledge, which knows its objects only as it were from a distance – in that sense "objectively" – is *caused by* what it knows, as the visibility of an object is caused by the object seen; practical knowledge is the *cause of* what it knows, as my intention to act is the immediate cause of my doing it.[20] And the *Comedy* taken as a whole and as an act of knowledge is both speculative – that is to say descriptive of the journey taken and recording it – and practical, for the poem

---

[20] *Summa theologiae*, 1a q14 a16 *corp*. We might be less sure than Aquinas that the distinction is as clear-cut as that, but it would be consistent with his account of it that acts of knowledge are speculative *insofar* as caused by the object known and practical *insofar* as it is the cause of what it knows, with many acts of knowledge in fact being complex mixes of both.

is itself the action of taking it. As of the *Comedy*, the knowledge is not one or the other, speculative or practical, at different times. It is always both. For purgatorial is his standpoint as penitent author in time, describing what he sees in Hell, Purgatory, and Paradise; and purgatorial is his standpoint as narrated, as one converted by the process he describes.

The Infernal Self-Knowledge

But what is this place that Dante must enter and step by step traverse? In due course, we will need to give thought to the question whether it is essential to Dante's infernal narrative that Hell is a physical place, an actual regime, peopled by the damned, a place physically constructed like a corkscrew winding its way down to its dead terminus in the inert body of Satan, for whom the place was originally created. But, for Dante, Hell is also a mindset that maps on to the place, the psychology mapping on to its topography and vice versa. Hell is always that conjunction. There is, then, a moral psychology of Hell, an infernal mentality that, though differing in degree, is common to all its occupants; and there is a topography descriptive of the physical place that their minds map on to psychologically. It begins with Francesca and Paolo's conventional infidelity, whose lust is, if a deformation, at least the corruption of an intense love and is for that reason the most understandable of sins,[21] and from there it spirals down ever

---

[21] At least this is so as Dante represents it in *Inferno* 5: What Dante attends to is the deformation of love that is lust. He ignores the far less forgivable sin of the injustice that Francesca's adultery does to her

deeper into sin's character as a final emptiness, down to the numb and loveless despair of the starving Ugolino who cannot even respond to the pleas of his innocent child, – "eat *me*," Anselmo cries to his father, and, being starved, the father eats the son, his hunger proving to be "a greater power than grief."[22] The progressive collapse of meaning is traced through the predicaments of personae of the condemned as they become ever more confined in themselves, ever more entrapped by a singleness of will, a self ultimately *self*-entrapped, persons ultimately self-obsessed. And the single most striking fact of all Dante's descriptions of Hell's inhabitants is that every one of them is entirely clear about what has them in Hell. None makes an excuse for what they did, and not one of them has any tendency to protest at the judgment that condemns them. They neither deny it nor excuse it. They are all entirely self-transparent, entirely open.

Scito seipsum, said the Delphic oracle, "know thyself." And it would be easy to suppose that every form of self-knowledge is always and everywhere salvific. Sartre, in his *Sketch for the Theory of Emotions*,[23] argues that all self-knowledge objectifies the self that is known in such a way that if you know you are guilty of sin *thereby* you are not; for your knowledge has already disengaged you subjectively from the thing known, and by way of making it into an *object* of your reflection you are affirmed as

---

husband, but that is because the sinners in Hell are all ideal types of distinct sins, persons defined by the one sin that has them in Hell.

[22] *Inferno* 33.75.
[23] Jean-Paul Sartre, *Sketch for the Theory of the Emotions*, trans. Philip Mairet, London: Routledge, 2013.

subject, your inert *en soi* becomes your choosing *pour soi*, and the latter frees you of the former. In this light the proposition "I am self-deceived" becomes self-refuting in the same way that the declaration "I am lying" means that you aren't.[24] But Sartre's generalization seems implausible, for it is easy to describe a state of moral consciousness that belies it.

Consider the introduction to the Pardoner in the Prologue to Chaucer's *Canterbury Tales*. The tale itself is a parable, or perhaps a caricature, of how to think in a correctly infernal way. He is of interest to us not because he is a perfectly run-of-the-mill shameless cheat and conman, at once fully aware of his vice and wholly unrepentant of it – though he is exactly that. In this, he is little more than a fourteenth-century version of the tout who sells overpriced tickets for the soccer Cup Final to last-minute hopefuls who are in despair of obtaining the regular article. The chances are that the tout's tickets are forged, but, gullible as you are, your hope when you pay the absurd prices is that somehow the forgery will see you through the turnstile undetected. Chaucer's tout sells "pardons," that is, by way of the supposed efficacy of the relics that he claims to possess (they are in fact bogus) he professes to be able to win a reduction in purgatorial time-out for

---

[24] The logic of Sartre's argument has a parallel in Aquinas, for whom the self cannot be a direct object of immediate self-reflection. It is known only indirectly, in what he calls a "concomitant" awareness whereby, in knowing its proper objects, the human intellect is aware of itself *as* knowing them. Otherwise than in that "concomitant" way, we know ourselves only as we know the self of others than ourselves, by way of a *diligens et subtilis inquisitio*, by "a searching and precise investigation" just in the way your friends or your psychiatrist know you. See *Summa theologiae*, 1a q87 a1 *corp*.

any such guileless penitents as will pay him the appropriate fees. Because the dispirited Pardoner's victims cling to a desperate hope, they can be counted upon to pay up; the Pardoner, on the other hand, is a splendidly joyful sinner, knowing that any such hopes are entirely vain. In short, he is an enthusiastic simoniac, a fraudulent dealer in spiritual goods, and Dante would have had him placed in *Inferno* canto 19 together with popes Boniface VIII and Nicholas III, heads buried in the ground, the soles of their feet aflame. In his being a simoniac cheat, the Pardoner's sin is routinely vicious and no doubt it deserves that punishment in Hell. But what in the Pardoner's cheating practice is notably illustrative of Hell's nature, of the defining infernal psychology of its inhabitants, is not so much the evil for which he is deservedly punished but the perfect fit between the evil of his life and his quite transparent, and utterly complacent, self-awareness of it. The Pardoner's self-knowledge has about it a certain kind of insolent honesty quite definitive of the psychology of the damned.

For while, as he admits, he plots to deceive the common gullible folk of his usual market, with his less gullible fellow pilgrims on the way to Canterbury his tactics need to be more subtle for he knows they are wise to his deceits and that lying to them won't work. Therefore, he turns the tables on their skepticism. With them he happily, even enthusiastically, admits his hypocrisy, cheerfully and openly he declares his bad faith, without reserve he condemns himself out of his own mouth, for he knows he is a hypocrite, and he is well aware that his fellow pilgrims know that his mask of virtue is but a stratagem of vice. Shamelessly, then, does he brag of his hypocrisy – "of course I am a fraud, as you know, but so what? At least I am smart at it," he says – if only in order to get his self-criticism in before they can accuse him of his venal practices: See, he declares, the hypocrite that I am: I preach that money is the root of all evil, and I do this as a way of cheating people out of what little money they have with the offer of false pardons that I know well they can ill-afford. That's how I make my living, by defrauding the gullible poor in the name of Christ, and you and I both know it. And the best part of it all is that in my very act of preaching I condemn my own practice, for in hypocritically preaching up my pardons "for coverteis," my "theme is and ever was / *Radix malorum est cupiditas.*"[25] What a jape! Thus does his preaching serve the purposes of the very avarice that he preaches against. The contradiction is internal to the act itself, and he absorbs the criticism as he boasts of its truth. But it is just here that Sartre's generalization seems wrong; for the Pardoner does not cease to be a hypocrite just because he admits to all and sundry, and especially to himself, that he is one.

There is something quite magnificent in the Pardoner's unreserved honesty. And the significance of it for our purposes is that in a single stroke he pulls off a remarkable combination: On the one hand, what he says is indeed true, for he is the hypocrite he says he is; and on the other, in brazenly admitting it, he succeeds in disabling the critical power of that truth precisely by way of the cynical openness of his telling it, precisely, that is, by his shamelessly not lying. All of it, the affirmation of the truth and

---

[25] Geoffrey Chaucer, *Canterbury Tales*, Prologue, lines 110–119.

the same truth's disablement, are done in the same act, and his venality is made impervious to moral criticism. His hypocrisy is without disguise, and the one thing he can say of himself before his fellow pilgrims is that with them at least his strategy is totally transparent, that he is completely honest and there is no *self*-deception. But neither is he lying to *them*. And what he shows by these stratagems is that, alas, the truth does not always set you free, not, at least, when you make it a practice to turn the truth full circle upon itself, like the snake that endlessly feeds on its own tail, regrowing its length as it is nourished by what it devours. Here, then, the Pardoner deceives *by way of* the truth.[26]

You might think (I do) that in the Pardoner's excess of self-reference there is a sort of philosophical parable of our times alongside Chaucer's parable of the self-subverting ethical. Pardoners abound. Chaucer's is a parable of our times bearing upon a second-order level of philosophical shamelessness, wherein by way of similarly bold devices of hyperbolic transparency philosophers seek to disguise their sins of thought. As a philosophy, it shows all the marks of a residual dependence on Descartes that is especially evident in our times among the advocates of radical deconstruction, a disposition to this day observable in that abiding cartesian obsession with clarity, with the certainty of the "clear and distinct idea" and its pure transparency, as the foundation of all true knowledge, though in our times it is evident mostly by way of reaction against it and in the negative form of the corresponding inference that if Descartes's

---

[26] See also Geryon, figure of fraud, *Inferno* 16.124–17.15.

case for certain epistemic foundations in the *cogito* fails, then there can be no external epistemic foundations at all, and therefore no ground for certainty, only an endlessness of self-reflection. Thereupon you are left with the Cartesian reflexive clarity itself minus the objective certainty that Descartes thought came with it, with only the cognitively self-disrupting act. It seems that such philosophers have constructed for themselves an epistemological version of the ethical Pardoner, the very excess of "critique" having become *self*-evacuating, the very surplus of the self-reflection destroying the self that is reflected upon. It is as if our ethical Pardoner and our purveyors of deconstruction are both a little too pleased with their auto-critiques; but they are respectively the moral and epistemological embodiments of the plight of the schizophrenic who once told me that the cause of his condition lay in what he called a default "x-ray vision." For, he said, in his schizoid moments he could see no given meaning *in* anything because he was compelled to see straight *through* everything, leaving nothing left on the other side to be seen, nothing but an endless succession of othernesses chasing one another down spirals of self-evacuation, equally of identity and of moral responsibility.[27]

Such is a philosopher's infernalization of the epistemic in parallel with the Pardoner's infernalization of the moral. And in either form it spreads. For, just as it is the strategy of the Pardoner to empty out the moral by

---

[27] It suggests that the conjunction of Descartes's epistemic prioritization of self-reflection with Hume's deconstruction of the *cogito* gives you the basics of a postmodern deconstruction – less *post*modern than modernism's apotheosis.

The Infernal Self-Knowledge

way of an excess of self-reference, so equally complicit in it is his audience, the Canterbury pilgrims. The Pardoner deceives none of them any more than he deceives himself; he hides behind no mask, which is why it is impossible to unmask him, the blatancy of his confession having undone all possibility of exposure. In any case, deceiving them was never the purpose of his strategy, which was so to tell the truth as to frustrate its power as criticism, to disable truth by its very excess, thereby to rip apart the interdependence of theory and practice. He says one thing, and his saying it does another, he says it all so as to have to do nothing. It is, as it were, a perfectly infernal form of autocritique. It is not the truth of what he says, then, so much as the blatancy of his saying it; it is the hyperbolic joke that does all the work, and Chaucer makes it clear that the Pardoner's ploy is, in the event, dramatically effective. As it turns out it is the outrageous theatricality of his performance that attracts the attention of his fellow pilgrims, and by the end of his tale they too are tickled by the degree of the Pardoner's cynicism. Getting the joke, they laugh at him and join him in admitting the sheer cynicism of his performance: They love it, as indeed at one further remove, do we. After all, Chaucer too is having such irresistibly knockabout fun. No truth is denied therein, no one is literally deceived, but the truth has been systematically disengaged from practice and everyone is complicit. In conjunction, pilgrims and Pardoner participate in a collectively cynical disablement of truth that issues in an absolute refusal of self-transcendence, in an enclosure in themselves so complete, having no outside point of reference, that it must, one thinks, be in its nature eternal. For a circle is endless when all you can do is traverse its finite circumference. The truth may set you free. But there is a form of cynically blatant truth-telling that is as good a deception as lying ever gets to be. Such brazenness is to truth, we might say, as pornography is to faithful sex. As with the one so with the other, nothing is hidden; the blatancy, precisely in its explicitness, does the work that hiding cannot. Thus is the Pardoner's prologue a succinct allegory of the psychology and epistemology of the condemned in Dante's Hell. It is the *contrapasso* of the ethical by way of the *contrapasso* of self-knowledge. Hell is where Pardoners and other such are forever at home. As Sartre says, here there is "no exit." One by one Dante's sinners tell their own tales; one after the other they are at once wholly honest and utterly cynical in the manner of their telling. Being self-entrapped there can be no escape. Hell is necessarily eternal.

Hell As a Place

You might, if you are theologically skeptical enough, leave Dante's Hell at that, taking the general interpretative view that whether or not there is a Hell makes no difference to how we should read the *Comedy*. For talk about Hell would retain its moral weight even were we to limit ourselves to saying that, while there is always the Hell we create for ourselves, and while Dante's *Inferno* proposes an allegory of it as if it were a place, you don't need to think of it that way to get the moral point. That objection, however, is hoist by its own petard. *All* talk of Hell is in any case allegorical. What else could it be? It is the mere prejudice of an individualist mentality that would toss all talk about an infernal *place* into some merely metaphorical trashcan as if by contrast with it talk about a Hell in oneself had a superior, because *literal*, sense. As allegories go it is essential to retain the sense of Hell as a social place, as a regime of sin – as a place we are objectively in before ever it became a place subjectively in us. The problem with Dante's conceit even within the allegory is that it remains hard to know with any degree of theological consistency what to make of Dante's description of himself as traveling in and through Hell while, not having died, he does not belong there forever condemned. For, being a place wherein you are forever as one condemned, is essential to its being Hell.

Dante's visiting Hell, his being "in" Hell but not "of" it, has a distinctively purgatorial character. And in that comprehensiveness with which its structural geography is described, and in its precision of detail, it is unprecedented – even Virgil's own pre-Christian journey through Hades in book 6 of the *Aeneid*, more so Langland's, Milton's, and Bunyon's Christian infernal narratives, are perfunctory by comparison. And for all of these, including Dante, Hell is a place essentially of eternal punishment, which means that Dante's being in Hell for a fixed time becomes intrinsically problematic, needing a theological explanation of its own. For Dante is not there in the way those are who are forever condemned by their refusal to repent; but neither is he there in the way that those holy women and men of ancient Israel were who, having died before the death and resurrection of Christ, can truthfully be said to have been "in" Hell for the nonce, but never "of" it by way of their personal deserts. They, at least, are there but not as eternally condemned. Thomas Aquinas and Dante seem to be of one mind as to the nature of the presence in Hell of the pre-Christian saints of Israel before they were released from it on Holy Saturday. "Before the coming of Christ," Aquinas says, "the holy Fathers [of the Hebrew Scriptures] were in a worthier place than that in which those souls [dwell] who after death are now being purged [of their sins] for they experience no bodily pain." In other words, though they are not eternally punished in Hell, they are not in Purgatory either, for "their place is adjoined to Hell, or even perhaps is in Hell itself: otherwise, when Christ descended to Limbo he could not be said to have 'descended into Hell.'"[28]

This, Aquinas explains, is what we have to say about the postmortem condition of the saints of the Old Law prior to their being released on Holy Saturday. For though they are in Hell it is for them no place of punishment, they truly are, after all, holy women and men, and personally they deserve none. But though not punished they are as yet unable to enjoy their desire's rest. They cannot be wholly happy while the achievement of their final goal is yet denied them, for not yet is there any world corresponding with their holiness that they may enter. Therefore, the final achievement of the happy destiny they have been promised, Heaven, awaits the saving action of the Cross and resurrection of Christ – for their virtue cannot be *meritorious* until that time.[29] In principle this solution secures the general point of theological doctrine in that it

---

[28] *Supplement to Summa theologiae*, 3a, appendix: *Quaestio de Purgatorio* a2 *corp.*

[29] *Supplement to Summa theologiae*, q. 69 a4 *corp.*

allows the theological possibility of what Dante thought Scripture affirms, namely that there were at that point some "in Hell" though they were there in hope, awaiting release. Their condition is therefore anomalous, for their presence in Hell is temporary, conditional, and not without hope, whereas it is in Hell's nature to be unconditional, final, and with hope abandoned. The theological problem is that consistency would seem to require that, wherever they are, it is not Hell if their confinement there is not eternal and hopeless.[30]

Thus far Dante seems to be of a mind with Aquinas. In canto 12 of *Inferno*, Dante encounters in the seventh circle of Hell a rampart reduced to rubble. Virgil is unable fully to explain its collapse to Dante because the destruction had happened since the last time he had been there, and so it is as new to him as it is to Dante; all he knows is that some powerful earthquake had destroyed the confining walls in that place and that some souls were thus dramatically rescued who in justice had no business being there at all, for they were "the stolen treasure of its highest place," seized by Satan who denied them their proper reward in paradise. "Moments before," that time

---

[30] Theologically what is needed is a third category, that of the virtuous, unbaptized adult pagans or Christian children who die before their baptism. In *Inferno* 4.30, Dante mentions the fate of unbaptized babies but seems to show small interest in the curious doctrine of Limbo as being the place where all such are. I was brought up on the penny catechism that offered Limbo as a solution to the problem, but that solution never made it into the authorized teaching of any Christian church. When I asked Herbert McCabe his view on the matter of unbaptized babies, he replied that he didn't know what was their fate, but what he did know was that God loves them infinitely more than their parents did or could.

> a tremor in every part
> Disturbed these fetid depths. The universe
> Must then, I think, have felt that love through which
> > It often turns (so some suppose) to chaos.
> At that same point, these age-old crags were rent
> And left both here and elsewhere as they are.[31]

Virgil, of course, is unbaptized, a virtuous pagan, and because his virtue is of a merely human kind he is ignorant of the theological significance of that harrowing of Hell when on Holy Saturday the risen Christ burst in upon it in retrieval of the holy men and women of Israel from the power of Satan. Virgil can know of that event only in the general terms of the chaos and disruption that the intervention of a perfect love once visited upon Hell's violent regime. Nonetheless, if only at a general level and while not knowing its name, Virgil does understand the dynamic of that disruptive power of love, for he sees that Hell itself in its very construction and in its nature is a sort of general *contrapasso*, a cosmic inversion. Hell turns the real upside down. If you are condemned to be in Hell then for all eternity perforce you see all things hellishly, including both Hell itself and the judgment which placed you there. For if stuck within those infernal conditions then infernal perceptions of them are entailed, and upon entering Hell the condemned are told that having chosen a love of their own they have rejected the "Primal Love" and must forever live with that rejection, their choices have been wholly defined by it.[32] Hell consists in their

---

[31] *Inferno* 12.40–45.   [32] *Inferno* 3.6.

knowing the nature of their rejection and in knowing that Hell is that rejection's regime, it is sin's order, it is the geography and the corresponding architecture of sin. And that is why the presence irrupting into it of a perfect love, retrieving its own from their captivity therein inevitably takes the inverse form of a destructive earthquake, the paradoxical truth being the reverse of Hell's self-misperceptions. For love's intervention reveals Hell's order to be in truth nothing but a vicious anarchy, the apparent order of its regime to be entirely bogus. Hell is disorder regnant.

At any rate, this result of an historical irruption of love into Hell was inevitable, Virgil adds, "as some suppose" – the "some" in question being philosophers of the atomistic school of Empedocles. For Empedocles maintained, as Kirkpatrick explains, "that the existence of created forms depended upon the constant collision of streams of atomic particles. On this view violence is essential for the existence of all we know," violence being the cause of all order, that "order" being no more than the uneasy parallelogram of equal and opposite violent forces held in equilibrium. Of such a Hobbesian kind is the infernal cosmology, and it is, Kirkpatrick adds, such "that any touch of love would" unbalance that violent equilibrium and "paradoxically reduce the world to chaos."[33]

Dante's Hell, then, considered as an order, as a regime, is in that sense "Empedoclean" in that it is the very articulation of violence: Hell is the politics of the Pardoner, emptiness as order, self-knowledge as self-destruction, sinfulness as polis. It is therefore that parody of order of

---

[33] *Inferno* 12, see Kirkpatrick's comment in his edition of *Inferno*, p. 360.

which alone sin is capable. And so, in as much as it is an order at all, it is but a centrifugal explosion of multiple hatreds held in precarious tension by the superior centripetal counterforce of Satan's repression. Hell is an assembly of psychopaths parading as regime, an assembly governed by the violence of the supreme psychopath, who is Satan.

The souls in Hell of those pre-Christian saints and prophets who are by prophetic anticipation destined to be saved, are in that sense "in it but not of it." For their presence in Hell is a destabilizing force of love that threatens disorder because, just men and women as they are, they are there temporarily and anomalously in a place whose nature is essentially eternal. Because they do not belong there, Hell cannot forever contain them. But although Dante too is in Hell, and though likewise he is passing through, his presence in Hell cannot be understood in the same terms as explain the presence in Hell of the holy men and women of the Old Law, not least because though his is a body "*of* death," as St. Paul puts it, his being not yet actually dead makes his premortem presence there impossible. For as Jesus said of the rich man in Hell, he may not return to earth to warn his brethren of the eternal price they must pay for their injustice to the poor. He has Abraham tell this "Dives"[34] – he has no name, he is *any* rich man – that there is a great chasm set between him in Hell and his family and friends in the world, "and that no one may cross over from there to us."

---

[34] Luke 16:19–31: The significance of the rich man being nameless (he disappears into his wealth) and the poor man being named (Lazarus has nothing but his own self) is entirely lost if "Dives" is treated as if a proper name.

And on the same grounds, Dante's literary anticipation premortem of death's requirement that is the condition of any journey to Hell is theologically impossible, ruled out on its own theological terms, in a way that no appeal to allegory can amend. Dante's theological dilemma is that he writes as if of a journey through Hell and out the other end of it, though the Hell he describes in such vivid detail is such that in principle you could not just pass through. For what you can visit and pass through can't be Hell. It's Hell only if you are condemned to be there for all eternity. Otherwise, it is Purgatory.

Therefore, Dante is faced with a theological dilemma unresolved by his spectacularly convincing narration of his journey through Hell. For the one part it seems that his journey may not be understood as only an imaginative psychological trip of his own contained within the scrutiny of his own individual moral experience, as if, that is, Dante is but visiting a place in *himself* where he feels condemned. Dante's Hell cannot in that way be reduced to no more than a place of bad conscience, the journey through it but a subjective bad trip. For his personal sin bears the weight of world-historical evil that has buried itself deep within him personally and within all human beings objectively, an evil that is embedded in a world, in a regime, of which he is a citizen. Therefore, Hell must have a politics. For the other part, then, Dante must imagine taking the journey that Virgil calls upon him to undertake even though such a journey is in principle inconceivable. And that inconceivability is not on account of its own inherent impossibility – though we will come to that question in Chapter 3 – but because even if it could exist it could not be Hell if, not being dead, you could visit it. You can't make a short-term trip to a place whose hellishness requires its eternity. Therefore, the imaginative ploy that is demanded by the nature of Hell's sin requires that visiting the place is impossible.

Here, then, we are faced with what necessarily is a fiction, the fiction of an impossible journey through Hell, that finds in Hell's very impossibility a truth buried in the imaginative construction of its counterfactual "as if" – the fiction of sin as if it were an independent, self-standing, regime. And that theological truth has to do with the nature of true repentance as distinct from an eternity of remorse, with the nature of a certain kind of redeeming self-knowledge, with a strategy of inhabiting your sins in such a way that, like Dante, you travel through them all one by one without at the same time infernally indulging them, but rather in repentance. For whether or not belief in Hell's eternity can be sustained, the imagination of it describes the would-be world created by a sinful consciousness, and, leaving the possibility or impossibility of Hell on one side, the imagination of Hell as a regime of sin, as a *polis*, a place with its circles and ramparts, a place with a diabolical structure of power distribution, is a theological necessity.

What to Make of Hell: Aquinas

What, then, are we to make of theological doctrines of Hell? And what are we to make of Dante's text, the cantica that is *Inferno*, the story of his journey through Hell?

As to the first question, the rarely challenged theological position in Dante's own times and places was that the conjunction of hope of Heaven and the possibility of unending despair in Hell and of the judgment whereby every person is assigned forever in the one or the other, is required by Scripture and tradition and is consistent: You can and should hold to the conjunction. And Dante in the *Comedy* takes that general belief for granted, where it becomes expanded in coherence and detail beyond all precedent.

For the one part, it was commonly agreed in Dante's time that on this side of death you could never be certain of how your life will be finally judged and where you will find yourself ultimately going. What is certain is that it won't be just on *your* say-so. For though, as Aquinas says, to be in a perfect state of grace guarantees entry into Heaven, and were you to be in that state you would know it, this side of death a perfect state of grace is not to be had; whereas, on the other side, you could die in a state of mortal sin only if you knew it, for honest subjective ignorance of one's sin's being mortal will excuse.[35] Such is how things stood in Dante's times within most Christian traditions East and West, Thomas Aquinas following the general consensus.[36]

But if the hope of Heaven and the fear of Hell correct one another and each balance the other out, still their relationship has also been uneasy, and in our own times they have come to seem theologically quite problematic. In fact, so difficult does it seem in theological circles today that for some, on the traditional Catholic side

---

[35] For further discussion of Aquinas on the conditions of entry into Paradise, see Chapter 5.

[36] In *2 Corinthios* 12, in *Saint Thomas Aquinas and Peter of Tarantaise: Commentary on the Letters of St Paul to the Corinthians*, Latin text and English trans. F. R. Larcher, B. Mortensen, and D. Keating, ed. J. Mortensen and E. Alarcón, Lander, WY: Aquinas Institute for the Study of Sacred Doctrine, 2012, section 445, p. 589.

Hans Urs von Balthasar,[37] and on the evangelical Protestant side Karl Barth,[38] such stark, unqualified forms of belief in an eternal judgment possibly condemning some to an eternity in Hell have become too hard to take, and both propose an uncomfortable settlement with the tradition. There is Hell, both say, because Scripture and those long traditions that include Dante, tell us so. But there is "probably" no one in it, says Von Balthasar weakly; for sure it is empty, says Barth more decisively. In either case there is compromise, and though you can understand why they say such things, it is unconvincing, falling somewhere between on the one hand the full-blown "infernalist" teaching that there is Hell and that there are at least some who upon death are there for ever after, and on the other the "universalist" case, according to which somehow, at least in the long run, all will be saved, and though there are in the meantime many hells to be endured whether this side of death or on the other side of it, none is eternal, none wholly devoid of hope.

Truly it is hard to know where to start with the currently emerging disagreements on the matter of Hell, but the least convincing narrative would seem to be Von Balthasar's "probably" – there *is* a place of eternal

---

[37] "If we take our faith seriously and respect the words of Scripture, we must resign ourselves to admitting ... an ultimate possibility (of eternal damnation), our feelings of revulsion notwithstanding. We may not simply ignore such a threat; we may not easily dismiss it, neither for ourselves nor for any of our brothers and sisters in Christ." Hans Urs von Balthasar, *Dare We Hope that All Men Be Saved? With a Short Discourse on Hell*, San Francisco: Ignatius Press, 1988, p. 237.

[38] See Karl Barth, *The Faith of the Church: A Commentary on the Apostle's Creed According to Calvin's Catechism*, trans. Gabriel Vahanian, ed. Jean-Louis Leuba, New York: Meridian, 1963, pp. 171–174.

damnation but probably there is no one in it. In general terms more intelligible, if only because it is at least consistent, is the position of the traditional majority that includes Dante, that as Thomas Aquinas has it, death is itself the judgment call: It is not just *upon* death that the story of your life is wrapped up. Death itself does the wrapping, all possible choices in life having already been made, the options covered; and when presented with your life's fundamental orientation, whether toward good or toward evil, in death it is settled with absolute finality.[39] That, Aquinas says, is to do with the very meaning of death: Death is the story told, over and done with, and once thus told in its final version it is free of room for doubt, free of self-ignorance, and, perhaps above all, free of life's self-deceptions. Hence death's judgment is beyond revision. For as the lesson of Chaucer's Pardoner's self-enclosed blatancy tells us, there is nothing in the character of those who are in Hell that allows room for their thinking, acting, or even willing, outside death's finite boundaries. Then, as that grim and relentless thirteenth-century hymn, the *Dies irae* of Jacopone da Todi, has it, you are presented with the book in which your life's final truth is told. It is a mirror holding your life up before your naked eye, for *this* is you, the *real* you, once and for all unmasked. It is the *liber scriptus proferetur*, the book in its final edition, *in quo totum continetur*, containing the whole of your life written out in full, nothing being omitted, nothing quietly edited out in the interests of a preferred self-image, there are no explanatory footnotes submitted in qualification, there is no appendix in

---

[39] Is the case of Trajan an exception? See Chapter 3, n. 29.

which you can claim that you didn't really mean it, no process of appeal in mitigation, for this book contains the record of your true intentions. Therein is the plain story, with nothing else except an index, headlining the book's contents, listing the names of the sins not repented that got you there. Thus, also, Dante's *Inferno*.

Would we be surprised at that outcome? In this connection, if in no other, Dante's *Inferno* can be seen as the imaginative narration of the formal theology of Aquinas, spelling out as story what Aquinas states as doctrine; and Dante imagines that if upon death it is Hell where you are to go it won't surprise you one bit. When in the end the awful clarifying truth is revealed, you will get it. For all that Francesca da Rimini and Paolo, damned for their lustful passion, hate without reserve their life yoked together for ever in Hell, they know they are where they belong, and, for all that they curse the outcome they know that justice has been served; whereas Piccarda Donati, called by vocation to be a consecrated virgin and forced by her family into an unwilling marriage, can scarcely credit her place in Heaven, such has been her life on earth. She is astonished. She feels rescued, snatched from the jaws. That is why she can calmly utter those words of acceptance, *e'en la sua volontade è nostra pace*: "it is in his will that is our peace." Free of envious comparison, her happiness may be smaller, but it is complete, as a smaller glass does not envy a larger when both are full.[40]

Your death, Aquinas says, tells your story, then, and in its final edition; or to put it in other terms, it tells you what you have really wanted, in that very

---

[40] *Paradiso* 3.43–57.

fundamental sense of the word "want" that is discoverable only when dug out from beneath the dense and tangled undergrowth of make-believe, fantasy desires, and self-deceptions. Dante thinks the same. You go where your life's story's end cuts through that undergrowth whether of false self-excuse or of false self-accusation, to the final truth that names where in the end you have wanted to go; and in one of the most dramatic ways of imagining the story of judgment, Catherine of Genoa in the early sixteenth century said that upon your death you are presented with three doors, opening into Hell, Purgatory, and Heaven; and wherever you go it is in no one's hands but yours. You will know which door to enter, for it is the total impetus of your desire that tells you, your death having cast the die.[41] It's a harsh conclusion, and it can seem a puzzle, even unfair, that just as there are last minute deathbed conversions that will save us, such as that of Buonconte da Montefeltro who is safe in Purgatory,[42] so conversely last-minute betrayals can catch us out in a final failure of repentance, as was the friar Guido da Montefeltro who is snatched by Satan from the hands of St. Francis who would have had him in Heaven, the fact that he had lived well enough before being of no avail to him.[43] How in justice, we ask, might a bad end mete out the final catastrophic judgment of Hell for eternity on a life lived for the most part at least moderately well, but caught out in a single momentary,

---

[41] *Purgation and Purgatory*, in Catherine of Genoa, *Purgation and Purgatory* and *Spiritual Dialogue*, trans and notes, Serge Hughes, London: SPCK, 1979, pp. 76–77.
[42] *Purgatorio* 5.88–108.   [43] *Inferno* 27.112–120.

accidentally mistimed, and uncharacteristic act of deliberate evil? The logic of Jesus's reply seems remorseless: "be you ready," Matthew's Gospel commands, for death comes "as a thief in the night."[44] And that seems to have meant that if it is but once that you have carelessly left a window unlatched it may be just then that you are burgled, for all that you have habitually taken care safely to lock the doors. It *is* rough, Jesus seems to say, but it's the justice delivered by your death, and as to that you were warned that you would not know the day or the hour of it.

So, Aquinas says, there is Hell. And in works early,[45] and in works late,[46] he is remorseless as he spells out how we must conceive of it. Hell exists in one of the more readily understood senses of the word "exists," for it is a real, physical, place: It has to be, he thinks, because human persons are kept there, and human beings are not persons if they are not present to one another in their bodies.[47] It is for this reason that he says in his *Commentary* on *I Corinthians* 15, that though the continuing existence postmortem of my soul is necessary for my survival after death it is not sufficient, *quia anima mea non est ego*, "I am not my soul"; and "were only my soul to survive death, then I would not," adding that a surviving soul is

---

[44] Matthew 24:43.
[45] *Summa theologiae*, 3a *Supplementum*, qq. 86, 94, 97–99. Note that the *Supplementum* to the *Summa theologiae* is an addition to the mature text that Aquinas failed to complete, put together after his death from earlier writings, in this case from the *Commentary on the Sentences* of Peter Lombard.
[46] *Compendium theologiae*, translation by Cyril Vollert SJ, Manchester, NH: Sophia Institute Press, 1947.
[47] *Compendium theologiae*, chapter 154.

"not I, nor *any* other person,"[48] no person at all.[49] And as to the nature of my body postmortem, there are theologians, he says, who do but "fancifully prattle"[50] and, so as to avoid the rigor of his earthy realism, speculate that maybe after death we have ethereal, nonmaterial bodies or some such. "Not so," he insists, for whatever my existence after death may be, in the final resurrection I will then "resume a human body made up of flesh and bones, it will be equipped with the same organs it now possesses,"[51] and it will be a body materially continuous with the body in which I lived before death. It is because those who are condemned to Hell are embodied persons that they can suffer from bodily fire and, he says, so they do.[52]

All that seems thus far to be coherent and rigorously consistent but also, and, most importantly, it has the merit of requiring theologies of the afterlife to work within a true understanding of death, one which takes death seriously. Death's judgment is indeed final and conclusive. But then comes the difficult part. All of us, saints as some few are, deadly sinners as unknown numbers are, and morally dull mediocrities – that's the rest of us – we will all live forever and one way or another bear the responsibility of our life's record, and, for repentant or unrepentant alike, at death the judgment of life is fixed not just for

---

[48] *In I Corinthios* 15, n. 924.
[49] That means: "they have the same identity as ..." Aquinas obviously doesn't mean that their *condition* postmortem is the same as their condition premortem. *Summa theologiae*, 3a *Supplementum* q79 aa 1 and 2.
[50] *Compendium theologiae*, chapter 153.
[51] *Compendium theologiae*, chapter 153.
[52] *Summa theologiae*, 3a *Supplementum*, q70 a3 *corp*.

then but unchangeably *for all eternity*. For those deepest dispositions of will by which we are judged are capable of change, may respond to new states of affairs, and more precisely remain capable of conversion and of obedience to existential choice, only *within* a time-bound life before death, for within life before death alone is there that indeterminacy of conditions that allows for choice. That is why in death the outcome is settled once and for all, not, that is, on account of some arbitrary decree of an omnipotent divine will, still less as deriving from God's vindictive and insatiable desire for ultimate punishment, but simply because of death itself, because of what death *is*. You may make light of death's finality in the way some do – Socrates in Plato's *Phaedo* for example – who think of death as no more than the blessed release of the soul from its exile in the body's captivity; otherwise, the alternative would seem to require Aquinas's conclusion that death ends all choices and fixes just one outcome for each, and that there are no further options, so that it is in life before death that anything determining eternal outcomes happens. From that point on the logic remorselessly carries all before it until it gets to that point where Von Balthasar and Barth stall and ask: *Can* this be true? Is it even possible? And that is the point at which Aquinas draws the conclusion that this destiny of the unrepentant sinner is irreversible, the pain and despair of a soul in Hell are in their nature eternal, as is the Pardoner's, who has emptied for himself the very language of repentance, having foreclosed all possibility of honest forgiveness by means of the transparency of a blatant, systematic, lie. How does Dante's *Comedy* stand in relation to this tradition?

3
Inferno as Anti-narrative

Is This True?

The theologian asks, can the theology of Hell on the accounts of Aquinas and Dante be true? The reader of *Inferno* asks, is Dante's narrative true only on condition that there actually exists a Hell of the kind that he and Aquinas describe, a place of eternal punishment for those who die, unrepentant, in sin?

An immediate reason for asking arises from the case proposed in David Bentley Hart's *That All Shall be Saved*,[1] in which in an intemperate polemic he declares there is not and could not be any such eternal damnation as Aquinas describes formally,[2] or as Dante's *Inferno* tells of it in the narrative of his journey through Hell.[3] Hart rules out doctrines of eternal damnation in Hell on the grounds that it is in flagrant inconsistency with Christian faith, perhaps the weightiest argument for that inconsistency being that doctrines of eternal punishment have no warrant in the New Testament sources;[4] and then, on moral

---

[1] David Bentley Hart, *That All Shall Be Saved*, New Haven, CT: Yale University Press, 2019.
[2] Ibid., pp. 19–20.   [3] Ibid., pp. 21ff.
[4] Ibid., pp. 92–129. To show that there is no positive support in Scripture for an "infernalist" doctrine of Hell is not by itself to show that Scripture rules such a doctrine out. Hart attaches little weight, and certainly no decisive weight, to the fact that almost uniformly the Western Church has taught some doctrine of eternal punishment of unrepentant sinners, as, for the most part, have the Eastern Churches.

terms, on the ground that belief in eternal condemnation in Hell and in a God who condemns unrepentant sinners to an everlasting stay therein displays a casually vicious cast of mind that, he thinks, better spirits even some among card-carrying Western Christian traditionalists don't in any serious way truly believe – witness the theological embarrassments of Hans Urs Von Balthasar and Karl Barth and others, at the thought of such doctrines.

But what is more to the point in raising these questions about Hell and judgment, is that Hart believes those teachings in their different formulations in Aquinas and Dante to be not only false, nor only testimony to a morally repugnant cast of mind and spirit projected upon a morally repugnant God; they are also simply incoherent and describe nothing that could possibly exist.[5] In short, Hart raises a critical question about the overall conceptions of divine justice that are proposed formally by Aquinas and are embodied concretely in Dante's narrative. My question is: *Were* Hart right in all this would that reduce to zero any theological interest in Dante's *Inferno*? Would the first cantica of the *Comedy* fail and hopelessly mislead theologically? And if so, would not

---

At the best, his argument that the scriptural texts adduced in support of traditional infernalism offer alternative noninfernalist interpretations is plausible, but hardly decisive. And what little he has to say by way of his peremptory rejection of Thomas Aquinas's teaching on Hell misses the point, that, for Aquinas, it is the *finality of death* as such that determines the outcome in eternity, not some arbitrary and merely willful divine decree. Generally speaking the least plausible critique of Aquinas's position is that it derives from some merely voluntaristic account of the exercise of divine will – though see note 28.

[5] Though that, of course, should mean that infernalism doesn't say enough coherently to be *even* false, as $2+2=5$ isn't false, the result of bad counting, it's just meaningless.

the poetic and theological purposes of the *Comedy* fall apart upon its first step?

Hart seems to think that in all three ways *Inferno* fails. The tragedy of the first cantica, he says, lies precisely in its powerfully imaginative reconstruction of that inherently vicious but also impossible terminal outcome of eternal torture for at least some members of the human race. Dante-author has Dante-pilgrim together with Virgil travel through Hell from top to bottom, observing its occupants and enumerating in detail their cruel and unusual punishments in an imaginative narrative that in many ways corresponds with Aquinas's formal teachings. Such teachings, whether poetically narrated or formally defended, cause Hart to ascribe to Dante-poet and to Aquinas-theologian alike – and therefore to their God – a moral sensibility that descends to levels so wretchedly cruel and morally perverted as to situate their imaginative powers and its work in that very place deep in the bowels of Hell to which Dante himself assigns the mythical Ulysses in canto 26 of *Inferno*; and there the poetic conceit itself manifests the same mentality it condemns in the very act of its description. On this account, Dante's *Inferno* is a story told on terms that are the same, but inverted, as those of Chaucer's Pardoner. For to believe in Dante's Hell of endless torment is already to inhabit the mental world of which *Inferno* is the fictional realization: The only Hell is in the belief in the minds of the likes of Aquinas and Dante. And their infernalisms are themselves pathological.

In that canto 26 of *Inferno* Dante describes the fate of the false counsellors, and in particular the fate of those who have betrayed the moral responsibilities of intellect itself. We could say that at stake in this canto are the values of the writers, the poets, the scientists, the historians, the philosophers, the theologians, and so, very typically, the values of the academics, of university people – more generally, then, of intellectuals. Ulysses is the intellectual's antitype: He sets out, Dante tells us, on a journey, on just the same quest on which the intellectuals have embarked, in search for "all knowledge and virtue" – our *universitas* – but in such a way as to betray the values he seeks in the very manner of his seeking them. Ulysses' voyage is a value-free fantasy, frivolously disengaging intellectual pursuits from any moral purpose – fittingly Dante has him reduced in Hell to a flickering flame, a fickle and cold light, a wonderfully precise image of us professors when we have surrendered to the ideal type of a morally rootless intellect and have become false counsellors. For in this endeavor of knowledge Ulysses ventures out beyond the ends of the earth and further out into uncharted waters, into an unpeopled universe, into a world, as Ulysses himself says, that is *sanza gente*, "where no one dwells" – such is an intellect torn away from its responsibilities owed to wider communities. This is not some vapid case against the abstraction required of specialization. But it is a case against the knowledge and virtue that Ulysses seeks having in this way been ripped up by their true roots in a repentant community of fellows, and, in his pursuit of this lonely Promethean quest, in his having ruthlessly abandoned all the responsibilities he owes to others, above all to his wife Penelope and their children, he is lost with all hands in a whirlpool of morally and intellectually empty ambition.

One might well think the opposite of what Hart credits to Dante, and that Dante tells of Ulysses' fate for a crucial reason of his own as poet-author of the *Comedy* and that is precisely in order to *distinguish* his own quest as poet from that of Ulysses, because he does need to know how to pursue that quest on altogether different terms, on terms of moral and spiritual responsibility that he will finally learn only from Beatrice as the climax of a painful journey through Purgatory. Only then will he be able to represent his journey of writing as being but a passing *through* Hell and out on the other side of it, if shocked to the core at what he has witnessed, himself morally unscathed by the experience.

But in truth, asks Hart, can Dante-author come out of his *Inferno* himself unscathed by what he has described therein? Hart's polemic would have us believe that Dante's narrative is itself an infernalism *about* the infernal, it is the authorial equivalent of Chaucer's utterly cynical Pardoner, Dante's *Inferno* being swallowed up in the same moral whirlpool that he describes Ulysses as having been swept into. For Dante's story of Hell – just in his believing it to be conceivable that the divine will would commit anyone at all to interminable pain therein – ascribes to the divine a mentality and judgment that belongs only within the Hell that it describes. And so, as one might say in the spirit of Hart's critique, Dante's God who condemns some to Hell, and the Satan who rules in sullen silence in the Hell God has made, have merged into one another in a shared debased narrative of the demands of justice and love. Thus do all distinctions between Dante and Ulysses, in particular the crucial distinction in respect of the moral character of their respective quests for all knowledge and virtue, disappear. And were that true then Dante's *Inferno* would deserve the same judgment that is sometimes visited upon Milton's *Paradise Lost*, namely of having in effect eliminated any other distinction between God and Satan than that of God's being in possession of an infinite degree of the same purely arbitrary and deeply amoral power that, if only in finite and diminished terms, Satan himself possesses.

Hart has caught *Inferno* in a very tight theological vice, though the theological and biblical grounds for his critique of the doctrines of eternal punishment in Hell need not concern us directly. Nonetheless, it must concern us whether Dante's literary imagination does truly depend directly upon a moral disposition so evilly perverted as Hart believes it to be. Does it? May we read *Inferno* on any other terms than those on which Hart judges it theologically?

Truth by Way of Counterfactual Fictions

Let us start again with Dante's narrative of a journey through Hell, and with a question about the nature of truth and falsity as relevant to fictional stories. What we need to know is whether, as narratives go, Dante's *Inferno* meets the minimum conditions required for a truthful one. I have in mind once again the sort of issue raised by Charles Singleton when he said of the *Comedy* that it is the construction of the fiction that it is not a fiction. At one level Singleton's point is trivial: after all, such is a general truth about any fictional narrative. It is true even of some impossible narratives, like *Gulliver's Travels*, in which the people Gulliver meets are either too short to exist, as are those in Lilliput, or else are impossibly tall, as in Brobdingnag. And as for the *Comedy*, even were it false to say that there is an existent interminable condition called Hell, the construction of a narrative describing it could be a defensible and illuminating thing to do; for a certain kind of improbable narrative, a demonstrably false narrative, and even a palpably impossible one, may be justified precisely in the light of the demands specific to truthful narration. As my friend and colleague in Princeton University, Philip Pettit, once said,[6] there may be a good test of the quality of a philosopher's argument in the quality of the novel that corresponds with it, in the plausibility of its correlative narrative. I suppose that on this account Sartre's novelette *La Nausée*, and perhaps even more so his terse little play *Huis Clos*, do stand in some such relationship of verification to the incontinently wordy *Being and Nothingness*, perhaps in the same way that Camus's *The Outsider* stands more concisely to his *Myth of Sisyphus*, or George Eliot's *Middlemarch* to her reductively Feuerbachian account of religion. And as, conversely, if you hadn't got Noam Chomsky's famous review to pull you back from the brink of the crude behaviorism of B. F. Skinner's *Verbal Behavior*,[7] you would be able to tell for yourself what was wrong with it from his truly awful novel-form rendering of it in *Walden Two*: The narrative's badness on its own is evidence enough against the

---

[6] When in the late 1960s we were colleagues in philosophy at University College, Dublin. Now that he is Professor of Philosophy at Princeton University, we are colleagues once more.

[7] B. F. Skinner, *Verbal Behavior*, Englewood Cliffs, NJ: Prentice Hall, 1957. See Noam Chomsky's famous review of Skinner's book, "BF Skinner's Verbal Behavior," *Language*, 35, no. 1 (1959), pp. 26–38.

philosophy it fictionalizes.[8] For if there are very few novels that are in some way direct products of their corresponding philosophies there are many that are tests of the plausibility of implied philosophical underpinnings precisely in the degree to which they succeed or fail to convince as narratives. And as to Dante's *Inferno*, notwithstanding Hart's arguments from Scripture and from his general moral rejection of doctrines of Hell, its character as an anti-narrative (as we might call it) would still serve a critical purpose. For while anti-narratives make a story of what is not so, sometimes even of what cannot be so and why, they do so in such a way as to disclose something that you wouldn't otherwise be able to see about what *can* be and about what there actually *is*. In short, we might be able to see the point of the *Inferno* as an anti-narrative whether there is a Hell in fact or not.

Anti-narratives

Anti-narratives abound in variety across a wide spectrum, and here I abbreviate the diversity to just three general types, one revealingly benign, the other two revealingly destructive. Benign is the story of the Fall of Adam and Eve in the book of Genesis, of which Christian exegetes from Origen in the third century to our times have known the formal impossibility, given that its narrative structure is self-contradictory. Nor is the contradiction hidden, merely implied. It is there on the surface, obvious for

---

[8] There is a good case for saying that the very possibility of the novel form, structuring in so many different ways as it does ineliminable dimensions of subjectivity and objectivity, is dependent on Skinner's behaviorism being false.

all to see. How, asks Origen, could Adam and Eve have experienced even the temptation to seek the "knowledge of good and evil" unless they had been in possession of that knowledge in the first place, still less possible being their having given in to the temptation in the event?[9] At one level the contradiction is simple and obvious: You must have already conceded to the fallen condition if you are to be tempted by sin's apparently better prospects.

Of course, you can't always formally resolve an apparent contradiction of such a kind; but that need not matter, for you can sometimes narrate one away, as the French theoretical anthropologist Claude Levi-Strauss said Genesis does, and sometimes that is *all* you can do. The lesson of Genesis is, he said, clear: There can be no consistent narrative account of the origins of sin, since any explanation of sin's origin – any account, that is, of a *first* sin – must presuppose that fallenness as a prior condition of its being committed, that being the reason why some will say that it is unbridled freedom of choice between good and evil that is truly "original," and that, given it, sin is inevitable.[10] Not that it was Levi-Strauss's purpose to

---

[9] *On First Principles* IV, 3, in *Origen Selected Works*, trans. and intro. Rowan Greer, New York: Paulist Press, 1979, p. 189.

[10] Jean-Jacques Rousseau in his way said something similar: The Fall, as one might put it in a deliberately paradoxical phrase, is a "fall up" into a fully reflective humanity open to all the possibilities of action, not a fall down from it into the dehumanization of sin. On this account the story of the origin of the knowledge of good and evil is the story of a true human nature, or true human "experience," as William Blake was to put it, from a prehuman condition of naive "innocence." This amounts to a sort of "theodicy" of freedom: If you want freedom you need to pay its price, which is the Fall, sin. In Chapter 4 we will see that Dante's understanding of sin represents the order of causality the other way round: It is sin that motivates the quest for just that false conception of freedom.

debunk the Genesis story; on the contrary, his point was show that you cannot just put it all down to some general proposition concerning a primordial freedom; for in its self-undermining character the Genesis story belongs with all such truly foundational and second-order stories that, told as if itself in a primitive first-order narrative, describes the origins and determining conditions of all subsequent first-order narratives. It is in the nature of the case that such narratives themselves presuppose the conditions of which they narrate the origin. And he argued that such is the way it is – and must be – with the narrative of the Fall. For its circularity goes with the character that such stories possess of being indeed *original*. Thus does Genesis tell a rattling good yarn that gets to a fundamental truth about human nature; but it is based on a contradiction that at one and the same time disguises and discloses the impossibility it contains. And for all that it is therefore a sort of self-refuting narrative it does a real job – that of illuminating by way of an impossible myth the foundational origins of a condition of human fallenness. And it does that job in the only way available, in an inevitable circularity that, because it is inevitable, is also benign.

In a similar way self-defeating but far from benign is the argumentative ploy of Thrasymachus in book 1 of Plato's *Republic*. What, Socrates had asked, is justice? "I will tell you," Thrasymachus retorts angrily, impatient with all talk of essences and definitions and foundations as is implied in Socrates's question; for, he says, justice is nothing materially constant, nothing definable in terms of given actions, for it is no more than the prevailing will of the strongest party, whatever that may be. In principle abstract definitions determining formal essences such as Socrates calls for are irrelevant. Worse than irrelevant, Thrasymachus adds, the pursuit of them is the last resort of the powerless seeking by way of appeal to the essential natures of things to wrest for themselves some control of their lives from the grip of the ruling classes – Thrasymachus is a sort of Nietzschean anti-essentialist *avant la lettre*, and in universities he is quite recognizable today. What answers to the definition of justice, they say, is not an essence that you could seek out in some spirit of objective inquiry, for there can be no such essence; nor in any way is it to be found otherwise than in the will of the de facto ruler, the one who as it happens has the power to define its content.

Justice, then, is exhibited only in a definition-defying tautology: *You* can't tell what justice is until there is someone powerful enough to enforce upon you *their* account of what it is, or you your account upon them. For to have any power at all to do a thing is to have more power than anyone else to do it, and, more specifically, to be in possession of first-order power is to be in possession of the second-order power to define what just power is. If rulers can successfully exert that power, then there is no more to justice than in their exercise of it. And if they can't do it then theirs is no justice, for there is no justice in impotence.

Plato's reply to this challenge takes him beyond book 1 of *Republic* into a further six books of Socratic argument – and extended as that argument is, it is worth noting here the general lines of it. Thrasymachus, Plato says, has proposed not so much a *morally unworthy* story of the republic's origins, though that is what Plato thinks indeed it is; nor does Plato respond to it by telling of *more adequately moral* foundations of a good society, not at first, though in due course he will; his first objection to Thrasymachus's brutal voluntarism is tactical and purely *ad hominem*: it is to deny him his merely willful attitudinizing. For all Thrasymachus's ranting on behalf of the superior will to power, in fact so vacuous is the tautology that defines it – you have *any* power only so long as you have *more* power than anyone else in relevantly similar circumstances – and so unstable in consequence is your hold on it – for everyone else's desire for power is a threat to the excess of yours over theirs – that his notion of power is far from establishing the possessor of it in preeminence; in truth it is the expression of a form of dependent weakness.

For, in a long sorites extending from *Republic* book 1 all the way up to book 7, Plato argues that the naked voluntarism of Thrasymachus's account of justice is conceivable at all only when in a manner that is self-defeating it is carried on the back of social stabilities guaranteed by other means and by other people. For in the absence of a stable social base in some sufficient proportion of the population, who, unlike the Thrasymachean ruler, have an interest in serving the interests of others for their sakes and not merely for their own, there is no social world within which the tyrant can exercise his power, nor can there be any power for the subject-peoples to subordinate themselves to. And in fact, the exercise of the Thrasymachean ruler's arbitrary and self-referring exceptionalism is itself parasitical in that it feeds off the conventional normality of the general, and it is powerless without that consenting social foundation. The tyrannical ruler is therefore like the thief who needs a stable property-owning society in which to carry out his theft, for without property assumed there is no stealing; he is like the adulterer who needs there to be an expectation of marital fidelity else there are no thrills to his faithlessness.

That being so, Socrates says, far from his possessing supreme political power, the power of the Thrasymachean tyrant is in fact utterly contingent and parasitical upon independent sources of social stability. When, therefore, in *Republic* book 2 Socrates invites Glaucon and Adeimantos to take up Thrasymachus's argument and to defend it in a calmer and more critically reflective way, their restated defense gets lost all the deeper in the self-refuting dilemma: For their defense rests on the proposition that the best form of life for me must be one in which I can count on everyone else subordinating their wills to the interests of the community, just so long as when they do it *I* don't. Were he, Glaucon says, to be in possession of the ring of Gyges that could render him invisible at will, such would be possible. But the point of what Plato demonstrates is, again, not that pure egoism extended universally is morally unworthy, or that there is in fact no Gyges's ring to be had; his point is that no society is possible at all on the basis that there is no more to it than the superior power of the tyrant, and in consequence no fixed theater on whose stage of routine moral convention he can play his arbitrary amoral part. Thrasymachus's is a fantasy of superior power impossible to exercise otherwise than in dependence on those prior conditions that others provide for him, those prior conditions being what he wills for others just so as not to have to will them for himself. The Thrasymachean "realism" is shown to be a fantasy just by its implications being clearly expounded.

Next, imagine a third anti-narrative that, like that of Thrasymachus, is far from benign, a narrative that likewise describes a state of affairs that is at once impossible and revealing. The logic of this sort of impossible conjunction is well articulated in one way in the person of Mozart's Don Giovanni and in more formal terms in Søren Kierkegaard's version of the same Don Juan in his *Fear and Trembling*.[11] For Kierkegaard's Don Juan is an entirely value-free person. He is not just *im*moral, though he will be when and where it suits him, just as he will act consistently with moral principles when that suits him; he is ideally *a*moral, careless of moral distinctions as such, and the word "moral" has a meaning for him only in scare quotes. Indeed, he, like the Thrasymachean tyrant, is not so much a person as an ideal type who is utterly without moral center of gravity, and, being altogether bereft of moral motivation, he is wholly shameless and incapable of remorse. And that is why, Kierkegaard says, there is no possible argument or motivation internal to his condition that can rescue him from it: He is forever fixed in it. Don Juan has no fixed ground on which even minimal moral levers can get a grip, for any reason Don Juan might have for behaving in accordance with a stabilizing and universally binding moral principle – for making the transition from his egoism to the minimum moral level of a Socrates, as Kierkegaard puts it – could not proceed from any motive available internal to the unmitigated egoism in which he is entirely enclosed, since just that motivation would subvert the moral motive supposedly derived from it. The principle here is that you can, on the

[11] In Søren Kierkegaard, *Fear and Trembling and the Sickness unto Death*, trans and notes, Walter Lowrie, intro. Gordon Marino, Princeton, NJ: Princeton University Press, 2013.

one hand, have a *self*-interested reason for acting in a way that in fact serves the interests of others, but such a reason gets you nowhere morally, its motivation of self-interest leaves you where you were, still stuck in your amoral rut. On the other hand, to have a reason that does get you from pure egoism to properly moral ought, a reason that gets you across the gap between the amoral libertine Don Juan and the morally principled Socrates, requires that you are already there, there being no bridges that can stretch across the existential gaps. For there is absolutely no such self-transcending openness within the enclosed, static, and morally empty world of Don Juan: You might say that he is pure psychopath. Only an unprecedented leap in the dark, Kierkegaard says, can get him to the other side. And that is why, if the condition of Don Juan can be taken to describe that of souls in Hell as Dante understands them, you would have to conclude with Sartre and Dante as to the inner nature of infernal logic. For both of them the hypothetical is valid: If there is a Hell then once in it there truly is, as Sartre says, "no exit," *Huis clos*. There is nothing in Hell to motivate a reason to be out of it.[12] If Hell is where you are going, Hell is where forever you are staying. There can be no non-eternal Hell.

Satan

Dante's *Inferno* is one of the most striking studies of evil, of its logic and of its psychology, in the whole of the

---

[12] Put in that way the proposition is a tautology: You describe Hell in such terms that there could not be any way out of it but only by construing its inhabitants as being so motivated that they could not *want* to be out of it.

Western canon. Dante in his own terms captures the logic of Hell's hypothetical perfectly: Once through the gates of Hell there can be no hope.[13] And because there is then no hope there is no possibility of moving forward, there are no possible leaps in the dark.[14] As to the infernal psychology, at the center of this Hell, its cause and victim, is the figure of Satan – a wonderfully impossible figure, impossible because he is the embodiment of a single, impossible, desire. Milton's *Paradise Lost* gives expression to that desire's impossibility in this its ultimate form when, thrust down to Hell by divine decree, Satan cries, "So farewell hope, and with hope farewell fear. | Farewell remorse: all good to me is lost; | Evil, be thou my good."[15]

Note here exactly what Milton's Satan says: He does not say, as a mortal human might, be *this* evil a good for me, may this adultery give me the missing pleasure, may this theft from the poor provide the financial security I seek for my billions' sake; and even the general defiance of our pathetically finite blasphemies is directed at a particular God. We humans are underperformers of evil because we are no angels, and the will for particular evils is all we are capable of within our limited agendas of evil action. Satan, though, wills the impossible, the infinite evil. Satan is not a simple sinner, a doer of this or that evil deed. Satan has one desire only, and that is to *displace* God

---

[13] *Inferno* 3.1–9.
[14] That is, unless appeal is made to an entirely arbitrary exercise of divine power to extract sinners from its clutches. If eternal existence in Hell is the natural outcome of a life lived then God's relieving people of the punishment that God created Hell to inflict upon them argues not for a merciful God but for a God hopelessly indecisive and pathetically incompetent, roughly Von Balthasar's.
[15] *Paradise Lost*, IV, lines 108–110.

and reverse the good. He is not to be satisfied with evil actions, howsoever many, not even spectacular world-historical evils on the scale of the Holocaust, for they too fall short of the evil that embodies a fallen angel's malice – they are focused campaigns of evil, too concrete, too particular, they are the targeted strategies that are the best humans can do in imitation of Satan. Satan is not just a *terribly* bad person, worse, say, than Hitler. Bad actions cannot be enough for Satan himself who demands a *universal* evil as the formal principle of his agency. Possibly the Holocaust is the nearest a particular human will get to a universal evil, and certainly as we know of such things it seems unsurpassably evil. But even the Holocaust stops short of a fallen *angel*'s defiance.

For if Satan seeks only the infinite evil his defiance is accordingly purely abstract and unconditional in character: He wants nothing at all that falls short of absolute evil, an evil that has not only no good consequences in fact but is intrinsically and intentionally without them, for he can will only to turn the tables on God absolutely, that is to say, not on anyone or anything in particular, not on any particular persons, states of affairs or conditions, but only in a formal defiance of the good itself. He is at the still center of Dante's Hell. There, the scope of Satan's desire is beyond even the dualistic aspiration of a Manichee – for the evil God of the Manichees wills to be an *alternative* God alongside and equal with the good God; and Satan's evil intent is the more absolute, since he not only denies the priority of the good but also all equality between good and evil. He wants to make the abstract unqualified evil to be the one and only true concrete. Satan therefore wills the reversal of the very order of existence itself and not merely to turn the moral world upside down with a bit, or even a lot, of very bad practice. Satan resents evil's being the subplot, its being no more than the privation of the good. Milton's Satan imitates Dante's, for their Satans want evil to be the real existent and the whole story and the good to be the fantasy. For that reason, Satan's desire is inherently impossible, what he desires has no possible object. For evil is essentially parasitical. And so is the devil, Dante capturing the logic of this with a characteristically telling image of an impotent Satan, no "roaring lion" he (as St. Peter had it) "seeking whom he may devour."[16] Dante's Satan is but a frozen, immobile, silent, sullen, cannibal, capable of nothing but the mastication of his own progeny. Dante's Satan is in fact the very opposite of the raging agent of evil. He is exactly as Dante has him, a being absolutely without agency. Paradoxically, there is nothing he can do, that is to say, he can do *only* nothing. For no agency is possible except in the light of some good to be done, and Satan would spurn all good. He is all impossible will. And because he is defined by his impossible will, Satan is impossible.

We human beings, hard as we might try, can't get to be that bad, we can manage only to be more or less evil, for not being angels we cannot achieve Satan's exalted level of pure evil desire. But we can absurdly wish for it. In every one of Dante's descending scales of *Inferno*'s evils, progressing in a downward sweep from Francesca and Paolo's lust in canto 5 to the malicious political hatreds of Ugolino and Archbishop Ruggieri in cantos 32–33, there is only the stale repetition of particular evils willed, the

[16] 1 Peter 1:8.

descending scales of Hell's evil marking variation only in the degree of malice, in the severity of the punishments, and in the ingenious savagery of the mind that devised them. Beyond that there are no true narratives *in* Hell because for those condemned souls within Hell memory has but one dimension: They can recount only the past. That is why their stories simply tail off – perhaps the most bitterly, hopelessly, inconclusive is Ugolino's, that culminates with the hint that, starving, he had fed on the corpse of his son before his own death. But none of them can have a resolution. For the condemned have no true future, nothing ever new, but only a single unchanging narrative within which they are forever trapped. Hell's is the true Nietzschean "eternal return." There is fascination for us in their stories, fascination in their degree of self-awareness, fascination too in Dante's construction of the vices into a downward spiral of progressive degrees of evil. We are fascinated because all of that evil we know as a possibility in ourselves. But the infernal sinners' consciousness of their sinfulness issues not, as it may for all premortem, in a well-grounded moral judgment of it: For though they know of that for which they are condemned they belong to no moral community that is the bearer of the judgment that condemns them. Here again the Pardoner's false-truthfulness says it all and serves for nothing. Every one of Dante's sinners is entirely alone, even when many populate the same *bolgia*. They know exactly what has them in Hell. And they know their sin only in those terms. They are, in short, enclosed by their failure of repentance, they are like cogs disengaged from the machinery, frictionlessly spinning in their own tight circle as endlessly as pointlessly. Only in Dante's account of his own journey with Virgil is there interest, because though *in* Hell he is not *of* it, and so he can learn from the experience of passing through; for the rest, the literary miracle of *Inferno* lies in the fascination we readers can find in Dante's tale of those successive conditions of an unutterable tedium that must be the worst Hell of all, a tedium more cruel than is the ingeniously constructed torturer's manual of a satanically efficient pain infliction – your head in the ground and the balls of your feet forever baked in the glowing coals,[17] the champing jaw of your political enemy forever clamped on the back of your skull.[18] The description of these physical humiliations is almost a relief from the truly ultimate pain of utter hopelessness inflicted in an eternally unchanging recurrence. The absence of historically successive time – for such time as there is in Hell consists in endlessly circular loops – rules out any possibility of change; and with the unending repetition of a past the elimination of all hope goes inseparably. That is why Dante's Satan has no narrative at all, he is anti-story incarnate, frozen stiff at absolute zero – the impossible temperature at which even the movement of atoms ceases and matter itself ceases to exist. As for whether there is, or is not, such a place as Hell, this is exactly what it would have to be like.

Absolute Evil

And whether there could be such a place, Dante is right about one thing to do with it, which some cheerful universalists seem too squeamish morally to allow. Dante's Hell

---

[17] *Inferno* 19. [18] Ibid., 33.

is not humanly unimaginable, and we need to know how correctly to imagine it. It is a condition to which you *could* come to consent, even aspire to it. It is not inconceivable that, like Dr. Faustus in Christopher Marlowe's play, you might throw all caution to the winds and flaunt a heroic infernal rebellion, a sort of ultimate two fingers to God, to God true or false, to *all* gods, and be willing to live with the consequences, knowing what they are. Faustus knows that Hell is the place to which he is increasingly committed by his compact with Satan, as choice after choice of evil removes from him the carapace of self-deception, drawing him to the point at which his will falls finally over the edge into that paralyzing void of empty clarity from which there is no longer any return. Poised just before that point, as yet on the nihilistic cliff-edge, Faustus believes that he is owed just one last dividend on his bargain with the devil; there he begs to see "the face that launched a thousand ships" – "Sweet Helen make me immortal with a kiss," he cries, even though by then he knows that Helen's beauty can no longer give him pleasure, not even the memory of it, for he has evacuated all pleasure of any power to attract.[19] Here is Marlowe's version of Dante's Francesca and Paolo. Faustus, like them, came to know that there is nothing to what he wished for but a fantasy in which he has now finally entrapped himself; and fantasy it was even when he made the originating fateful bargain, though then he but deceived himself about the moral abyss to which he was opening himself. Now, too late, the veil of

---

[19] Christopher Marlowe, *The Tragicall History of Dr Faustus*, Act 5, scene 1, in *The Complete Plays of Christopher Marlowe*, eds. Frank Romany and Robert Lindsey, Harmondsworth: Penguin, 2004.

self-deception is torn away. And what are we to say about Faustus's condition of mind, and, more relevantly, about the psychology of Dante's condemned? Is it impossible? Can they not knowingly will to be in Hell? To be thus trapped by your own desires, bound by your free choices, enclosed in circle of willed self-destruction – is that a condition impossible positively to desire, at least as a price willingly paid in pursuit of a fantasy of freedom? Is not the possibility of willing it always there, whether on the margin of moral thought or at the center of it? Is not the *will* for a terminal condition of self-entrapment all too possible if in the meantime there are rewards enough in an infinite defiance?

Is it possible to imagine yourself willing what Dr. Faustus says he wills? Is it impossible that Pope Boniface VIII or Pope Martin knowingly pursue what they know will have them in Hell? Or, to put the question in that other way that I envisaged in the case of Kierkegaard's Don Juan: Can Marlowe's play work? *The Tragicall Historie of Dr Faustus* is an imperfect but terrifying drama; Faustus scares the wits out of you, and so he should, just because it *is* possible to imagine willing what he wills, because we know today what Marlowe knew at the end of the sixteenth century: That two centuries of voluntarist philosophies had in his time turned into the shape and form of a society and of its accompanying social morality for which an ideal of pure willing is its primary ethic. But as to this figure of the naked will, if it is possible to will thus absolutely as Faustus does, is what Faustus wills possible? I ask, that is, not about the willing but whether its object, the thing willed, is realizable. For the pursuit of an ideal act of pure willing, of wanting will to be ultimate, demonstrably is possible, as Marlowe's play convincingly shows us. And showing what that world would be like that corresponds with so unconditional a will is perhaps the point of Dante's *Inferno*. The world entailed by that will is Hell. As Dante journeys through Hell, he takes you one after the other not just through a cycle of vices but through the ever-deeper pit of evil to which the pursuit of them brings the sinner. The journey tells of the desires that take you all the way, as it were, down to that ideal type of willing that is, paradoxically, the wordless, meaningless paralysis of will that is Satan.

But is the *thing willed* possible? To that the answer must be, no, it is not. For though you can will to be in Hell, the thing willed, Hell, is not possible. Hell is a fantasy, a telling anti-narrative, and the fantasy in Marlowe's play is the same as that of Kierkegaard's Don Juan, and of Plato's Thrasymachus, it is the fantasy that wills an impossible freedom for itself, it wills a condition of purely abstract personal autonomy that is as impossible to realize as a general choice for humans as it is for Satan, because its realization *for me* requires, as it does for a Thrasymachean pure will, the existence of a world in which *others* provide the non-egoistic theater, the stage on which I can play out the pure drama of my unqualified egoism. And so it is that such an act of pure psychotic and morally empty willing is possible only *within* a stabilizing moral world as its condition: As one might put it, a manic Hitler is possible, even conceivable, only on condition of a default commonplace and nonpsychopathic general compliance, as Hannah Arendt said.[20]

---

[20] *Eichmann in Jerusalem: A Report on the Banality of Evil*, Harmondsworth: Penguin Classics, 2006.

Inferno as Anti-narrative

Given that the *narrative* of *Inferno* works as a story of progressive moral collapse, does Dante think that the narrative requires that the Hell he imagines exists in reality? Probably *he* does. But does it in truth? Even if it doesn't exist is it impossible to envisage Dante seeing the point of composing an anti-narrative, a story that needs telling of an impossibly evil will? For even if it could not be true as described, nonetheless it vividly contains a truth about the psychopathology of evil and of the infernal regime that it entails. What is without question is that his description of Hell tells explicitly of the *world* that goes with that *will*, a description that teases out in analogical detail the intimate connections between the shape and form of a social world and the shape and form of an individual will that is the impetus calling it into being, exhibiting, therefore, the social logic of a wholly evil will. However unlikely it is that Dante is to be read on such a supposition as to fact, what we can say is that there is a point in it either way, and though it is clearly not up to us to read Dante just as we like in some fit of postmodern *jeu d'esprit*, or on other grounds to force the poetic narrative to conform to some universalist presumptions as to what actually or possibly exists, still *we* can legitimately read *Inferno* as an anti-narrative, impossible but frighteningly illuminating, because to do so is at least not inconsistent with what we must concede is essential to Dante's purposes – and you wouldn't have to change a word of *Inferno* in consequence of doing so.

And those purposes are to spell out what things would be like were we to imagine Dr. Faustus, Don Juan, Francesca da Rimini, and Paolo impossibly getting exactly what they ask for. Dante says that thus imagined they tell us – in fact the whole of *Inferno* says just this and really nothing else – that there is not and never was anything at all that answers to those desires as they know them, nor could there be; and Hell is the construction of the counterfactual fantasy made by the would-be but impossible choices of its inhabitants. Were it to exist, necessarily it would be a place of eternal frustration from which there could be no recall.

Indeed, Dante's Hell does have all the apparatus of a self-sufficient regime. It has a power structure, it has its hierarchies, it has its enforcers, and it has its ideologies: It *looks* like a very evil regime, the one and only regime that fits with a wholly evil world, a world that, as Dante describes it, is to all appearances, complete and self-sufficient. But all that is pure illusion.

For Dante's Hell shows that a self-sufficient regime of sin alone is impossible. That is common ground between a theology that allows for Hell within a dispensation of divine providence and a theology that, like Hart's, rules Hell altogether out as entailing a morally and conceptually repugnant theodicy. The condemned in Hell tell of the personal journeys that brought them there, the stories telling of their sin from the inside of it, the trajectory that their particular sin followed. In Hell, they do not come to see that they were mistaken about their desires in the way that we are when in our premortem existence we discover that we don't in the event want something that in anticipation we thought we wanted, and so repent of the false construction of desire that had impelled us to make wrong choices. What Dante imagines for Francesca and Paolo is that they get *exactly* what they wanted, to be together for all eternity in the lust they longed for, floating like dry leaves on the fierce hot winds of their own desires, wafted first this way and then that until, no longer able to repent of that desire, they are trapped in the fantasy-world that is the product of it. It is, then, not the frustration of guilty desire that makes their hell intolerable; on the contrary, what is intolerable is their being trapped wholly on the inside of their fantasy's being eternally met. As we all know, sometimes the true disaster is when we *do* get just what we want, the sheer contingency of premortem life mercifully ensuring that for the most part we don't in fact get it and can learn before it is too late. So it is that within the unconditional nature of their desire it is *they* in Hell who desire its eternity. They can't any longer repent of it, and *Inferno* tells of the world that desire creates, the world you would have to live with were you to desire above all a known evil and get it.

Far from unhappily guilt-ridden, then, Dante's Francesca and Paolo are at once wholly sad and entirely without remorse. Their misery is not the unhappy consciousness of persons who know of and admit to their moral failures and are forever condemned by them. But it is just for that reason that the doubt arises as to its possibility in fact. For you can construe Francesca and Paolo as being in an irreversible trap only upon a construction of them as having no desires other than those the satisfaction of which got them there. Hell's people would have fallen into a trap that could hold them forever in its grip only if they were no longer persons, but only personalized embodiments of a particular sin. That is why their condition is eternal. For persons can always know their guilt; and for as long as you can know your guilt the possibility of repentance must remain open. Therefore, were you to insist, as Aquinas does, that persons in Hell do retain some remnants of conscience,[21] then you will have to accept as a consequence that they are held there forever only because an infinite punishment is imposed upon the finite creature willy-nilly, that is, because God holds them there so as, contrary to their essential natures, they cannot in fact repent, come what may – or that, even if they do repent, it will be of no consequence to their eternal fate, because it is too late. For Hell to be a fate necessarily eternal Hell's people would have to have become nothing beyond the guilty *fact* of their sin, which, as it were, they incarnate, being *wholly* defined by it.

Accept, then, Dante tells us, what must be accepted as moral and psychological fact. Life *is* like that; it is such that you can envisage Hell's awful possibility as something you might choose. It is possible to hate, reject, even despise, the mentality of the universalist who tells me that I am damn well going to be saved whatever I say or do about it. And can I not want to tell those universalists that that is where I mean to go and that they cannot trick me out of it by way of their universalist fantasy? Dante's *Inferno* is the narration of that apparent choice, and if your last word has been to make that choice then that will have been the end of the matter. But, if it is right to interpret him so, Dante sets out that idealized mentality

---

[21] Aquinas maintains that the condemned in Hell can regret their sins but only in as much as they are the cause of their punishment. They do not properly repent them: see *Summa theologiae, Supplementum* q 98 a3 *corp*.

of evil in such a way as to make apparent in the whole sweep of the *Comedy*'s narrative that, as, bit by bit it sets out the dramas of salvation, so bit by bit as he progresses out of Hell through to Purgatory the choice of Hell is evacuated of any meaning because Hell is the place of meaning's evacuation; and in the end his journey serves to demonstrate its impossibility – whether Dante likes that conclusion or not, understands it to follow, or doesn't. And it is just because those supposed inhabitants of Hell died willingly unrepentant, and just because they wished to exist forever as if defined by their guilt, as if they were no more than abstract and impossible embodiments of a psychopathology, that their condition cannot possibly exist. Theirs is a fantasy of defiance that can never be fulfilled. But then as we know, human beings are up for even an ultimate fantasy.

Even if we do begin there, in a position contrary to what seems to be Dante's substantive belief, with the proposition that no such infernal world is possible, then not all is lost for Dante's narrative. For then the story of *Inferno* appears as the construction of an antitype, it tells of an impossible state of affairs that illuminates the truth it inverts precisely by way of its inversion; and then we see that its role within the *Comedy* not only does not require that there is any such place, but more: Its role for the reader is that you can now see it as demonstrating just that impossibility, the impossibility of a state of affairs that could exist only within an unrealizable fantasy of evil, and that, in truth, the evil is in the fantasy. In that finite fantasy of sin, the condemned but mock Satan's absolute embodiment of evil, willing in their pathetically finite way the impossibility that Satan, in his malice, wills unconditionally.

Postlude: Is Aquinas Inconsistent?

And so, as finally we come back to where we began, with that *theological* assertion, unchanged throughout Aquinas's writings, of the real existence of an eternal Hell, we meet a paradox: As with Dante, so on Aquinas's own account, the Hell he described is shown to be impossible. Undoubtedly Aquinas himself *is* a stout infernalist and does not doubt Hell's existence: He thinks that eternal damnation in Hell is possible, indeed is warranted by Scripture. Even were it plausible to imagine Dante being open to persuasion and to abandoning his prima facie infernalist position – universalism is at least *consistent* with *Inferno* – there seems not to be any such way round for a reading of Aquinas. And yet it seems not impossibly inconsistent with Aquinas's known views, indeed in one important connection it seems to be entailed by them, namely that the eternity of Hell is indefensible, since it is on his *own* account of Hell that souls eternally in Hell without the possibility of parole would be not persons; they would be at best person-fragments, actually existent "Horcruxes," as Harry Potter would have called them, bits and pieces of persons incapable of meeting on their own necessary conditions of personal identity, as bits and pieces of metal and rubber don't add up to parts of my bicycle until put back together in due workable form, or as a surgically removed arm is no one's – functionally it's not even an arm – until surgically reattached to a living body. And in the same way such infernal person-fragments would be unable to meet conditions for continuity of personhood between premortem and postmortem selves. If in Hell Denys Turner cannot be a person at all, then in Hell there can be no such person as the Denys Turner who died. And if there can be no such persons in Hell, then there can be no such actual place as Hell for a person to be in, not even a place empty of people, as Von Balthasar and Karl Barth suppose.

But why on Aquinas's own account would Denys Turner in Hell not be a person at all, and so not Denys Turner? The reason is that, on Aquinas's own say-so, among the conditions for being any person, howsoever evil, is the possession of a minimum of fundamental moral orientation, an ineradicable tendency to the good. Just as on the side of speculative reason there are ineradicable conditions of truth – such as those set out by the principles of contradiction and identity – so on the side of practical reason there are fundamental orientations toward the good that go together with simply being a person at all, with not being that pure antitype that is the idealized psychopath.[22] Such is the principle that "the good is to be done and evil avoided" together with "all the other principles that go along with it,"[23] the first and most general principles of the natural law, or for that matter of any sort of law.

On the side of speculative knowledge, the principle of noncontradiction is a principle *constitutive* of all possible thought, not, to employ a Kantian distinction, merely regulative of it, as if you could, like Walt Whitman in a mood of grand and speculative defiance, declare yourself to be "large" and, thus "containing multitudes," happily contradict yourself at will. You can't workably defy

---

[22] Of course, it is true that not all psychopaths are nothing but psychopaths; but for a psychopath *when* in a psychotic condition there is nothing else outside it.

[23] *Summa theologiae*, 1–2ae q94 a2 *corp.*

the principle of contradiction without self-entrapment into fundamental obedience to it: Contradiction and consequent meaninglessness will catch you out as you compose your self-deluding skeptical strategies, for, like some infallible sleuth whose undetectable presence bears down upon every thought or proposition you could possibly entertain, the principle is always there behind you however quickly you turn around to catch it at work and, having thus caught it, could then "happily contradict" it.[24] As Aristotle puts it, the attempt to deny the principle of contradiction serves only to confirm it, since for the denial to have any meaning it must obey that principle first.

And Aquinas agrees with this. Moreover, he adds that the equivalent is true of practical reasoning: It too has its ineradicable starting points without which there can be no moral thought at all, one way or another. You can make all sorts of moral moves, ranging across a spectrum from those of the pure, untroubled, sure moral elegance of the saintly, through the heroically gritty and inelegant struggles of the strong-willed who by the skin of their moral teeth hold out against temptation, down through the morally weak, who would resist temptation if only they could but don't seem able to do so, down

---

[24] Such principles are not direct *objects* of knowledge in the way that I know which way *you* are facing – say toward me – for I can see that. They are known "without observation" in the sort of way in which I know which way *I* am facing – say, toward you: I don't *observe* which way I am facing, that knowledge just goes with the facing itself as an intentional act. Thus, the principle of contradiction is operative *within* any coherent structure of thought. It cannot be correctly stated formally without its truth being assumed.

the slippery moral slope further still through the plain ignorance of the morally immature to the self-delusion of the chronically morally benighted, and so finally to the moral rock-bottom occupied by the entirely morally dumb: Aristotle takes you through all these moral states in book 7 of his *Nicomachean Ethics*. But of the condition of the psychopath he says nothing, except for the mention in book 1 of a Persian king Sardanapalus, who, in the legend, so delights in the pairing of the colors red and green that he arranges daily for slaves to be bloodily slaughtered on the lawn in front of his palace just for the aesthetic pleasure of the contrasting color scheme.[25] But Sardanapalus is not at the bottom end of the scale of moral decline; he is simply off the moral scale altogether. In short in his Sardanapalus is the nearest Aristotle gets to our psychopath. Were such an ideal type of a person to exist, he wouldn't belong within any moral world at all, which means that there would be no world of its own of any kind for him to occupy, but only an imaginary one parasitical upon a world constituted by others who are properly moral agents. And that, for Aristotle, is to say that there isn't enough of a human being in him for moral thought even to begin to engage.

And it is the same for Aquinas. What he calls *synderesis*,[26] the general capacity for moral distinctions that underlies our particular judgments of conscience, operates at the

---

[25] *Nicomachean Ethics* I, 1095b 18–21. I think it is possible I invented this account of Sardanapalus. But if so, I am quite pleased with my invention.

[26] He borrows the term from St. Jerome's corruption of the Greek *suneidesis*.

practical level as the principle of contradiction does at the theoretical: As absolutely you can't think at all without obedience to the one, so absolutely you can't be a *human* agent without at least implied obedience to the other.[27] That primitive practical orientation toward the good is, Aquinas says, what puts you on a moral scale of any kind, and without it you are not on the scale of personhood at all. And so, *before* there can be any practical judgment for good or for ill, whether you hit the mark of the morally heroic or collapse morally into a settled condition of vice, or anywhere in between, the judgment of good as being prior in itself, and that of evil subsequent and dependent, simply cannot be unconditionally eradicated; and ineradicably implicated in that judgment is the orientation of will to the good. It is thus that *given* that orientation no human being is immoral beyond recall; and *without* that orientation no agent is more than in a purely biological sense human – if *physiologically* continuous with the person that existed premortem, not on that account *personally* identical with them. For that degree of moral sense is ineradicable in a human. In short, it is Aquinas himself who shows that there are minimum *moral* conditions for being a person, and that an eternal existence in Hell would be possible only for those in whom those conditions are no longer met *at all*. It follows from this that to conceive of God willing some human beings to be eternally punished therein without possibility of amendment is to conceive of God punishing them by willing their destruction as human, and of Hell being a version of Harry Potter's Azkaban, populated by organisms that once were persons

---

[27] *Summa theologiae* 1–2ae q94 a2.

but are persons no more.²⁸ In short, either the souls in Hell are persons, in which case they can truly repent, or else it is by God's eternal decree that, whether they would repent or not, they are stuck with an eternal punishment. And that, as Hart says, is a pretty unpleasant God.

It is here that the doubts begin to intrude as to the consistency of Aquinas's moral psychology, his account, that is, of the necessary conditions for human moral agency on the one hand, and the description of the condition of the souls in Hell on the other. For it seems hard to match them up with any consistency. Either the souls in Hell are not moral agents, in which case they are not persons at all and so not the persons who died in sin, or, if they are moral agents, then they cannot be held in Hell otherwise than by a divine decree that requires repentance's being simply forbidden them, coming too late. Dante can at least potentially resolve the conflict by demonstrating that there would be theological point in the hypothesis

---

²⁸ Commenting on a draft of this chapter, Nate Gadiano, then an undergraduate student in Princeton University, responded that souls in Hell do retain a grip on moral conscience: They would have to if they are to be human at all, and this does appear to be Aquinas's view – see *Compendium theologiae*, cap. 174, where he says that souls in Hell do retain freedom of choice. But if that is so it should follow that the will to repent cannot be ruled out in the nature of the case. If, however, on Aquinas's account it is too late for souls in Hell to take up that option of repentance, then, contrary to what his position seemed to be in the account of it I proposed in Chapter 2 – that those in Hell are self-condemned – it can only be because it is laid down by God's decree that Hell's punishment is to be eternally irreversible, regardless. But this can only make things worse for the theology of God underlying the infernalist position, leaving it wholly vulnerable to Hart's critique. Gadiano has been of immense help to me by way of commentary on earlier drafts of this manuscript, but on this matter I am unpersuaded by his defense of Aquinas.

of an unchangeable infernal will, even were it impossible in fact.[29] Aquinas doesn't resolve it, though I think he too could have done so: For it is on his own principles of moral psychology that a noninfernalist way is open to him. You can make sense of Dante's narrative of a journey through Hell, of his encounter with the damned, of his converse with souls held captive there by way of their own self-condemning desires, telling *within* the narrative he constructs for them the tale of their damnation; and Dante can tell of all this as if in a coherent story, and he could do so for good reason even were it no more than the fictional construction of a conceptual impossibility, an anti-narrative. Of that impossible narrative Aquinas attempts to describe the consistent practical reality: But in doing so he sets up the contradiction that goes along with it, making to be impossible that which Dante could say is but an idealized and telling narrative, though it be contrary to fact and even impossible.

How, then, are we to answer the first question I raised at the beginning of this chapter, about the existence of

---

[29] Vittorio Montemaggi has suggested that Dante in fact allows for the possibility of Hell's judgment not being irreversible, as in the case of Trajan, whom Dante allows has been rescued from Hell and is in Purgatory, see *Paradiso*, 20. In the Middle Ages there are other legends than Dante's of a soul's being postmortem rescued from Hell, for it is there in the legend of St. Erkenwald told by the fourteenth-century Middle English *Pearl* poet. Such speculative cases, however, serve more to confirm the irreversibility of death's judgment. For both Trajan's case and that of St. Erkenwald's recovery of a pre-Christian king from the grave require their being brought back to life, thereupon being baptized, and then dying again, the second time in grace, if they are to be thus redeemed. In short, both legends require an impossible second death precisely so as to confirm the intrinsic nature of death's judgment, not so as to allow exceptions to it.

Dante's Hell? Perhaps it is that there is no such place. And as to the second: On the supposition that there is no Hell what are we to make of Dante's *Inferno*? To that the answer is that it is at least a powerful and necessary conceit, a fiction that portrays a moral faction, a possibility of which there is a hint at the end of *Inferno*. Hand in hand with Virgil, seeming to climb down on the scaly thighs of Satan's inert body, Dante comes to see that in truth he was upside down all the time and is now climbing the right way up to the foothills of Mount Purgatory – that Hell therefore is life's judgment upside down and Purgatory is the truth of Hell when turned the right way up. For it is on those now ascending slopes that the anti-narrative of eternal despair in Hell is retold, its truth now rescued from the infernal suffering, and made secure in the time-limited story of Purgatory's hope.

PART II
PURGATORY

4
Purgatory and Purgation

Choice

Dante's journey through Hell may, then, be a fiction. But even if it is, in that fiction is contained the *Comedy*'s literal truth that leads into its existential core, a faction. Vittorio Montemaggi says that at that core of the *Comedy* as a whole, central to the poem's intent, is a moral demand – he even speaks of the *Comedy* as above all a drama of "human encounter."[1] And that is true. Everything in the *Comedy* is organized around Dante's personal dramas of interaction with the human persons he meets, and by hearing them tell the dramas of their lives. It is in the manifold movements of that drama of human encounter that the structural dimensions of Hell, Purgatory, and Paradise are embodied. The *Comedy* is a play, the plot of which is told by its characters in their interactions with Dante himself; but among the *dramatis personae*, crucial to the conduct of the play's drama, are we readers ourselves. The *Comedy* tells of a moral challenge internal to its narrative. But the telling itself is a moral challenge to its readers.

The *Comedy*'s "existential" core is, however, far from existential*ist*, just as Dante's moral purpose is far from reducible to a moralizing ethical program even when, as often, he is castigating the moral performance of the

---

[1] *Reading Dante's* Commedia *as Theology*, Oxford: Oxford University Press, 2016, pp. 20–30.

Church of his times.² His purpose is to make a call for nothing less than the conversion of Church, often explicitly, and always, explicitly or implicitly, of person. And that purpose's medium is a fictional journey. As I said in the Chapter 1, it is not as if "the facts" were one thing and "the moral demand" another, as if each were definable without relation to the other, for it is fact reimagined that by itself entails the moral demand, not some moral purpose tagged on to it from other, logically independent, sources. As Dante sees it, judgment of human action is embedded in the very shape of the universe itself. We will see more about this in Chapter 6.³

It is no doubt true then that, as Montemaggi says, the *Comedy* does have direct ethical implications for the reader too, who from the outset is confronted with a drama of a free choice to be made between the only two ultimate outcomes to a human life, between being forever after death either in Hell or else in Paradise. Readers may, of course, simply see Dante as describing what those choices are, leave it at that, and pass on. They may even read of that drama with sympathy and understanding of how such writing works, though they are themselves unchallenged by it. But when they do it is they who are making an abstraction from Dante's complex whole if they suppose that any call the narrative makes on a personal response is an extrinsic addition of something further to

---

[2] Griffin Oleynick argues for the influence on Dante of the so-called "spiritual Franciscans," enthusiasts for the most radical forms of Franciscan poverty and in consequence bitter critics of the corruptions of the contemporary Church, see Oleynick's *Dante's Franciscan Way*, New Haven, CT: Yale University Press, 2014.

[3] See Chapter 6, 'A paradisal politics.'

the plain meaning of the narrative itself. Those final outcomes are what a lifetime's free choices, brought together by Dante in precis, have been the choices *of*. What is more, that character of the "ultimate" is not only temporal, as if the fact that both repentance of sin and unrepentant persistence in it are always possible prior to the moment of death entails that nothing is final until that last moment, all time before being a space of contingency, free of relation to the ultimate. Dante supposes that the choice between life and death is quotidian, ever bearing upon that "meantime" that is our mortal life. That is why Dante's distinction between Hell and Purgatory is based, broadly, on the distinction, commonly made by moral theologians of his day, between how you die, whether burdened with the weight of "mortal" or of "venial" sins, distinguished as between those sins that here and now do bear upon the ultimate choice between life and death, and those that do not have so conclusive a bearing and are no more than the provisional failings consequent upon one's personal ignorance or other moral immaturities. Death, and so the ultimate, can on this account catch you out at any time; therefore, being ready *all* the time is called for.

The choice between eternal life and eternal death is, then, always being made at every moment within life, and, as we have seen, that is so whether or not there is a Hell as the Christian traditions have generally believed. But which ultimate choice is irreversibly made is not easily predicted and known. Though within a life there is indeed but history and contingency, it is possible, Aquinas says, to think of one's salvation as reasonably likely and one may, indeed must, hope for it. But the certainty of it in advance is presumption. And there is that uncertainty either way, not merely in the possibility of our having in fact chosen Hell, our optimistic self-deceptions notwithstanding, but also in the possibility of Heaven, notwithstanding our guilt-ridden self-recriminations. And, Dante says, it is true that there are exceptions to death's final judgment, Trajan, as we saw, being one of them: It is at the intercession of Gregory the Great that he is retrieved from Hell's grip after his death, is then restored to life, baptized, "and so," Beatrice tells him, "believing, blazed forth in such fires | of love in truth that he, on second death | was fit to make his way to this great game."[4] Likewise Ripheus: "by that grace that drops like dew (upon him) ... God ... opened his eyes, | grace upon grace, to when we'd be redeemed. | In that redemption, he believed. And so | he did not suffer any pagan stench, | but stood as reproof to those who stayed."[5]

Those exceptions of Trajan and Ripheus apart,[6] on the general point Dante is at one with Aquinas: All is predestined, and one death is all you get and it is final, its judgment an unfathomable mystery. We cannot know ahead who is saved and who is not. "How remote," Dante says, is predestination's root even for those in heaven. For even those blessed have "faces that, in looking up | cannot *in toto* see the primal cause. | And so you mortals, in your judgments show | restraint. For even we who look on God | do not yet know who all the chosen are."[7] And in several pointed instances Dante tells us that you cannot be certain

---

[4] *Paradiso* 20.115–117.   [5] Ibid., 20.18–126.
[6] See note 30 in Chapter 3.
[7] *Paradiso* 20.130–135. Though as Kirkpatrick points out (*Paradiso*, p. 416) Dante does appear to know that Trajan and Ripheus are in heaven.

of salvation even in your own case: Dante notes that upon their deaths some have been initially surprised at where their final judgment has placed them, only to see in no time at all how it was wholly appropriate. Such is the case of Folco, a onetime great sinner who in Paradise came to see that he no longer had need to remember his sins; "we don't think back to that," he says, for in heaven his guilt for a past life is swallowed up in forgiveness. Rather, he may smile as he reflects on "the art that makes beautiful the great result."[8] And surprised by an even less predicted joy than Folco's – given her own judgment of her life's failures – is Piccarda Donati, abducted by her family and forced into marriage in betrayal of her calling to a life of chastity as a nun, who can hardly believe the merciful judgment of her life that nonetheless places her in Paradise.[9]

However, if life's ultimate outcomes, whichever they are, are not conclusively predictable before death, they are not arbitrary; it will always be possible to read them retrospectively as having been wholly fitting and just. Not one, even among those in Dante's Hell, complains, vainly protesting as if at an injustice done as to their personal fate, they apparently dare not; and not one among them denies that they are in the place that corresponds with the true intent of their choices as upon death they have come to understand them to have been. In short at that point their self-perception tallies exactly with the final judgment delivered. That is why inscribed upon the gates of Hell are the words declaring that place's origin and meaning: "justice and a primal love made me," it says.[10]

---

[8] *Paradiso* 9.103–108.   [9] Ibid., 3.70–87.   [10] *Inferno* 3.1–9.

And as for heaven, Piccarda may not have expected to be saved, but in Paradise she is far from thinking of herself as lucky to have got away with it, as if arbitrarily and without merit to have caught the merciful eye of God in an unexpectedly forgiving mood. Her delight in finding herself in Paradise at all lies in her having discovered the truth of her life to have been otherwise than the judgment her own ill-formed conscience had delivered; and her happiness is enhanced, she tells Dante who wonders about it, by her being assigned to the lowest sphere of heaven. For that, she now knows, is exactly where she should be, and no higher. When speaking of the nature of prayer's discernment Aquinas says that it is *quodammodo interpretativa voluntatis humanae*[11] "in a certain way a hermeneutic of a person's (real) will"; and so it is with the last judgment of a life, which reads the true intention of a person's desires fully and finally understood as having been thus and thus. So it is for Piccarda. For her the place in heaven where she finds herself is a true judgment of exactly where that same "justice and a primal love" would have her, and so it is, she says, that "in his will is our peace."[12]

And it is in the divine wisdom that finally relieves Piccarda of a guilt-ridden false self-judgment that we can see how Dante's understanding of human free choice is far from that of the libertarian freewill philosophers, or those of the existentialists of our times, for whom choice is most free, and most human, when it comes from no antecedent cause but my causelessly unencumbered free will, my responsibility extending directly only into those

---

[11] *ST* 3a q21 a4 *corp.* [12] *Paradiso* 3.85.

consequences of my actions that I anticipate and formally choose, my freedom of choice being "free of" any external agency, even, or perhaps more especially, of any causal agency of God's. For, says the libertarian, choices can be "mine" – accountable to me – only insofar as they are free; and they can be free only insofar as I alone am their cause, my freedom being essentially the work of a God-free agency.[13] On that account, in a general sense "existentialist," my continuing identity, the story of my life, is mine just in as much as it is the story that I alone tell of me, that being the record I tell spelled out in life's trajectory of those free choices. As Jean-Paul Sartre said,[14] even those surreptitious, slow-growing, accumulated, half-conscious, acts of self-deception, seeming to emerge unwittingly from my *mauvaise foi*, are in truth ultimately chosen, for my refusing to choose, howsoever unthinking and habitual, is still choosing to refuse to lead an examined life.[15]

An existentialist understanding of my freedom as coming from nowhere and nothing, from, as Sartre puts it, *le néant*, lies at the extreme end of a libertarian doctrine of self, freedom, and identity. But the options are not reduced to an exclusive two, as Sartre seems to have believed, namely that between an absolute and unconditional freedom of choice and the determinism

---

[13] See my brief discussion of the position of Alvin Plantinga in my *Thomas Aquinas: A Portrait*, New Haven, CT: Yale University Press, 2013, pp. 150–156.

[14] *Being and Nothingness*, trans. Hazel E. Barnes, New York: Washington Square Press, 1984, Part I, chapter 2, "Bad Faith," pp. 86–116.

[15] *Existentialism is a Humanism*, trans. Carol Macomber, preface Ariette Elkaïm, New Haven, CT: Yale University Press, 2007.

of a robot, any claim to an ambiguous space between them being created only by my self-deceptions. For Dante, we are ultimately judged as to the extent of our responsibility, that is to say, *insofar* as we are free, and with what degree of freedom we have acted is often, perhaps more often than not, unclear to ourselves, or even *especially* to ourselves. Thus Piccarda Donati. *Her* judgment of responsibility for a failed vocation got it wrong, her place in heaven showing exactly how to get it right: securely there, but in the lowest place. Only there can she be at peace. All bad choices are possibly forgivable, for many such choices come from a place in us of which we are at best only partly aware – as Aristotle had acknowledged we are none of us more than partly responsible for those states of character out of which we act.[16]

In principle, then, it is those for whom *only* their own choices matter, those for whom, as Sartre says, there is nothing morally relevant but their free choices made "out of nothing," who will go where their choices take them. Hence, as we saw in Chapter 3, there is a sense in which they do get what they have wanted, like it or not in the event. And that is what Hell is, the place where dwell forever the ultimate choosers: For they have insisted upon its being *their* choosing that settles the final judgment, not God's forgiveness, which, Piccarda had come to understand, saw deeper into her freedom than she herself understood. Those in Hell are hoist on their own petards, since for them there is no other lifting gear than their own choices.

---

[16] *Nicomachean Ethics*, 3, 1114b 1–5.

Augustine and Life's Story

Dante's conception of the personal freedom that settles a person's fate is, then, quite other than that of such libertarian existentialists. That is not to say that Dante has no alternative account of the place of free will.[17] Following a long tradition from Aristotle to Aquinas, Dante acknowledges that there is a kind of freedom in the will's being able to turn to evil, but only in a secondary and subordinate way, for nothing can destroy the will's primary orientation to the good. Nor is this primary orientation to the good merely formal in the sense that whatever you choose, howsoever evil it may be, necessarily you choose it *as being* in some way good, no matter in what degree its goodness is disproportionately little by comparison to its evil. In that formal sense, even Sardanapalus sees at least some aesthetic good in his mindless slaughter of the innocent. Dante's point is not in that way purely formal. When Aristotle says that "the good is what all things desire"[18] he means not only that for any object of desire there is some good in it, but that there are some actual goods that are the natural objects of desire for anyone at all, and that there is a primary orientation to a final good that goes simply with being human. In Dante's context Robin Kirkpatrick calls it a "natural" desire that is always there, never altogether obliterated, though it can be lost behind layer upon layer of habitual obfuscation. It is that orientation toward such "natural" goods that Aquinas and others called *synderesis*, as we saw in Chapter 3, and it is this natural desire for the good that Virgil tells Dante lies

---

[17] See *Purgatorio* 17 and 18.   [18] *Nicomachean Ethics* I, 1, 1094a 2–3.

at the center of this complex relationship between the good and human freedom, and must be set in contrast with those desires that can lead astray from the inherent orientation of nature:

> The love of good, he said, when this falls short
> Of what it ought to be, is here restored.
> The oar that wrongly slackened strikes once
>   more ...
>   Neither creator nor created thing
> Was ever, dearest son, without (he starts)
> The love of mind or nature. You know that.
>   The natural love can never go astray.
> The other, though, may err when wrongly aimed,
> or else through too much vigour or the lack.[19]

That is to say, within the complexity of human freedom as exercised by rational agents choice may in practice go wrong, the oarsman may catch a crab; for human freedom is such that the choices of the rational human being can always be misled by self-interested and self-deceived redescriptions of what is at stake, such that when human choice

>   wrongly twists towards the ill,
> Or runs toward the good to fast or slow,
> What's made then works against its maker's plan.[20]

And it is therein that is sin, which, Kirkpatrick comments, "as Virgil presents it, is not directly an offence against God but rather against ourselves, in so far as rational love chooses to ignore the promptings of the natural love that,

---

[19] *Purgatorio* 17.91–96.   [20] *Purgatorio* 17.100–103.

unfailingly, impels our existences."[21] The journey of Purgatory, then, its plot, is that of the recovery and return of the rational will to its natural object, which is God; and here, as before, the journey described is the journey thereby taken, Dante the narrator is once again the Dante narrated, and in that sense *Purgatorio*'s plot is the *Comedy*'s plot. That is why, when John Frecerro explains that there is indeed a personal "confessional" trajectory and structure to Dante's *Comedy*, one that parallels Augustine's story as he tells it in his *Confessions*,[22] he insists that for both Augustine and Dante it is a journey not of their invention, of choice, but of discovery – or perhaps better, it is a journey of *re*covery, of restoration, of that natural will that lies deeper within the self than ever simple free choice of the will can access.

Given the overwhelming influence of his theology in the Middle Ages it may seem remarkable that Augustine in name is absent from the narrative of the *Comedy* until the very end in *Paradiso* canto 32:35, where Dante sees him in the company of saints Benedict and Francis. But that company should alert us to Augustine's influence's being far from a marginal adjunct to Dante's theological profile otherwise defined. For Augustine's near invisibility in the *Comedy* is like that of the air we breathe – as your dependence on it is unnoticed until you are denied its oxygen and you gasp for the want of it, so is Augustine's theology for Dante. Augustine's *Confessions* is more

---

[21] Robin Kirkpatrick, *Purgatory*, vol. 2 of Dante, *The Divine Comedy*, Harmondsworth: Penguin Books, 2007, p. 403.
[22] John Frecerro, *Dante, the Poetics of Conversion*, ed. and intro. Rachel Jacoff, Cambridge, MA: Harvard University Press, 1986, pp. 1–2.

like the map itself of Dante's journey, less a particular place of interest on the way, his influence being in the character of the story as a whole, not as a bit-part played within it told on other terms. In this way Frecerro is right that for Dante even the personal confessional character of his journey is properly understood as Augustine understood his, not as autobiography, that is, as an author's tracking of his own individual psychological trajectory in isolation from its representatively theological character, or at least not merely so. Dante himself, says Frecerro, "speaks of Augustine's life as giving an 'essemplo,' implying the transformation of personal experience into intelligible, perhaps even symbolic, form." He adds: "it is the exemplary quality of the *Confessions* that distinguishes it from its modern descendants" as does the combination of the living flesh and blood *persona* of Beatrice with her evidently Christological, and so typological, significance in the conversion episode in the last cantos of *Purgatorio*.[23] In both Augustine and Dante, Frecerro adds, "*exemplum* and experience, allegory and biography, form a confession of faith for other men."[24] These pairs are not, for Dante, terms of contrast.

The events of Augustine's story, the "autobiography," are in this way representative of universal truths concerning divine providence, and the two connect because the weight of their universal significance is born by the precise and particular events that he records. And there is in that emphasis an epistemological preference distinctive of the way Augustine tells the story of his conversion in

---

[23] See Chapter 5, "Remembering a 'first' self."
[24] Frecerro, *Dante, the Poetics of Conversion*, pp. 3–4.

Confessions.[25] For even if the significance of the events of his conversion is, as with all significance, universal, that universality does not, as Plato thought, belong properly to an "Idea" or "Form" existing separately from its individualizations. It is rather where Aristotle said the universal exists, in the individual event, in the time-bound and historical. For Augustine too, history's meaning is known in its contingent events of time and place and person, and therein as in a glass darkly, catching but a shadow of that significance that is known in full only in the providential mind of God determining those events. For Dante, as for Augustine, their stories are told by God first and by them only when, as by their conversions, they become able to own them as theirs. For Dante and Augustine, life's stories are as much told by providence as by our telling of them, for we are more Hamlet within the play than Shakespeare its author,[26] and until that final moment of reckoning that is death no one gets to know the whole story even of their own lives. For the ultimately compelling story is not told until then, in a truth-telling that is otherwise known as a judgment, the "*last* judgment" of them all.[27]

---

[25] One uses the word "autobiographical" here with caution and qualification. The point about Augustine's *Confessions* is that it is of course the story of his life, but it is the story that is told by God and by grace, who has made Augustine for himself and Augustine's heart will not rest until it is in God that he rests. *Confessions* I: 1.

[26] Within the play Shakespeare determines when Hamlet acts freely causing things to happen with intent and when unfreely and as determined by other causes than his own will: Shakespeare is Hamlet's God.

[27] It seems reasonable to say that, rather than that it is only the last act of sinners – their final persistence in a sin – that condemns them, as if nothing in life before then can count at all when caught out in an unrepented sin at the last minute. It is of course self-evident that it is

Nor is this play between the personal and the typological incidental. In Dante it *is* the *Comedy* as a whole, just as in Augustine's *Confessions* it is the whole meaning of a life. In both, the *historia* is told as they have come to understand it, Augustine's conversion being told in a narrative that extends over the first nine books of *Confessions* wherein he recounts the frustrating experiences of his failure to grapple with the meaning of his life's narrative. But that narrative leads eventually into a process wherein alone a full, authentic discovery of it becomes possible. That discovery is his conversion, and it turns his life upside down and the causal order of events back to front, and the story that is told after the conversion transforms the way he tells the story of all that precedes it. For after his conversion he sees how he must retell the story in entirely different terms from those in which, before his conversion, he had understood the events that led to it.

That final conversion is famously dramatic, the drama being intensified by its having been provoked by the trivial accident of his overhearing the chant of children at play in the neighboring garden – out of the blue he hears them sing *tolle lege, tolle lege*, "take it and read, take it and read," and he picks up the epistle to the Romans, reads, and, bursting into tears, it is all over. It is not as if Augustine hadn't already been reading intensely and debating the Scriptures before that decisive event. He had. But *his* literary and interpretative skills as a rhetorician had got him nowhere; it was rather by way of a chance event,

---

the last act before death that finally stops the story of a life short; but it is then that a final judgment of the *whole life's tendency* is made, one that is unavailable to subsequent revision.

entirely gratuitous, that the eternal work of providence intervened, and the trivially contingent became the bearer of the world-historical. That disproportion between the accidental occasion of it and its overwhelming significance casts a spell, and to this day we are spellbound by it. No wonder Augustine himself weeps for joy. No wonder do we upon hearing him tell of it.

The sheer contingency that bears the weight of a life transformed is set in telling contrast with that series of failed philosophical conversions that preceded it. Aquinas tells us not to set chance and divine providence in opposition, for he says – it seems paradoxical to some – that God can, and sometimes does, bring about his providential way precisely by way of chance.[28] Just so for Augustine. In those subsidiary and partial "conversions" that Augustine records there is no such arbitrary suddenness. There is carefully modulated progression that begins in his liberation from the "hissing cauldron of lust"[29] that was Carthage by way of the austere metaphysical and moral dualism of the Manichee Bishop Faustus, and though traces of that dualism will remain with Augustine throughout his life as typifying his imagination of evil, not for long will it stay with him as formal doctrine. For Augustine quickly learns from Cicero to see evil as simple failure – if evil is not nothing, for it is real, then for certain it is not a Manichean agent either, for it is no more than privation, and is a cause only in the sense that being deprived of food is the cause of my starvation. Nor will

---

[28] *ST* 1a q 22 a4 *corp.*
[29] *Confessions* III: 1.1. Latin: *sartago flagitiosorum amorum*. Lit. "a sizzling pan of shameful loves …"

his liberation from the Manichees by way of Cicero's ethically universalist stoicism satisfy him any better, not until the philosophical writings of the late Platonists show him how a Ciceronian degree of moral stability has its foundation only in what he calls the "true immutability of truth" itself.[30] But as much as the philosophical weight of their idealism bears down on him even the *platonici* could not enable Augustine to overcome his persistent weakness of will.[31] Each of these, Faustus, Cicero, Plato, offered, at the worst, as in Faustus, a false start, and at best a merely philosophical conviction, as with Cicero and the Platonists. But none could finally and comprehensively meet the needs of this *vir desideriorum* of this man, like Daniel the prophet, of many passions and of unconstrained desires.[32] For a man of intellectual and speculative disposition such as is Augustine, what is no more than mere "opinion" (as Plato called it[33]) is all too easily changed. But, he knows, change so cheaply won is never going to be conclusive. He is a philosopher, a practicing academic, and the price of an academic's intellectual conversion is low enough and easily paid, for academies are places where the cost of doing so is institutionally reduced. But the price of the academics' conversion of their most intimate passions is all the higher for their routinely mistaking the one for the other.

For this reason, when reading those first eight books of *Confessions* in which Augustine recounts the successive phases of his failed conversions one might be led to think that his true conversion was far from coming

---

[30] *Confessions* VII: 17. [31] *Confessions* VII: 17. [32] Daniel 10: 11.
[33] *Republic* VII, 517aff.

out of the blue, that all the time it was on the cards, and you could see it coming on its way as if it were the concluding peroration of an upward trajectory of self-transcendence into God. Such is the blessed illusion of conversion's true narrative. Though you could not in advance have told what outcome will come of it, post-factum you read the whole story backward, retelling it as if the outcome of conversion had been inevitable, there all the time from the beginning. Then it is that at once surprised by the conversion's radicalness you somehow also say of it, "of course, exactly so," it *fits*, "all along that was where it was going," the surprise on the one hand and the "exactly so" on the other coming in strange conjunction; and the realization of its character of the "exactly so" comes readily, as if in a moment that reminds you of what you somehow *already* knew all the time. It's a platonic instinct to think that way, for Plato believed that the moment of resolution, of knowledge achieved, appears as an *anamnesis*, as a moment of *un*forgetting, a clearing away of the accumulated debris of false memory, allowing the truth that was always there to be uncovered.[34] That remembering demands the revision of the narrative that led to it, so that the whole story is changed upon an instant, its trajectory now making sense in the terms of its outcome. And contained in that insight of Plato's there is a general truth about narratives, autobiographical or historical. All truly radical change demands that history be rewritten in the light of the new result it achieves. It *is* a revolution just on that account, for revolutions

[34] *Phaedo* 88a.

essentially change the past, and anything they change for the future follows from the revised story. And if the outcome doesn't seem post-factum to have been implied all along then it wasn't a revolution at all, as Karl Marx so sensibly observed.[35]

Conversion

In an individual life we call such revolutions "conversions." The connecting link between the before and the after of Augustine's conversion lies in the persistent dissatisfaction of this *vir desideriorum* with a merely finite goal to his desire: Only an unlimited object, God, could satisfy the intensity and profusion of Augustine's passion – in that sense his conversion is a point of arrival at a place of resolution where beforehand he had known only that there was *somewhere* else to go. But where? It won't capture the radical nature of conversion to think of it merely in terms of Augustine's discovery of God. For God was not so much that passion's object as its cause, present *in* the seeking itself, buried so deeply within Augustine's desire that he could not recognize it until, upon conversion, it reveals itself. Then it comes to him just like the gift that you didn't know you wanted until your lover, who knows you better than you know yourself, presents it to you. Then it comes, as the theologians say, as "grace," because it is freely given and wholly unexpected, and so *gratis*;

---

[35] Marx gets this. He is no historical determinist, but he does know that when revolution comes it is then that you can see how it had been "on the cards" all the time.

but it is also received in gratitude, for it carries with it that sense of the strangely familiar that G. K. Chesterton's world traveler experienced, who after the long and difficult journey discovers the Brighton pier from which many years before he had set out to have become magically transformed upon his return to it, the difference being made by the point of departure's having become the journey's point of arrival.[36] It is a recognition; it is as Plato says a "re-cognition," a remembering; or as Augustine says, it is *tam antiqua tam nova*, new-old news.[37]

For prior to his conclusive conversion in the garden in Milan it had seemed to Augustine as if in addition to his own created will there was some other agency at work that was not his own but a will as if "outside" and working upon his own, even perhaps a will opposed to his own. It was a God held at a distance from himself, a finite object of desire given and known, the God of a finite identity, definable and knowable in advance of the search, and so directing it. Then to the unconverted Augustine it seemed that it was he who was truly "within," for it seemed to him that it was his story of his selfhood, constitutive of his own identity, that he was recounting. But now the converted author of *Confessions* can record how all the time he had misconstrued the nature of the search for God. It had seemed to him that it was God who was outside, distant, his searching having set God apart from his own identity, from

---

[36] Chesterton, *The Everlasting Man*, San Francisco: Ignatius Press, 1993, p. 9.
[37] *Confessions* X: 27.

that which constitutes his own identity as Augustine.[38] But now, converted, Augustine must invert the total trajectory of his life; now he has come to know that "it was you who were within me; it was I who was outside myself,"[39] and the two wills, his and God's, have at last become one in a single act, at once God's doing and Augustine's being done by. It was only God's action that could achieve in Augustine a conversion radical enough to turn what until that point had seemed to him to have been but the *historia* of his seeking God to be revealed now to have been all the while the *historia* of God's seeking Augustine, both *historiae* true and neither exclusive of the other. And it took the accident of the children's chant in the garden for that hidden intentionality to be revealed to him as the overt truth. The transforming jolt's suddenness, its being so out of the blue on the one hand, and on the other its seeming to be "just so," so perfectly right, fitting, a coming home: *that* is why he cries those tears of joy.

It is therefore integral to Augustine's understanding of the nature of conversion itself, that, Frecerro says, he will not separate the psychological movement of the experience of it from its generalizing typology, which, he says, is precisely the retrieval of a true self from a psychologically introverted, self-limiting selfhood of his own

---

[38] Dante, like Augustine, typically thinks of this *false* self as an *external* self, offering a threat to his deeper, more "interior" selfhood, as for example, in *Inferno* I: 49–60, where he is harassed by the she-wolf of false desire, "gaunt, yet gorged on every kind of craving" (*Inferno* 1.50). Neither, though, sees interiority and exteriority as *inherently* opposed, though they both know all too well how human beings in practice get to oppose them to one another.

[39] *Confessions* X: 27: *tu autem eras intus et ego foris.*

construction. Therefore, *Confessions* is specifically not an *auto*biography, as if the self who writes and the self who is thereby described were one and the same. For Augustine, navel-gazing is not the way into self-knowledge, his is no inner eye gazing into some abstract interiority. For Augustine, you know yourself not by introspection, for that is precisely how you will be deceived, but in your choices, and in the acts of God that by grace cause them. Now it is no longer he who is the narrator, no longer a self whose identity is constituted by his narrating, for he is now essentially a being-narrated, a story retold by God in and through – *by means of* – his free choice. And it is here that one can see why the influence of the *platonici*, for all their decisive role in his intellectual conversion, had failed him emotionally. Platonism might have pointed him in the direction of the transcendent goal of conversion, but with it came no power to heave him over the brink of contrary desire and so actually convert him.

Even when in *Confessions* VII: 17 he tells how Plato has brought him intellectually to the point of belief in an immaterial God, he remained, if persuaded intellectually – *in ictu trepidantis aspectus*, he says, "in the shock of a trembling glance" – nonetheless unable yet to give himself over body and soul to the truth he saw therein. For even here Augustine is still telling his story on his own terms, and those terms must ultimately fail him. It is for this reason that he adds, in a strikingly downbeat coda to his account of the role of the Platonists in his slow journey to conversion, that they could give him the conviction but not the courage of it: "I did not possess the strength to keep my vision fixed," he says. "My weakness reasserted itself, and I returned to my customary condition. I carried with me only a loving memory, and a desire for that of which I had the aroma but which I had not yet the capacity to eat."[40]

And when in *Confessions* VIII he is at last on the edge of the final, true, conversion, now known to be a conversion only to Christ, now intellectually convinced that Christianity's truth supplants that of the *platonici*, persuaded moreover by Ambrose in Milan that the Christian Scriptures can be rescued by means of allegory from what had seemed to him to be their literary and rhetorical awfulness,[41] even then he was unable to take the step into the personal commitment that it called for – like a man who hesitates on the seashore on an cold day, Augustine can put in a toe in the ocean but can't get himself to take the plunge. It is then that he prays indeed for chastity – "but not yet."[42]

Augustine and Dante at the Point of Conversion

The parallel between Augustine in the garden in Milan in *Confessions* VIII and Dante poised on the brink, high on Mount Purgatory, is hard to miss, for Dante's predicament, granted a crucial difference that we will examine in a moment, is in this respect the same as Augustine's. Teetering on the edge of the chasm, both hold back, and both are reduced to tears by their failure to take the leap into its unknown depths. Both, supremely articulate as they are, lose their voices under the stress of their guilt. Dante tells us that,

---

[40] *Confessions* VII: 17.   [41] See *De Doctrina Christiana* 2.16.
[42] *Confessions* VIII: 7.

> A crossbow triggered under too much stress
> snaps its own string and splinters at the arc.
> Its shaft thus hits the target with less force.
> I burst in that same way beneath the load
> and, shedding streams of sighs and sobs and tears,
> my voice came slack and slow along its course.[43]

"Weeping," Dante confesses to Beatrice that soon enough after her death he had forgotten about her, and

> mere things of here and now
> and their false pleasures turned my steps away
> the moment that your face had hid itself.[44]

And so, standing before her now, he is

> [a]s little boys who stand there dumb with shame,
> eyes on the ground and listening to what's said
> aware – very sorry – of what they are
> so I, too, simply stood.[45]

Dante's model is Augustine's conversion taken into equivalent narrative detail. Augustine was converted but not before God "lashed me with the twin scourge of fear and shame in case I should give way once more,"[46] just as Beatrice lashes Dante; like Dante, the most articulate of poets, who, confronted by Beatrice's challenge, is "dumb with shame," so too does Augustine the orator lose his voice, his lungs weakened, and he is disabled in the very powers that defined his identity as a rhetorician and in those powers of acute self-description on which his pre-conversion selfhood had heretofore relied.[47] Here

---

[43] *Purgatorio* 31.16–21. [44] Ibid., 31.34–36. [45] Ibid., 31.64–67.
[46] *Confessions* VIII: 11. [47] *Confessions* IX: 4.

again their narrative powers fail them and so they are forced to abandon their self-told stories, their stories *of* themselves told *by* themselves. And just as in both cases their personal identities are tied in with the possession of the rhetorical powers that had made them the writers that they are, so it is those very skills of expression, forensic advocacy in Augustine's case, poetic creativity in Dante's, that are rendered impotent. There is only one way forward: They will be able to reclaim their lost rhetorical powers only on condition of their embracing an entirely new life, a *vita nuova*. If they are to be able truthfully to tell the story of their conversions, they need to become new writers; and if they are to become new writers, they need to become new selves; it is all circular, both the same thing, the conversion itself and the ability to tell the story of it being mutually enabling, each possible only on condition of the other's actuality. *Everything* is at stake for them, both as persons and writers; for Dante, poetry and persona, for Augustine, rhetoric and self-knowledge, are inseparable. Only the converted can truthfully narrate the prehistory that leads to their conversion, not for the trivial and tautological reason that the unconverted have yet no conversion to narrate, but because by their conversions they have a new story to tell that require new powers of narration adequate to the telling of it. You can tell the story of conversion only from the end. As Hegel said, the owl of Minerva flies after dark, when the daytime's deeds are done.[48]

---

[48] G. W. F Hegel, "Introduction," in *Elements of The Philosophy of Right*, ed. Allen W Wood, trans. H. B Nisbet, Cambridge: Cambridge University Press, 1991, p. 23.

Akrasia, and Telling the Story of Conversion on Your Terms

These parallel accounts that Augustine and Dante tell of their immediately pre-conversion predicaments therefore describe states specifically of *unresolved* desire, of commitment postponed, of a form of desire that is closer to the wish than to the will, closer to what at a second-order level they want to want when as yet they don't have the first-order strength of purpose demanded of them truly to want it. They are both still, or perhaps, once again, "lost in a dark wood." These accounts tell of how things seemed to them at the time, of their predicaments as they understood them then as being like that of St. Paul who wills the one thing but his unconverted flesh would have him do the other; and so he says "I do not understand my own actions" for, "I do not do what I want, but I do the very thing that I hate."[49] All here is conflicted desire. Whereas Augustine could reflect that when in Carthage there was indeed something that he sought but then he didn't know what it was, for wallowing in the city's fleshpots he had misidentified the truth of his desire, now in Milan it is the other way round. Now he knows what he would want if only he could but finds in himself a source of resistance to it, having no power to seize upon the object of his desire. Now, it seems to him, his predicament is no longer that set by his failure of self-knowledge. Now what he sees himself to be failing in is strength of will. But in that self-conception too he has yet to learn that he is wrong.

[49] Romans 7:15.

Frecerro says that the terms in which Augustine describes his moral paralysis in *Confessions* VIII fit better with Aristotle's account of *akrasia*, or weakness of will,[50] than with Plato's account of moral weakness, as somehow a failure of knowledge. Plato had thought it impossible that those who truly know what they ought to do could fail to act accordingly. For, he said, it is a matter of definition that of those who fail to act as they think they ought it cannot true that they *knew* that they ought to act in that way. Theirs, he said, could not have been the true *episteme*, the true knowledge of the truly virtuous, but only weak "opinion," mere *doxa*, by which latter Plato meant something like our hopeful, merely wishful, thinking. In short, he said, you cannot act contrary to knowledge, for any judgment you fail to act on is shown thereby not have been an act of knowledge at all, for knowledge conquers all. This, Aristotle complained, makes an analytical truth out of a material claim that is simply counterintuitive, being at odds with the obvious way of looking at things, *tois phainomenois enargos*.[51] For, Aristotle said, we all experience ourselves doing what we know we shouldn't, and in such a case it is in every ordinary and legitimate sense of the word "know" that we know both what we are doing and that we are wrong to be doing it.

Aristotle thought his disagreement with Plato about *akrasia* was stark. Nonetheless in the account of Augustine's narrative of his failure of moral nerve there is no

---

[50] Aristotle doesn't have anything much like our modern notion of will as a power altogether distinct from and independent of intellect and reason and in itself nonrational. The better translation of his Greek is something like "reasoned desire."

[51] *Nicomachean Ethics* VII, 1150a 7–11.

need to set them entirely at odds with one another in the way that Aristotle thought was necessary, for there are more ways than one in which we morally fail, some being better explained in Plato's way, others in Aristotle's. And of the two narratives of moral failure in *Confessions*, the first, in book VII. 17, seems better to fit Plato's conception of it, the second, in book VIII, is better accounted for by Aristotle's.

You might say that when in *Confessions* VII: 17 Augustine tells the story of his wavering conversion to Platonism and of how, though he was theoretically convinced by the arguments of the *platonici*, those arguments failed to take a firm grip on his practical life, it does seem plausible to ask whether his failure to change his life accordingly didn't in itself show that the conviction had fallen short of true "knowledge," was not *episteme*, just *doxa*, the shallow habit of a fleeting thought in pursuit of the plausible, no more than that illusory claim to knowledge and of truth that keeps a prisoner chained in a cave facing flickering shadows cast on the back wall of the cave in the twilit world of mere opinion.[52]

It might well seem that those are the terms appropriate to Augustine's predicament in *Confessions* VII. But in *Confessions* VIII his description of his now resolved acceptance of Christian truth won't yield so easily to the Platonist's account of his being in a cognitive state of mere opinion. For he is now fully convinced that the truth is to be found in Christ, and, Frecerro says, his failure to take the final step of conversion might seem to fit better with Aristotle's account of *akrasia* as being

[52] *Republic* VII, 514aff.

a failure of *desire* of the good, more with a weakness of will than on a Platonic account with lack of intellectual conviction. For in book VIII Augustine has come to see for himself that as he stands on the threshold of conversion, knowing that he should cross it but unable to do so, then it was his will that failed him and his vision, for all that it pointed to the truth of Christianity, was inept in consequence of will's failure. And his sense of guilt at the failure bore personal witness to the fact that truly he *did* know what he should do. But he could not take the step because, he said, he did not have the strength of will to do it. So, at the point of crisis, it seemed to him.

Conversion of the Will

But if it was in some such terms that Augustine understood his predicament while he was on the edge of conversion, it was not in such terms that, once converted, he came to see his predicament to have been. His conversion enabled him to tell the story of it in other terms than of the strength or weakness of his will, for he came to see that his perception of his unresolved condition of mind and soul in the garden in Milan as being *akrasia*, a failure of will, fell short of the complexity of his pre-converted predicament. It is here that the importance becomes acute of distinguishing between a conversion story experienced from the inside of it provisionally at the time, and that which is told definitively from within the converted perspective of the new life wherein his vision is finally transformed. From within the crisis in the garden in Milan it had seemed to Augustine that it was "will" that was failing him; but from the standpoint achieved by his eventual conversion it seems rather that that account of his moral predicament was inadequate to the deeper truth of it.

It is here, though, that we should first note a difference between the two crises of Augustine and Dante, the one, Augustine's crisis of book VIII of *Confessions*, the other, Dante's crisis in cantos 30–31 of *Purgatorio*. For whereas Augustine's crisis seems to be caused by a failure of will and so of moral weakness – he knows what he should do but cannot get himself to do it – the Dante who emerges from the painful cleansing trials of Purgatory, the marks of the seven Ps now removed from his brow, is a man not troubled by the thought of moral failure at all, and in this respect his problem is the opposite of Augustine's. Far from seeing himself as falling short, Dante thinks he truly has met the conditions of his renewal as a poetic author and person, because now that the names of the vices have one by one been removed from his brow, his trial of moral failure seems to him to be over. It is, then, as one who in that way is beginning to think of himself as the hero of a moral success story that Dante arrives at his point of crisis, just as Augustine meets his crisis in a story of a man defeated, an inadequate moral failure.

But *eadem est scientia oppositorum* as Aquinas says:[53] Terms that are distinct belong with one another in a common family of distinction at some level or other, for in general judgments of sameness and judgments

---

[53] See, for example, *ST* 1–2ae q54 a2 ad1. Usually he is quoting Aristotle, *Peri Hermeneias* 6.17a 33–35.

of difference go hand in hand. So it is that Dante and Augustine do indeed differ, but only on such common ground as is occupied as much by the morally firm as by the morally weak. For they differ only as to where they are on the *same* scale of moral strength, Dante believing himself to possess it, Augustine knowing only the lack of it. And if both are in crisis the cause is the same for both, even though approached from the opposed ends of the common range, Dante thinking of himself as having made it to a level of moral achievement that defines that of which Augustine in the garden in Milan has fallen short. Or so it seems to them at their respective points of crisis. Both, however, discover that they are mistaken, and for the same reason.

It is because Dante and Augustine share a common set of terms descriptive of their opposed pre-conversion predicaments that Dante's persistence in the arduous journey up the slopes of Mount Purgatory seems to him to be a moral achievement: as, compared with Augustine's weakness of will, it is. That being so, the question arises why, Dante now purged of sin, does Beatrice so violently humiliate him upon arrival at its summit. In what way, thus relieved of the hold of the vices upon his will, has Dante not met the condition set for him when at the end of *Vita nuova* there appeared to him that "miraculous vision in which," he says, "I saw things that made me resolve to say no more about this blessed [Beatrice] until I would be capable of writing about her in a more worthy fashion."[54] Why, then, does he still lack the capacity, moral and

---

[54] *La vita nuova*, chapter xlii, ed. and trans. Mark Musa, Bloomington: Indiana University Press, 1973, p. 86.

literary, to write the *Comedy* itself? How have the painful progressions in the company of Virgil through Hell and through Purgatory failed to prepare him for entry into Paradise together with Beatrice? How is it that the real progress he had made by way of his journey through Hell, where the fate of Ulysses had taught him what in his former life his poetic self he had risked morally, still wasn't enough? Above all, how is it that the journey in Purgatory that has taken him progressively through the stages of "purgation" required of his becoming able to write worthily of Beatrice, has left him still falling short? How is it that these two reformations have *not* brought him to a condition of worthiness for entry into Paradise, are *not* yet the conversions required of the poet-author of the *Comedy*?

Beatrice's challenge confronts smug Dante with a wholly unanticipated crisis. He is stunned, humiliated. We as readers are caught equally unprepared. To be told at this point, now two thirds of the way through the narrative of *Comedy*'s journey, that we have arrived only at the beginning of it, takes some adjustment of perspective, and Dante makes it clear that the adjustment is entirely necessary. Beatrice confronts Dante with an unpalatable truth. He is still far from having met the conditions of person and of poet that he had laid down for himself in that vision of her at the end of *Vita nuova*. And Dante confronts the reader with the same unexpected truth. Just as Dante misconstrues the nature of his journey, so have we. What is more, it is the very success with which he has up to that point pursued his journey of personal moral reform that prevents him from seeing that he has *not* arrived. If Dante's journey thus far has been sufficiently arduous to persuade him – and we readers are perhaps similarly persuaded – that he has arrived at its proper destination, now he must learn that, on the contrary, it is just such confidence, and with it the illusions on which it is grounded, at which Beatrice now directs her ire. For it is that self-confidence that will hold him back.

There is an old story of moral and spiritual development that Dante tells in his own way, and it is not a uniquely Christian one. It is told by Aristotle himself in the *Nicomachean Ethics* in the distinction that he makes between the strong-willed person and the truly virtuous person. The weak of will, he says, do of course contrast with the strong of will, the morally feeble, the *akrates*, with the steadfast, the *enkrates*; but, Aristotle says, *both* the moral backslider *and* the morally steadfast in turn contrast with the truly virtuous. For strength of will exercised merely in control of wayward desire is in itself no virtue, he says, not yet, or even, sometimes, not at all; for mere willpower can as easily amount to no more than mere stubbornness, as is illustrated by the silly joke of the Sophists who, Aristotle says, claimed that stupidity plus moral weakness gives you virtue, since if stupidly you think that you ought, say, to commit adultery but lack the strength of will to go ahead with it, then in the event you will have acted well.[55] Thus those strong-willed persons who can through gritted teeth hold firm morally, though by inclination they would act otherwise, and those who can't get their teeth sufficiently to grit and can do no more than in shame and disappointment grind them are, for Aristotle, together on

[55] See *Nicomachean Ethics* VII, 2, 1146a 18–22.

the *same* page of moral underdevelopment, as are Dante and Augustine respectively. In Aristotle's terms *both* lack virtue. Both are, as it were, *self*-asserters only. Dante the *enkrates*, the "continent," and Augustine the *akrates*, the "incontinent," are both poor performers morally, the one with grim effort gets himself to do what he knows he should, thinking on that account that he is a moral success, the other would rather do what he ought but lacks the strength to carry it out and knows he is a moral failure. Both measure their performance by the same standard of degree of willpower, and it is therein that is their common failure, holding them both back, both having missed the moral point. For in construing their predicament in terms of their own moral agency, of its strength in Dante's case, or of its weakness in Augustine's, they have but reinforced the problem. The problem is not Augustine's weakness of will; nor is Dante's strength of will the solution. The problem – the obstacle to their conversions – is in themselves, in the very notion of their conversions being a matter of *their* agency, of their *wills*. And whether in the form of Augustine's despair at the lack of it or in the form of Dante's presumption in his possession of it, their true conversion, the discovery of new narrative of a new life, is held back. All they know is the old story and come what may they are sticking to it. But they cannot be converted just insofar as they do.

Beatrice's Challenge

Dante's discovery that his constancy of will achieved through the disciplines of Purgatory is but a pale image of virtue at its best, and at its worst a false image of it, shatters his complacency. In the harshest of terms Beatrice humiliates him. She knows she must do so because of his presuming to have arrived at the end when he has only just made it to the beginning: Dante's self-righteousness is grimly self-confident. Therefore, it is as one "stern and proud," that she looks on him; with "sovereign strength" she "spoke her fieriest words" directed at his willful and humorless self-righteousness:

> Look. I am, truly, I am Beatrice.
> What right had you to venture to this mount?
> Did you not know that all are happy here?[56]

It is not virtue, she says, until it makes you happy, and so he confesses, that his "eyes fell" and upon looking down into Lethe's "spring clear brook" he sees in his own reflection the morally stunted person he still is, and in shame he had to look away. So hurtful had Beatrice's scolding of Dante seemed to her companions that they plead on Dante's behalf, "Why, donna, cause him discord such as this?" they say. Beatrice is unmoved. She insists that Dante has not yet begun to face up to the gravity of his betrayals of her when after her death he had "turned his steps to paths that were not true," so that even her prayers for Dante "came to nothing."[57] She goes on: So little heed had he paid that she had had to call upon Virgil to drag him through Hell itself. But, she adds, the way back for Dante will pass not only through Hell, nor only through the purgative trials one by one of all the vices, neither being yet enough, for from where those trials have left him there is no way forward. If in his judgment he complacently imagines he has

---

[56] *Purgatorio* 30.70–78.   [57] Ibid., 30.130–135.

passed the tests required of him then where he is is where he will forever stay, a self-satisfied prig. As such he is not ready to pass beyond Purgatory, for, Beatrice replies to her companions who had pleaded on Dante's behalf that she should ease up a little,

> God's high decree would shatter ... if he
> should pass by the Lethe and go on to taste
> the food of life, yet leave unpaid the tax
> of penitence, which pours out flowing tears.[58]

Christian theologians of Dante's acquaintance for centuries before him and ever since his times still, have known of this starting point, this spiritual stage in the *itinerarium mentis in Deum* at which Dante has arrived, and of its dangers; and in common they knew of the error, intellectual and spiritual, of confusing an initial clearing away of the accumulated moral clutter with achievement of spiritual maturity, of thinking that the starting point is a point of arrival.

Long before there are distinct doctrines of purgatory as a postmortem place or condition, there are Christian doctrines of spiritual purgation in *this* life, as a merely preliminary stage of spiritual development, for, as in the late fifth century the Pseudo-Denys had said, a first stage of purification is to no good purpose if it does not lead to higher stages of illumination and ultimate union with God.[59] And in turn, 800 years before Dante, he draws upon a tradition

---

[58] Ibid., 30.136–145.
[59] *Celestial Hierarchy*, 3, 165C, in *Pseudo-Dionysius, The Complete Works*, trans. Colm Luibheid, Paulist Press: New York, 1987, p. 153. This is a liturgical pattern as Andrew Louth says, but soon enough in the hands of Western Christian commentators it becomes detached from that connection and more a pattern of individual spiritual progress. See Louth, *Denys the Areopagite*, London: Geoffrey Chapman, 1989.

that begins as early as Origen's account in his *On First Principles* of the necessary purgations required as the condition of being able to read even the Scriptures themselves with any degree of adequacy to their true meaning.[60] In Dante's own times Meister Eckhart preached that those who seek God in the ways and means of ascetical practice will find the ways and lose God, "who in 'ways' is hidden."[61] Three hundred years after Dante, Teresa of Avila, knowing next to nothing directly of those long theological traditions, can in just the same spirit admonish the sisters of her Carmelite reform who, she says, having cleared the spiritual decks of obvious faults and sins have settled down comfortably, secure in the third of the seven "mansions" which, all taken together, stake out the itinerary of the mystical life: "with humility present," she says, "this stage is a most excellent one. If humility is lacking," she adds, "we will remain here our whole life – and with a thousand afflictions and miseries."[62] Miserable, she says, are the angry, censorious mentalities of those merely pious sisters of hers who, believing themselves to have made it to perfection have called a halt to further progress, adding that it "is very characteristic of persons with such well-ordered

---

[60] *On First Principles*, IV, chapter 2, in Origen, *An Exhortation to Martyrdom, Prayer, On First Principles: Book IV, Prologue to the Commentary on the Song of Songs, Homily XXVII on Numbers*, trans. and intro. Rowan A. Greer, New York: Paulist Press, 1979, pp. 178ff.

[61] Meister Eckhart, *Sermon 5b: In hoc apparuit charitas dei in nobis*, in Meister Eckhart, *The Essential Sermons, Commentaries, Treatises and Defence*, trans. and intro. Edmund Colledge and Bernard McGinn, Paulist Press: New York, 1981, p. 183.

[62] *Interior Castle*, III: 2.9, *Collected Works of Teresa of Avila*, vol. II, trans. Otilio Rodriguez and Kieran Kavanagh, Washington: ICS Publications, 1980, p. 313.

lives to be shocked by everything"[63] and to be irritated by the "imperfections" of her sisters: They do but parody the attitudes of genuine virtue believing that their pious poses contain the substance of it. They are, she says, but invulnerable prigs. And it is in just that same spirit that Beatrice challenges Dante's complacency. The warning, constant and insistent in all the best Christian ascetical traditions, has its origins and gets its authority from the parable Jesus told of the man who had had a devil cast out of his soul and, thinking himself secure, thereupon tidied up his inner life and having set his house in order had on that account become wholly at the mercy of seven more devils. The result, Jesus adds, was that "the last condition of the man was worse than the first."[64] So much for the complacent illusions of the comfortably well-ordered life. Dante before Beatrice is just such a person.

Viewed in some such terms it is not hard to understand her fury with Dante: She had hoped to have unsettled him radically enough in that vision of her that he had reported at the end of *Vita nuova* only to discover on Mount Purgatory that he has complacently settled down again into a condition that is not a place of arrival at all but a mere staging post, in effect refusing the demands of conversion by way of a complacent and merely moral containment of it. It is as if, to put it in Aristotle's terms, to constrict the demands of the good, and in Dante's terms, the imperatives of love, by way of the control mechanisms of the merely continent who, happy in their achievement of self-discipline and self-control, have just on that account become quite closed to conversion. It is, after all, unsurprising that in a cantica

---

[63] Ibid., III: 2, p. 315.   [64] Matthew 12:45.

called *Purgatorio* its climactic scene should thus turn on Dante's discovery of the true nature of purgation, that it must *self*-transcend, go beyond what Søren Kierkegaard called the Socratically ordered universal moral principle on the way to "the infinite demand" of faith.[65] Purgatory is no place to stay and has no meaning except as clearing the ground for a total transformation of self, and as of self so also of authorship, that goes far beyond anything that Dante had been able to conceive in advance. Beatrice's call in *Inferno* canto 2 upon St. Lucy and on the Virgin Mary, answers the despairing plea that Dante had addressed to Virgil at the prospect of the arduous journey demanded of him: "But me? Why me?" he had asked in anguish, "Who says I can? | I am not your own Aeneas. I am not St Paul ..." At that point at the beginning of his journey Beatrice reassures Dante, giving him at least enough encouragement to set out with Virgil on the journey that Aeneas had taken through Hell. But at that point Dante had no idea what the final cost of the journey was to be, nor has anything in the journey through Hell and Purgatory thus far prepared him for what Beatrice will now demand as the price of entry into Paradise. In short, Beatrice shows Dante at the *end* of the journeys through Hell and Purgatory that he has not yet undergone the true conversion that is called for as the condition of entry into Paradise, a conversion for the want of which he will be unable to write the *Comedy* itself.

It is not, of course, that Dante had made no progress at all. He did at least know how the rediscovery of his

---

[65] See Søren Kierkegaard, *Fear and Trembling*, Problem I, in *Fear and Trembling and the Sickness unto Death*, trans. and ed. Walter Lowrie, Princeton, NJ: Princeton University Press, 2013, pp, 107–129.

selfhood in Purgatory must be distinguished from Hell's eternally repeated infinity of self-reference, where reflected feedback on the self becomes the self's substance, where the *self* becomes the Hell. But he does not yet understand just how radical that difference is. Indeed, it seems clear that for Dante-author what he has Beatrice calling for now is a crisis of theology as much as of person, and it is one far more demanding than some theologians of his times envisaged, who thought Purgatory's pains could be distinguished from Hell's merely as pains suffered hopelessly are distinguished from the same pains suffered remedially. For such theologians, Hell's and Purgatory's pains are the same pains, just *experienced* differently.

Aquinas puts it this way and one wonders about it. Possibly, we saw Aquinas to say, Purgatory as such – and not just the purgatory of the pre-Christian saints of Israel – is even the same place geographically as Hell. At the very least Hell and Purgatory are in "close proximity" and, above all, the fires are the same in either place, for it is "the same fire torturing the damned in Hell that purges the just in Purgatory,"[66] adding that "in itself" (*quantum ad substantiam*) Purgatory's fire, like that of Hell, is eternal, though in Purgatory it is temporal in its reformative effect.[67] Gregory the Great, he adds, is of the same view: "just as it is the same fire that melts gold and reduces straw to smoke, so it is by the same fire that the sinner is burned and the elect purged."[68]

---

[66] "[I]dem ignis sit qui damnatos cruciat in inferno, et qui iustos in purgatorio purgat," in IV *Sentent*, d 21 q1.
[67] Ibid., ad 1.
[68] Though Aquinas admits in the same passage that Scripture settles no questions definitively on the matter.

Aquinas's understanding of Purgatory is, however, very hard to make out with any consistency. On the one hand he is clear that Purgatory is a place of hope, whereas Hell's suffering is essentially eternal and therefore essentially hopeless. On the other it is just that distinction which puts pressure on the proposition that their fires are the same; for if, as Dante clearly believes, they are essentially different it is because Hell's fires' hopelessness pervades its every experienced moment; and to say that the suffering of Purgatory is the same as Hell's, except that, Purgatory's being temporary, there is hope in it, seems to fail entirely to capture the difference. And if it seems wrong to represent Aquinas as saying that Purgatory is just Hell with a different attitude, as if, like Ludwig Wittgenstein's duck-rabbit, what it is depends on which way you look at it, it is not at all clear what he is saying.

For in so far it is in any way true to say that the fires of Hell and Purgatory are the same fires, eternal in the one case and temporary in the other, it is at best trivially so – in the sort of way that telling the truth and telling a lie might be said to be the same because they are both acts of telling. If that is so it's not the sameness that is of significance. Or perhaps it would be as if to say that Purgatory's being distinct from Hell in duration is like saying that a marriage vow with built-in conditional escape clauses is just a limited version of the indissoluble sacrament's infinite and unconditional commitment, and that they differ only as to the commitment's timespan. But again, the comparison misses the substantive point, for the difference in timespan is caused by difference as to the *nature* of marital commitment and not the cause of it. Correspondingly, the supposed "sameness" that consists in Hell and Purgatory's both being igneous places becomes an empty and pointless abstraction, and the point moot. There may be living flames and conflagrations in both Hell and Purgatory, but it seems but an empty thought that since some of those in Hell are suffering the pain of *some* fire, and it is only some who are thus described – the simoniacs in canto 19 of *Inferno*, their heads eternally stuck in the ground and the soles of their feet aflame, or the barrators in canto 21 who are stuck for ever in boiling pitch – and since fiery too is the condition of the penitent in Purgatory, whose soul, like the lover's in the Song of Songs, is *liquefacta*, melting in the "fire of love," therefore they can be said to be enduring the *same* fire. For, their common deployment of the same igneous metaphor notwithstanding, their narratives tell entirely different stories in wholly diverse universes of thought, in vocabularies between which there is no possibility of translation, none between those who are said to burn eternally in tormented guilt in Hell and those whose sins are burnt away by the passion of the love of God in Purgatory.

Hence, if we insist in saying with Aquinas and Gregory the Great that the fires of Hell and of Purgatory are the "same fire," it will be so only in the way that the description of two events in the abstract and without reference to any enclosing story might be said to be the same event. There is no possible non-eternal Hell, and Purgatory is not to be understood as if that is what it is. Concretely, like Aquinas, Dante does distinguish Hell and Purgatory as between worlds as radically opposed as are the registers of despair and hope; but for Dante that distinction makes *everything else* different as between the one and the other, and so as between their respective "fires." Far better theologically than Aquinas's abstract and misleading metaphor of Hell and Purgatory as sharing a common fire is, Kirkpatrick says,[69] Dante's very different conception of Purgatory as the place of the joyous recovery of virtue, the recovery of an original excellence, the place where the soul is returned in happiness to its true self and to that self's true world, yet to be encountered in the Earthly Paradise. The hope of the souls in Purgatory is not an attitude, a different *take* on the fires of Hell, to be adopted in accordance as one merits.[70] Purgatory's "fire" is the searing joy of a transformed vision. Hell's is but ash. And the difference is not a matter of will at all. It is, Dante says, a matter of memory.

---

[69] Kirkpatrick, *Purgatorio*, p. 481.

[70] There is another, more charitable, understanding of Aquinas's position on the "sameness" of Hell's and Purgatory's fires, namely that they are "the same" in that it is the single, one and the same, love of God that is the cause of both, though the experience of that love is hellish torture for those who have rejected it, whereas the penitent souls experience it as a refining fire that will bring them eternal happiness. I could make sense of that account of the "sameness" of Hell's and Purgatory's fires, but I don't find the evidence of such an understanding in Aquinas's texts – though admittedly they are early writings in the *Commentary on the Sentences* unrevised in the incomplete *Summa theologiae*.

5
Hope, Memory, and the Earthly Paradise

The Conversion of Memory

Augustine in *Confessions* book VIII and Dante in *Purgatorio* canto 27 are morally paralyzed, though Augustine knows it and Dante doesn't. Why in their different ways are they held back? What more do their conversions demand of them?

For Augustine, the "more" needed is something that is not within his power to provide. Truly he hesitates on the brink of conversion, his situation is fraught with tension, and resolution will come to him not at will but gratuitously, by way of a grace given at the instance of the voices of children at play next door. For his living purgatory has done its work and the conversion he now knows he needs far exceeds his strength to achieve. It will come as pure gift. Anxious as he is, his life's crisis still unresolved, he just has to wait for it.

Though paralyzed and rendered helpless by his sense of weakness – or perhaps just because of it – Augustine is open to grace. In contrast, Dante in *Purgatorio* 27 appears to be closed to it, for he seems to think his own purgatorial work has done all that is needed, having steadily pulled himself up one by one through all the vices, expunging the marks of them all from his brow. In truth, though, Beatrice tells him otherwise. She makes clear to him that his conversion is far from done, and there is no simple step further along the path already taken that will complete it, and that he is now called upon to retell his story from its beginning to its end, and in different terms than those in which has understood it thus far. He doesn't seem to understand that a new life is not a simple moral achievement, for it demands that new story; and what shows he hasn't understood this is his grim determination. Simply, Beatrice tells him that his joylessness, his failure to smile, shows that he is still playing the old game and is closed to the new. G. K. Chesterton in one way does get the greater radicalness of this sort of pivotal moment right: Dante's Brighton pier itself hasn't changed but it is so entirely new to him upon his return to it after years of peregrination abroad that it is no longer now what it was when he first set out from it; and in his different terms Plato too gets it right in that, he says, all true knowledge is acquired by way of a kind of *anamnesis*, by a process of "unforgetting," by the recovery of ancient memories long lost in the dark forests of false desire. In both Chesterton and Plato, the truth is in the origins to which all conversion is a kind of return upon the culmination of a long journey back home. That is why when you get back to Brighton, new as it seems, your smile is also that of recognition. Dante, by contrast, is satisfied with the progress he believes he has made in his journey through Purgatory thus far and he gives no thought to revising the past which he has left behind in Hell. He seems to think that he is now fit to move on from his Purgatorial rejection of Hell directly into Paradise.

Beatrice allows Dante no such complacency. She has told him that the Dante he thought he had abandoned when emerging from Hell still clings to him, and the act of spurning it had cut only superficially into the tissue of his false selfhood, the selfhood of sin's making. Asked of him now is a root and branch transformation of how he is to remember himself, a transformation therefore of how differently he is to tell the story of his journey to the summit of Mount Purgatory, and by retelling it to recover those primordial, deeper truths of self and identity that, given to him in the act of his creation, were lost in the subsequent catastrophe of sin. In short, he needs a new identity; or rather he needs to rediscover his true identity, for he has lost sight of it, hidden as it is below layer upon layer of a distorted self, a self of sin's construction. He has yet to learn that sin is not merely moral in its consequences. For though those seven "deadly" sins were indeed directly confronted and, in a way, one by one "purged," removed, in the arduous progress up Mount Purgatory, that journey was only the beginning of Purgatory's work. In canto 29, the imagery of contrast between Hell and Purgatory is telling. Hell was an inverted cone that spiraled down in ever tightened circles into Satan's empty silence at its core; Purgatory is the same cone the right way up, expanding as it ascends through the same vices as Hell's in reverse order, now redeemed. On the one hand, Hell was a terminus only for its inhabitants. For Dante, it was a place to travel through, and though indeed it was a place of conversion it was but negatively so, a place in which Dante's rejection of sin's rejections is achieved, the negation of Hell's negations one by one realized. Purgatory on the other hand is not a terminus for anyone at all, which is why Dante's treating it in canto 30 as if it were an achievement completed is so forcefully challenged by Beatrice.

In principle Purgatory is no place of arrival, whether for Dante alive or for those there who are dead. It is a place of learning wherein a transformation is achieved that cuts more deeply still into the tissue of Dante's selfhood than anything thus far achieved by his overcoming each of the vices in his peregrination of Mount Purgatory. Now a transformation more subtly cognitive is required of him, wherein fundamental distortions of self-perception, of identity, are challenged. It is no longer the sins he has done, his "actual" sins, that continue to burden him. He must confront the deeper damage from which those sins proceeded that has been done to his very selfhood, he must confront sin at its origin in him, the place whence the actual sins come. And it is this damaged self that must go if ever his true story is to be restored to memory – and that will take his being drowned by Beatrice in Lethe's waters, in the waters of self-forgetting. Only then will he have learned now at last to smile.

Self-Knowledge as Repentance

Dante of course has already told us that not all ways of remembering sin are ways of repentance. He has shown that the transparency of the memories of those in Hell, their very lucidity, have served only to reinforce a self-deceived complacency in sin, for those lost therein seem to be nothing without those memories, they cling to the recollection of their sins and their sins cling to them. Their memories are no more than pathological obsessions. Hell's sinners, like Chaucer's Pardoner, are so completely turned in upon themselves as thereby to have emptied themselves entirely of personal substance. They are in a perverse sense entirely honest, the self they see is pressed upon them with ghastly clarity, it is a self that is trapped in Ulyssian whirlpools, eternally wheeling round in diminished circles of lucid despair – circles, being endless in circumference and finite in radius, are Hell's mockery of eternity. The souls in Hell see nothing because they see through everything, the very excess of self-reference having destroyed the self thus known. They are therefore infinite in solitude. Their self-perceptions are like an absurd parody of the Cartesian philosopher whose identity, Patrick Masterson says, is not merely given in the speculative thought-experiment – the "I am" given in the "I think" – for that identity has become entrapped there in an endlessness of self-reference, in a self whose identity needs no others, wishes there weren't any others, because, as Sartre said, *les autres* have become *l'enfer*,[1] every other person being a negation of his own self, *his* hell.[2] Sartre's *L'être et le néant* is, Masterson says, the historical outcome of the Cartesian *cogito ergo sum*. But he adds, it is also the *logical* outcome of it. And so it is that the geometric circularity of Hell's *bolgia*s is a telling metaphor of their endless, but also pointless, self-obsession.[3] Theirs is the loneliness of the long-distance runner, except that they

---

[1] Sartre's existentialism is in this way the *reductio ad absurdum* of the Cartesian "cogito": Start with the "I think" and you will be ever after imprisoned therein.
[2] See Patrick Masterson, *Atheism and Alienation*, Harmondsworth: Penguin Books, 1972.
[3] Hell, too, is spiral, a whirlpool whose whole energy sucks you down, though it is also a system of concentric circles, and you cannot escape from the circle to which you are assigned. Purgatory is in every way Hell's inversion: It is an ascending spiral the energy of which is precisely to enable release into Paradise.

are forever running on the same spot. Therefore, in Hell all do indeed "know their sins" – in fact they are obsessed with them; but they know nothing else; and for all that they may regret sin's consequences they cannot repent of the sin itself. They are as a result immensely sad. This, the "punishment of loss," is, Aquinas says, "the chief suffering of the damned."[4]

I was once told when I complained about it that it is not cruel to confine a goldfish to a life within the perimeter of a small clear glass bowl, for the capacity of its memory is so small that it is in a constant state of surprise at the endlessly interesting view of its surroundings; for in want of memory its outlook, being never ancient, is ever new. I have no idea whether this is true or not – it probably isn't – but while the goldfish may be overexcited despite its world being confined to a tiny wholly transparent bowl, the cognitive condition of persons in Dante's Hell would in one all-important respect have to be the exact opposite experience of the same bowl. For Hell is filled with persons cursed with nothing but perfect recall of the past; what they lack is a future, they endlessly know what endlessly is going to happen, every time the same. And what is worse, contrary to what some say about the impossibility of identical repetition, Hell's fate would be, on this account, repetition eternally identical, the experience of a repetition that accumulates no new meanings. Its "same again" would be *exactly* the same, again and again, a trap, memory operating only repetitively. And as with Bill Murray's character in Danny Rubin's *Groundhog Day* where every day the same events are identically repeated,

---

[4] *Compendium theologiae*, chapter 174.

what for my hypothetical goldfish is endless delight at life's endlessly new vistas must become in a human utter despair, their hopelessness unalterable, their loneliness complete, their memory a curse.

Hell's pit is, then, the place of memory's turning in upon itself in an ultimate vicious circle, and circles are two-dimensional. Its world is entirely static. Once you are in the circle to which by your sins you are assigned you spin endlessly around it, there being neither any further up nor any further in. The very different geometry of Dante's Purgatory likewise matches its very different nature. It is a cone-shaped mountain that is traversed in a spiral from bottom to top, and then beyond. Three-dimensional, then, the spiral combines, as the Pseudo-Denys said,[5] the endlessness of the circle with the purposive directionality of the straight line, a line that is going toward an end that lies altogether beyond it. The whole movement of Purgatory is therefore provisional. It is a movement toward an essential "beyond" that is essentially eternal,[6] and the course of its journey is that of hope.

For this reason, when the souls in Purgatory revisit their pasts theirs is no infernal identical repetition. It is a place of progressive recollection. The repentant recall their pasts and retell them in the mercy of God, and their pasts resurface, their lives are renewed, their stories retold. Purgatory's spiral process therefore is in the formal geometry of hope, in that Purgatory's time-bound stay, once done, turns into its other, into Paradise forever

---

[5] *Divine Names*, 4, 704D, in *Pseudo-Dionysius, Complete Works*, trans. Colm Luibheid, New York: Paulist Press, 1987, p. 78.
[6] See Chapter 7 for further discussion of this eternity.

gained. For its being the place of entry into Paradise is the very meaning of Purgatory, its time-bound character lying not just in Dante's short-term premortem journey through it, but in its essential nature as time-limited, for all penitent souls, postmortem.

Nonetheless, now in *Purgatorio* 30 Dante is reminded that the transition from Purgatory to Paradise is to be no uninterrupted journey, as if his Purgatory's test had already been passed. As yet, Dante is a long way from having met Purgatory's condition of exit. Emerging at its summit, now about to be brought back to an original innocence in the restoration of the Earthly Paradise, Dante faces a new crisis that, as before in the very first canto of *Inferno*, once again demands of him a revision of narrative. This time it is Beatrice, not Virgil, who calls for a retelling of the story of how Dante got there; and now it is as when lovers enter a new life with one another, the old story disappears, and even the "facts" of the past cannot remain the same given the new world that they now enter upon. For Dante, the challenge of the story's retelling demands far more than what Virgil had called for when in *Inferno*'s first canto those savage beasts in the dark forest had threatened him. It requires more even than that which he himself had understood was called for when in *Vita nuova* he came to see that his lyric poetry must come to a halt until he had learned to understand Beatrice, his poetry's inspiration and gift, in an entirely new way. Hence, it is that although he has tracked his path through the trials of Purgatory, and though the marks of the seven deadly sins have each been wiped from his brow so that it had seemed to him that he had at last grasped what it would take to be worthy of Beatrice, he is told by her that even now he knows no such thing, that he is as yet far from being able to see her anew, as, now raised to Paradise, she truly is and always had been.

Purgatory and Learning How to Remember Well

For if the unalterable condition of the damned, Hell's "eternal return," is a mockery of Purgatory's time-bound hope, Dante is soon to learn by how much the more does Hell's eternity stand in stark contrast with the true eternity of Paradise.[7] Purgatory is no goldfish bowl; its movement is not that repetitive traversal of a finite circle, it is sequential, a finitely time-bound process placed between two "eternities" of wholly opposed natures, those of Hell and of Paradise, of eternal repetition and eternal renewal; and that would be true even if Purgatory takes but an instant of time, a process complete in a moment after death.[8] Instantaneous or time-bound, it is still a process inherently finite. It began as a journey of transformation of Dante's moral self that Virgil had been able to guide Dante through, as one by one all the marks of the vices that reign in Hell have been wiped from his

---

[7] See Chapter 7, "The Two Eternities."
[8] It really makes no difference to the doctrine of Purgatory whether, as in medieval times, you could perform pious acts that, if done appropriately, could reduce the time assigned to a soul in Purgatory (and even, if plenary, could complete it all in one go) or whether, as I recollect some theologian of our times having said, it could all be over and done with in a moment, in the "twinkling of an eye," the *intensity* of the pain of which is the measure of the degree of need for purgation. Images are images, and you need as many as possible lest any one of them gets to stick at the expense of all the others. Why not both?

brow. But in those for whom death has left the residual damage done by those vices as yet unexpurgated – this being what the medieval theologians called the *fomes peccati*, the "dry tinder" of sin still so easily set alight by the least temptation – there remains a sinfully weakened disposition that survives the willed repentance, like the sick person in recovery, the body still debilitated though the fever itself has gone.[9] And Aquinas says – Eleonore Stump reminded me of this[10] – no one may enter upon the beatific vision short of their perfection in grace, that is to say, not until they are in receipt of all the gifts of the Holy Spirit, including among them the gift of fortitude, the strength of final perseverance. For, Aquinas says, it is by way of the gifts of the Spirit that

> [a] man's mind is moved by the Holy Spirit, in order that he may attain the end of each work begun and avoid any perils that may threaten. This surpasses human nature: for sometimes it is not in a man's power to attain the end of his work, or to avoid evils or dangers, since these may happen to overwhelm him in death. But the Holy Spirit works this in us, bringing us to everlasting life, which is the end of all good deeds, and the release from all perils. A certain confidence of this is infused into the mind by the Holy Spirit, who expels any fear of the contrary. It is in this sense that fortitude is reckoned a gift of the Holy Spirit. For it has been stated above [Aquinas is referring to *Summa theologiae* 1–2ae q68 aa1, 2] that the gifts have to do with the Holy Spirit's movement of the mind.[11]

Such is Aquinas's way of identifying theologically what it takes to pass through the true test of Purgatory. The gifts

---

[9] See *ST* 1–2ae q82 a2 *corp.*   [10] In private conversation on Zoom.
[11] *ST*, 2–2ae q139 a1 *corp.*

of the Spirit are not an achievement of the person who possesses them; final perseverance is not a virtue whose achievement is won by passing a moral test, though there is a moral test and there is no step forward without having passed it; it is more that you cannot begin to respond to what is called for until you have passed a test of wisdom, the supreme gift of the Holy Spirit. And in this much at least Søren Kierkegaard is right, that you can't anticipate this final perseverance that is the work of Abraham's faith by way of the moral achievements of a Socrates, for perseverance to the end is a gift wholly unmerited, not given in what we do to win it; and that is true even if it is not given without such efforts. The still moralizing Dante doesn't know he needs this grace of perseverance. Thus far he has set his goal in terms of what *he* can achieve and, as he thinks of it, in terms of what he has already won for himself.

There is, therefore, no hope for Dante in this spiritual condition – that is to say, there is no true purgatory for him if he will not allow grace to move him on, for as matters stand he will be left with the remaining traces of Hell's self-obsessions still unexpurgated. For of Dante's state of mind at this point in Purgatory Aquinas's description of what Purgatory is like would hold true. For at canto 30 Dante's is a moral psychology that still belongs within the spiritual world of Hell, a place of sin and of Hell's punishment, even if it is only, and absurdly, Hell on a fixed-term punitive sentence. But this, we saw, *is* absurd because the hellishness of Hell *consists* in its endlessness. Just as Dante's journey through Hell properly understood is Purgatory, so Purgatory thus misunderstood is but Hell.

In any case, Dante cannot stay stuck in the rut of a punitive psychology of this kind. But neither can he move on until he submits to a moment of total vulnerability, and it is this requirement that differentiates Purgatory in every way from Hell: for in Hell all is eternally enclosed in an impenetrable carapace. In Purgatory all is openness, confession in both senses of the word, as the admission of sin and as the profession of faith, and so the mood is that of openness, passivity, vulnerability. Purgatory is pure *apologia*. Therein too lies the exact nature of the paradox that if the gifts of grace require that vulnerability on Dante's part it is also true that the vulnerability which is the condition of grace's reception is itself the gift of grace.

This is the reason why Dante's Purgatory is emphatically not a sort of fixed-term Hell. It is, rather, a condition whose primary purpose is to be a site of recovery from sin's beguilements – beguilements primarily about sin itself and principally those consisting in the false persuasion that it is sin's reality, sin's judgment, that comes first and last. It is in this way precisely that Dante's Purgatory is, as Robin Kirkpatrick says, nothing like Hell at all. It is a place of joyful recovery of a primal reality of which sin knows nothing, namely of "the happiness and love that the Creator had located at the heart of the human person. Since *Purgatorio* [canto] 16, Dante has repeatedly emphasized that the impulse in God's creative act is happiness, and that human desire constantly seeks to recover the initial happiness of creation."

Here is no guilt-ridden pain: Dante had suffered pain enough in his slow hard progress up the slopes of Purgatory, for guilt is what souls bring to Purgatory and Purgatory's purpose is to be rid of it, to achieve the recovery of a capacity for happiness that sin has destroyed. That is the reason why, as we saw in Chapter 4, Beatrice "scathingly condemns Dante for daring to come in tears to a place where human beings are meant to be happy."[12] The only tears permitted in Purgatory are tears of joy upon acceptance of that truth. It is a place of joy's recovery, the joy of a person's having been unconditionally redeemed, the joy of a grace received. But therein lies the exact nature of the paradox of Purgatory: If the gifts of grace require that vulnerability on Dante's part, it follows also that the vulnerability required cannot be his achievement, the vulnerability itself being the first work of grace. For even Dante's free consent to that grace will be the work of the grace he consents to, as Aquinas says.[13] And this seems to be the meaning of Beatrice's violent remonstration: Dante must be *dis*abled first if ever he is to be, by grace, *en*abled.

Beatrice's Anger

Therefore, Dante's only hope lies in an act of total submission to Beatrice, and Virgil, who represents for Dante the highest achievement of moral reform available to human powers, must now disappear without a word of explanation, for nothing in Virgil's experience permits the anticipation of what must happen next; and if Virgil does indeed know that he must now leave the scene, his work done, he knows no more than that. Therefore, he leaves Dante, and Beatrice must take his place as Dante's guide. It is here, then, that Dante faces the real crisis of

---

[12] Kirkpatrick, *Purgatorio*, p. 481.   [13] *ST* 1–2ae q 113 a 3 *corp*.

the *Comedy* at a pivotal point in its narrative. For his hope now lies in Beatrice's intervention, anything left within Dante's own power having ceased to be a means and is now only a block to further progress.

It is for this reason that the change Beatrice calls for is so shocking. But the shock is needed, and Beatrice insists that she must break down Dante's resistance in a way that seems to him at first to be catastrophic – it reduces him to those pathetic tears of humiliation. It's not just his being made to feel a moral failure in a routine way that humiliates him. What crushes him is the discovery that it is just this sense of his reliance on a *moral* achievement that is now causing his failure to recognize Beatrice as she reveals herself to him. A crisis faces him, and it is in this way that Kierkegaard does get right this need for "more," a more that goes well beyond anything Dante had achieved by way of the removal of the marks of the vices from his forehead as he makes progress through Purgatory – for in Kierkegaard's terms that is no more than a "Socratic" achievement of moral stabilization. Now it is a destabilizing leap of faith that is called for, there being nothing in what Dante himself brings to the crisis that will resolve it. He has been missing the point, and he still is, being unable still to see that what is required of him is the *loss* of that would-be self who aspires to the self-defeating ambition of a self-salvation.

Kierkegaard's dialectic of faith therefore captures well enough a sense of the radicalness of the demand that Beatrice places upon Dante; but it does not do justice to the complexity of that challenge, nor does it explain why Beatrice's excoriations are so fierce. She insists that Dante should have been prepared for that further step, for, unlike Kierkegaard, who thought that there is no continuity bridging the gulf that divides the Socratic moral universal from the dark night of Abrahamic faith, Beatrice judges Dante negatively precisely because the journey of moral reform through Purgatory should have prepared him for the more that was demanded of him, a more that goes beyond all that the journey of purgation, just completed, could achieve in him. He had failed to understand that this further demand was already contained *within* the lesser demands that he thinks he has met, and that failure to understand the further demand was itself the evidence that he had not understood even those lesser demands. That is why, Beatrice tells Dante, he has thus far *altogether* missed the point of Purgatory. Instead of a path forward, Purgatory was in danger of becoming a trap, because in Dante's clinging to the belief that he had achieved what was demanded of him he had allowed it to become one. As a result, his progress through Purgatory stutters to a halt.

The Purgatory's Supererogatory

"But I am right to exaggerate!" protested Professor Paul Williams, my colleague at Bristol University where I once taught, when we had laughed at some or other characteristic rhetorical extravagance of his. "I am right to exaggerate," he had said, and right indeed he was. It was we his colleagues who were mistaken, and it was his hyperbole that was just the thing called for, as it is in some crises, moral or spiritual, when the supererogatory is the minimum required, when not to exaggerate means you have entirely missed the point. Such is the general nature of the martyrs' responses to the threat of a death imposed. For martyrs know that what is called for is a total sacrifice and that the meaning of it is contained in an instant of choice where truly it is all or nothing, when anything at all short of the heroically supererogatory action of the saint is total failure, when a negotiated compromise is complete betrayal.

It is, after all, a truism of Christian belief and practice that we can add as a general point to Stump's, that Heaven's gate is open only to those who, one way or another, have died for their faith in perfect charity,[14] which is to say the same thing as she in another application. It is in fact precisely for the want of our having died well that a purgatory after death is needed to complete death's full meaning. The Church's saintly confessors are canonized only because they are martyrs by other means, in that theirs was a martyr's will. Entry to Paradise is given to those alone in whom, in one way or another, the supererogatory has become the default. The purpose of Purgatory after death is the achievement of that canonization of which the rest of us have before death fallen short.

Dante's moral reform, achieved painfully in that long steep climb up Mount Purgatory from Hell's depths, has done all the work that the recovery of human virtue can achieve. But it leaves him still short of what was required of him, for he has not yet fully embraced death in the relevant sense, that is, in an unconditional freedom of spirit;

---

[14] And notwithstanding the terrible deformations of this truth in some contemporary forms of politicized belief, it is a truth of faith that Christians and Muslims share.

it is thus that in truth he has not yet died in unconditional happiness And though Aquinas is right when he says that natural human virtue doesn't *entail* the supernatural[15] – for what the natural entails must on that account be itself natural – to say no more than that is to fail to capture the supererogatory moral force of Beatrice's challenge to Dante. For Beatrice makes it clear that she too has every right to exaggerate, that the need to exaggerate *beyond* the satisfaction of the humanly attainable moral demand is already there as called for from *within* that moral demand itself, if only negatively and as known only by way of an indeterminate sense of the inadequacy of the merely moral. For the minimum test determining whether Dante had truly understood the force of Purgatory's challenge is that he should understand the ascetical-moral to be insufficient even on its own terms. Duns Scotus seems to have understood the theological point of Beatrice's challenge more clearly than does Aquinas, for Scotus seems to grasp that you can know that you fall short in some indeterminate way even when you do not yet know explicitly the standard by which you

---

[15] Aquinas says that "the human good is twofold: (i) that which corresponds with our own nature; (ii) that which exceeds the abilities of our own nature …" and that the first does not meet the requirements of the second. Hence "it is necessary for there to be some sorts of completeness in us that exceed the abilities of the principles natural to us and that order us to our supernatural end. This could only be the case if God infused in human beings certain supernatural principles of activity on top of the natural ones." *Quaestio disputata de virtutibus in communi*, a 10 *corp*. That supernatural grace beyond the natural capacity is necessary to the life of virtue does not entail, but could be consistent with, the natural knowledge that such grace is necessary. At least in this text Aquinas leaves that question open.

have failed – as when you know quite well that you are not as happy as you should be, but not yet in what such greater happiness could consist. It is, Scotus says, "quite unsurprising [*non inconveniens*] that there should be a [human] power that is naturally ordered to an object to which it cannot naturally attain, that is, [an object] it can naturally and on its own terms be ordered to which is beyond its power to achieve."[16]

It is in some such terms that Beatrice appears to be accusing Dante of a failure to understand that more was asked of him than merely the achievement of a certain kind of moral stabilization. For without that further demand of a more radical conversion acknowledged and met the moral achievement itself becomes a sort of failure, a form of spiritual stationariness, a condition complacently closed in upon itself. And even though, when he emerges from the slopes of Purgatory onto the plain at its summit, he could not then have known in precise terms exactly what that more is that was still needed, he could have known that Purgatory's work is not yet done; and because he could have known it he should have known it. And because he should have known it but doesn't, he cannot yet be perfectly happy. Thus Beatrice.

Scotus's instinct, then, is that contained even within the world of a purely natural morality there is a sort of inkling of the implicit significance of that further demand of the supernatural, if only by way of a sort of negative anticipation of a truth that we have not yet been able to grasp,

---

[16] John Duns Scotus, *Ordinatio*, Prologue, quaestio unica, n. 92, cited in William A. Frank, "Duns Scotus and the Recognition of Divine Liberality," in *Archa Verbi, Subsidium* 4, ND, p. 53.

something that Keats was to call a "negative capability,"[17] the ability to grasp that there is something more called for of which we do not yet know the nature – perhaps not even its name. For by nature we can know ourselves to have fallen short even if we cannot know by what measure we have done so, or what it is that would make up what is lacking. Such was the knowledge actively present in those moments of unspecific unhappiness that Augustine experienced in Carthage and then later in Milan when he knew well enough that he had failed but not by what measure he had done so, being, as then he was, ignorant of the nature of the conversion that was called for.[18] It's a case akin to having a word on the tip of your tongue that you are unable to remember, though when it does come back to mind you know that it was just that word which you couldn't recall. And this seems better to explain Dante's predicament as Beatrice so forcefully puts it to him: After all, the pagan poet Virgil had been capable of knowing it in the way that did the atheist Keats, as it were "negatively," when he came to see that he could take Dante no further, and, in knowing that much, he knew that there *was* a further called for – though as a pagan it was beyond his power to comprehend its nature. That is how he knew that it was time to leave the scene, and without a word he leaves a complacent Dante to the mercy of Beatrice's ire.

---

[17] He describes it as the condition of one who is "capable of being in uncertainties, mysteries, doubts, without any irritable reaching out after fact and reason." Letter to Brothers George and Thomas, December 22, 1817, in John Keats, *The Complete Poetical Works and Letters of John Keats*, Cambridge: Cambridge University Press, 1899, p. 277.
[18] *Confessions* III: 5.

This is the challenge that Beatrice thrusts so violently upon Dante, and it is the arrival point of the *Comedy*'s whole tendency. It is not just an episode within a drama; it is the Archimedean point on which the *Comedy*'s universe turns. Dante either responds adequately to Beatrice's challenge, in which case the *Comedy* is possible, or else he cannot do so and there can be no further narrative to be written. What is more, had Dante failed to respond to that challenge, the narrative even of the sixty-seven cantos of *Inferno* and *Purgatorio* that had preceded this point would have had no significance, they would be, as it were, the self-deleting text of an inconclusive and meaningless plot, to be tossed into the trash can of literary and theological false starts. You can see implicitly why this is the narratival logic of the poem from the failure of the practice, as misleading as it is common in our schools, of reading *Inferno* for the first time on its own, detached from the other two cantica,[19] apparently just for the sadistic fun of its ingenious tortures, reducing its worth to nothing better than a higher literary equivalent of the snuff movie: *Inferno* is an essential moment in a redemption story. And Dante the author knows this truth about his text just as he describes the Dante-narrated as seeming thus far to have failed to understand it within the text.

It is here that the tension between Dante-author and the Dante-narrated is most acute. For this Dante-narrated was at that point not only a moral failure. Because of that moral failure he was a failure as poet-author, incapable

---

[19] I say, "for the first time," because when you know how to situate *Inferno* within the setting of *Purgatorio* and *Paradiso* then, but only then, can you make any sense of *Inferno* "on its own."

of writing the *Comedy* in any part, never mind the whole of it, though of course it is just in representing this failed Dante in the text that Dante *succeeds* as its author. For he writes of this failed poet and a failed man from the standpoint of one who has in fact passed the test that in *Vita nuova* Beatrice had set him. How else could he have written about his failure in *Purgatorio* 32?

It is for this reason that, very dramatically, Dante reveals his name, thereby marking that point at which we know that his writing the *Comedy* is an act which saves him both as poet and as person. In both connections Dante is called back by Beatrice to his baptism. It is then alone, when he has responded to Beatrice's demand, that Dante-narrated and Dante-narrating have finally become one and the same person, one and the same "Dante." Here at last the Dante saved by Beatrice in the poem composed and the Dante saved as its author by way of the act of its composition are united in one and the same "Dante."[20]

Or is he? I ask at this point because it is at this critical moment at the end of *Purgatorio*, if anywhere, that an alternative, even perhaps an opposed reading of the *Comedy*'s entire narrative trajectory is possible. You can read the crisis, as I have, as leading Dante-author to a surrender spiritually to Beatrice, therein quieting his authorial voice as poet so that he may speak the theological truths that underpin the structure of the *Comedy* in and through her voice. But why not see the crisis as demanding a volte-face

---

[20] In this way Dante goes beyond Aristotle's distinction between *phronesis* and *techne*, prudence, intelligent moral judgment on the one hand, and art on the other: for it is by way of his poem that Dante is converted just as it is in his poem that he describes it. Here are prudence and art in mutual entailment.

of a wholly opposed kind? Why not understand this turning point in the light of the fact that it is he, Dante-author, who, wholly in control, puts the imperious words of command into Beatrice's mouth: He is the author of Beatrice-guide, not Beatrice-guide the author of Dante. Were we to read this critical juncture of the *Comedy* in such terms, would it not follow that it is just here that we are called upon to grasp that if Dante-authored submits to Beatrice it remains that it is Dante-author, the poet Dante, who creates her in the first place. It is *his* Beatrice, the person he has reconstructed from the recollection of a former juvenile fantasy, who submits to Dante's call in the ironic construction of what, until this point, seems to be the reverse direction of narrative, the narrative of his abject obedience to *her* imperious command. After all, it is Dante-author who remains in control – of course he does, he *is* the author – and in introducing his own name at last it is he who in his standing as poet-narrator moves into the foreground so that his standing as the theologian correspondingly recedes, and the movement from the one to the other becomes that of theology's retreat as it dissolves finally into Dante's own poetic resolution.

The Waters of Lethe and the *Fomes Peccati*

How might we decide between these conflicting readings? Most obviously by observing that there is no need at all for some such general polarization between literary and theological values. Most especially we do not have to set the two allegories, that of the theologian and that of the poet, at odds. From the first chapter of this study and thereafter, I have argued that Dante had no interest in doing so and that we as readers have every reason to follow him. Here Dante admits to his name. Here is Dante who at last is thrust forward as author; he is the same author whose journey to a truer conception of authorship is narrated, and it is at exactly this point in the narrative that the identity of author and authored is achieved. Here Dante the poet and Dante-theologian emerge as one and the same Dante, no poet without the theology, no theology unless by way of poetry. And it *is* an achievement, an outcome won, a purgation described, and a purgation achieved by way of its description, a summation of both in the passive moment of the drowning described and of the active work of the author describing it.

Here then is the point in the narrative at which the resolution of the fundamental crisis of the *Comedy* can no longer be delayed, nor the poem's theological and literary meanings any longer concealed. Dante now makes it clear that he had been unprepared to meet Beatrice because he hadn't been ready for Christ. And this is not because Dante simply identifies Beatrice with Christ, though it is because what it takes to understand who Beatrice really is exactly what it takes to understand how Christ is the mover of the whole story. Beatrice isn't Christ, even allegorically. But she is an *alter Christus*. Beyond that, it really doesn't matter which way you put it: You shake the theological kaleidoscope, and you get one or the other pattern, the love-story with Beatrice or the story of conversion to Christ, the story of Dante-theologus or the story of Dante-poeta. It is the *kaleidoscope* that is the reality just in its containing those many meanings that are within the shake of a hand of one another. And either way the pattern is that of a conversion story, one in which, as we have learned all along in one way or another, and now definitively, *amor* and *caritas* converge, the personally erotic passion for the historical Beatrice who makes a poet of him, converging with the typologically formal representation of the *caritas* of the Church which makes a Christian of him; for they have become one in Dante's love of Beatrice in Paradise.

As we saw in Chapter 4, Dante is at this point in Purgatory faced with a new and more drastic crisis and he is quite unprepared for it. He was nowhere near understanding what it will cost him personally to be able to respond to Beatrice's examination of him, as relentlessly she presses on with accusation after accusation detailing his betrayals of her: "Since you grieve at what you're hearing, raise your beard | and, looking up, you'll feel still greater pain."[21] For the paradisal future of which baptism is the sacrament, breaks in and disrupts, but only so as to require the reenvisioning of all the continuities leading up to this point and create the truer narrative. Only then will Matelda and her accompanying ladies plunge Dante into Lethe's waters, the river of forgetting, the classical Styx, which Dante knows from Virgil divides the underworld from the Elysian fields. This is no passing metaphor. Dante must be denied the oxygen of the old life delivered by his power of memory, for memory's narrative strategies have shaped the pre-conversion identity which had been reinforced and held in place by such moral reformation as Dante's hard journey through Purgatory had brought about. Beatrice knew that she had to break that narrative thread connecting all that he had experienced in

---

[21] *Purgatorio* 31.67–69.

the journey from the dark gate into Hell to the high peak of Purgatory, and the breaking of the thread will demand of him a trauma of forgetting, an abandonment of all those traces of nostalgia for his old life's self-reassurances. It will take the riddance of those *fomes peccati*. It requires an expurgation not only of Dante's actual sins, for required is the expurgation of those *remnants* of sin, the residual damage that they have caused. In short, what is called for is the expurgation of the sinful *self*, before Dante can finally leave Purgatory and enter Paradise.

Again, we recall Folco's words – "Here" in Paradise "we do not remember our sins," and he smiles – though what he says is not quite true, for in a way the point is that in Heaven he can and does remember them. This "forgetting" of sin is no simple amnesia. Folco's memory of them isn't somehow shuffled away to be suppressed. The difference made by this "forgetting" is that now he smiles.[22] Now he can remember his sins no longer as threat, no longer a burden on conscience, the memory of them no longer seduces, for his sin's hold on him has been finally broken. Now he *may* remember them, for no longer has he any need to deny them, self-deception having ceased to be either necessary or even possible.

For if his sins do remain on the edge of memory they are without threatening effect upon it, no longer having any part to play in the construction of his identity otherwise than in that they have been forgiven. Here, then, is that other transparency, that of the celestial, wholly opposed to the despairing clarity of the souls in Hell, for it fills the soul with hope. Dante is forgiven, or rather, as he now comes to

[22] On smiles, see Chapter 7, "The Demotic Celestial: Smiles."

see, he has broken through the fog of sin to the consciousness of his having always been forgiven before ever he had sinned. And therein is the new reality: It is a moment of singular passivity. And it is because of it that at the thought of his past sins Folco can safely smile, for Freud's "cunning of desire"[23] that had hitherto been able without fail to find the means to sour even the best, most positive, sense of self, can no longer have its wicked way with him. Lethe has made such sinful tokens of identity redundant.

And it is this stripping away of memory's narrative power that had left Dante initially in that state of panic, at a loss to know where his selfhood had gone, questioning how he could manage without his given patented story that he had carefully assembled piece by piece, sin by sin, as he made his way through Purgatory. Here again is the dialectical shape of the *Comedy*'s narrative revealed. Just as the journey through Hell is realized as Purgatory, so in turn is Purgatory fulfilled in its outcome and in its way too is "abolished," being recovered in an entirely new, paradisal, meaning.

It is not just at the personal level of his actual sins that Lethe now causes Dante to forget. If we are to understand Dante's sense of alarm at the gravity of the crisis that he must face it is essential to see that he does not moralize about it all in the exclusively individualistic way characteristic of our times. Hard as it is for him to forget his actual, live, sins, sins ever on his conscience, it was harder for him by far to forget sinfulness itself, sin in its general causal condition and in the impersonal power with which it imposes upon Dante and all human beings in

---

[23] Ernest Gellner, *The Psychoanalytic Movement: The Cunning of Unreason*, London: Wiley Blackwell, 2003.

common, like a *dead* weight. The task of self-forgiveness overwhelms Dante, for a forgiveness so unconditional – the sheer terror at the thought of its depending on no action of his other than on an unconditional trust – can be even more disturbing of self than a trust too little. It is now clear to him that the true heroism demanded of him is that he should finally abandon this self of sin altogether. And the absolute and unqualified nature of this forgiveness panics him. Insecurity had revisited him at the prospect of losing the comforting complacency of a moderately and on balance more-or-less decent life now morally in order, and it is a quite natural fear – after all, one knows of few descriptions of what the condition of things in the beatific vision would be like that do not repel, precisely for the want in them of a tolerable human ordinariness. I recall when a teenager the effort it took to get myself to prefer Bach's music to Tchaikovsky's at a point when I discovered that I ought to do so because my musically sophisticated older brothers and sisters whom I much admired all did; and as I tried to figure out why the formally contrapuntal Brandenburg Concerto No. 6 ought to be preferred to the rather noisily vulgar drama of the 1812 Overture, the *fomes*, the dregs, of my childish musical tastes clung on to me until I learned first how to prefer Bach, and then how to like both, and no longer the one at the expense of the other.[24] Until then I had but second-order wanted to first-order like something that I didn't in fact first-order like that much at all. Therein

---

[24] Mind you, I yet have to overcome the feeling that it is just what I like so much in Bach that makes it so difficult for me to like anything much in Wagner.

was conflicted desire, a problem of self-identity to be distinguished in form from the kind of conflict faced when there is something that you want but are not sure that you are willing to pay the cost of getting it. For in this case the analogy is not so much with the ascetical cost of achieving ultimate happiness, more a matter of desirability in principle of what seems to be heaven's austere form of it, and so of wanting to want its felicity because called upon to do so while doubtful of the appeal of its tediously severe uneventful eternity. For heaven's eternity seemed lacking in the frisson of risk and drama, and to be deficient in, among other things, simple fun, to fall short in the matter of jokes. And there is no heaven for the doubtful, or for those who do not know what they want. Act 3 of George Bernard Shaw's play *Man and Superman* captures the instinct here – it's a bad play but the idea is good – in having the conversing pair apparently from Heaven and Hell turn out in fact to have come respectively from Hell and Heaven. For their shared endlessness would, it seems, be the interchangeable common factor,[25] and it is possible, for that reason, not to be all that certain which of the two you want.

Those instincts are the spiritual force driving the natural and spontaneous theology of the *fomes peccati*, of sin's "dry tinder," a sort of nostalgia for sin's undistinguished and rather petty ordinariness, whose presence is observed in a person's lived experience of sin's being "original," so-called because told in the earliest legends of humanity, where, ever since, it has infected one's sense of shared humanity and not just one's own individual will.

[25] See Chapter 6, "The Two Eternities."

Thus does the vulnerability to sin remain in the form of the *need* for a sort of reassurance that not too much is demanded even by way of future happiness. For we are like the women of Canterbury in T. S. Eliot's *Murder in the Cathedral,* who "do not wish anything to happen," preferring to heaven's unconditional demand to be but "living and partly living," in a more comfortable mediocrity.[26] And Dante had possessed no power of his own to get past that experience by any means presently available to him. For it was on sin's own seductive terms that Dante had been in danger of turning the purgatorial experience into a form of ultimate entrapment, wherein the sinful self reaches an uneasy truce with its sin, but mainly on sin's terms. Such would have been Purgatory betrayed; and Purgatory betrayed is Hell.

Therefore, Dante seems to be in peril because he can no longer himself do anything about this predicament. For a fallen will *is* fallen just in that it cannot lift itself out of its fallen condition even if it would want to. What Dante now needs is not more *purgation*. A more extended purgation will get him nowhere further, being nothing but a higher form of masochism. He needs a different conversion, a conversion not of will but of understanding, a new vision, an *illumination*. If Dante is to become a new person it will be only by entering into a new world, a world that he cannot enter short of death to the old world and burial in the waters of Lethe which requires his abandoning the familiar narratives that record his old self's clinging nostalgias, and his rewriting of the bad draft of

---

[26] T. S. Eliot, *Murder in the Cathedral,* Part I, Harcourt: New York, 1963, p. 19.

his life's narrative from beginning to end. It will require not a mere moral reform. It calls for a change of identity; and the change of identity requires a change in the nature of the relationships by which identities are established and recognized; and together it requires a new birth, a change that reaches down into the place where sin first found a home, and then further, to the place that is absolutely primordial, because it is *pre*-lapsarian, the place that is and always was beyond the reach of sin, the place within the self where the Creator's eternal will first touched the creature in time and remains there ineradicably forever after.

Remembering a "First" Self

In this way one remembering lost gives way to another remembering regained, a remembering of a self that is more antique, more original, and so more fundamental even than sin's remembering of a heaven lost, a hard-won recovery of origins that with reason Plato called an *anamnesis*, an "unforgetting." Julian of Norwich, caught up in a "showing" of love, saw "all that is," not in herself alone, but in creation as whole, and it was as small as if it were a hazelnut, its hold on existence so precarious that it seemed permanently to teeter on the edge of nonexistence. And yet she saw that in truth its existence is secure because it is made and unconditionally sustained by an infinite love eternally given. That love is all that saves the creature from the nothingness from which it came – which is as well, because, given our human contingency, love is all that *could* sustain it. And in that showing, made by love, she "saw not sin" – not even the thought of it – though, being herself on this side of death, she still experiences sin's "sharp pain," for her premortem experience is not yet the guilt-free memory of Folco in Paradise. It took Julian's being buried for decades in an anchorhold,[27] in a place of forgetting, to achieve a presage premortem of Folco's conclusive loosening of sin's grip. Only by that anticipation of death was there a restoration to a reality deeper in meaning within her than sin's reach, already there waiting to be recovered. That is why she "sees not sin" anymore, for she sees into the place in the soul where there is no sin to be seen because sin, poor devil, is unable to find its way into it.

What Beatrice causes Dante in Purgatory to see is that his sinful self is, in fact, a fantasy self, a false self, but above all a *falsifying* self, and with it comes its own false world that is told by sin's story of how things stand. It's not personal sins that reach down that far; they can be confessed and absolved, for they are but the phenomena, the trappings, of a fallenness, in which personal guilt obsessively calls attention to itself, distracting thought away from the harder part of sinfulness, which is the *fomes peccati*, the traces of loyalty to sinfulness's world, loyalty to a residual sinful cosmology. This is a deeper falsification by which sin creates the image of itself as primary, preceding all else. It is a falsification that buries the true self under layer upon layer of illusion until even the doctrine of salvation is itself buried under it and the work of redemption itself comes to be understood only on sin's falsifying terms, as a remedial

---

[27] Literally. The rite of initiation into an anchorhold was the ritual of burial, anticipating that true death that otherwise must succeed our merely physical death, getting your Purgatory in first.

afterthought, a sort of desperate backup plan, the original plan having gone so badly awry in Eden's Garden. It is that theology of sin as *the* primordial reality which Dante is now learning from Beatrice to resist; and Matthew Treherne reminds me that the commentators on *Purgatorio* 16 sometimes go so far in pressing Dante's downplaying of sin as to have him denying sin's reality as anything more than politically induced theological heist.[28]

That, I think, goes too far, though it does indeed seem certain that Dante is least at home theologically with Augustine's understanding of sin's "originality" according to which sin is embedded in all human nature prior to any actual sin that in their freedom human beings may have intentionally committed. When in *Purgatorio* 16 Dante asks Marco Lombardo whether the origin of evil is to be found in the stars or in the freedom of the will, Marco responds that the source of moral evil is in the latter, though he has no doubt that "the stars" have their role in influencing human behavior, an answer that fits in a general way with the views of both Aristotle and Aquinas. Both maintained, as Aristotle put it, that the actions of human beings generally proceed from the dispositions of their current "state of character" for which they are indeed in some degree responsible, but only up to some point determined by complex and ever-changing combinations in each human act, of choice, general ignorance, upbringing, habit, circumstance, and mere fortune – the "stars" – all playing roles in ever-shifting combinations.

Now, Dante says, we must *add* to the list, as Marco Lombardo does, that "bad government | is why the world

---

[28] Commenting on an earlier draft of this chapter.

is so malignant now | It's not that nature is corrupt in you."[29] There is, however, no need on the strength of that statement to attribute to Dante the quite general proposition that bad government is the one and only source of the world's evil – else Dante would be left bereft of an explanation as to how it is that "government" is itself so routinely bad: For he clearly doesn't think that bad politics *invents* evil even if it powerfully sustains and multiplies the damage sin does; and in any case, as we saw in Chapter 3, there is not and cannot in principle ever be a comprehensive account of the origin of sin and evil in the world that does not presuppose just that which it seeks to explain. It is for that reason that at some point you do have to describe sin as having an "original" character, in that we have no general explanation in terms of a prior condition that entails it.

To advert to that fact is one thing; a quite different proposition, not entailed by the first, is that sin is the *defining* "original" human reality. For the common medieval tradition of reading the Genesis narrative maintains that it tells the story of a "fall" precisely from an original condition of innocence, in short that sin, sinfulness in general, is precisely *not* original, not the first thing to be said, even less is it the last. Furthermore, it goes with his rejection of *that* notion of original sin that Dante resists the other, very odd, but remarkably common opinion that the reason why there is no need for a *narrative* of sin's origin is that human beings, being free, are anyway bound to make evil choices, on the inference that since the will's freedom makes evil action *possible* it is on that

---

[29] *Purgatorio* 16.103–105.

account alone *inevitable* that they will: You don't need a story to explain it. The logic here seems to be that of what the philosophers call an "omega inconsistency": Necessarily there will be sin, but that necessity imposes no compulsion on anyone to commit it. Hence, the fall is only allegorically represented in the Bible as a catastrophic *event*; in truth you need no event to account for what is, by virtue of human freedom, inevitable.

That, as a general principle, cannot be sustained consistently with much in Dante's theology; in particular, it would make wholly unintelligible any doctrine of Paradise, and there are no grounds in the exchange with Marco Lombardi in *Purgatorio* 16 for concluding that Dante maintains any such proposition. On the contrary, the narrative of *Paradiso* presupposes as a given that once in heaven it is impossible to fall again, though the redeemed there are *maximally* free. That seems to be the point of Folco's remark that in heaven the Purgatorial theology of sin fades away unremembered to be replaced with a memory of the Garden of Eden as the truly original condition of things. And as to *Purgatorio* 16, the key to that exchange is indeed Dante's rejection of the proposition that it is *nature* that accounts for political sin, for bad government causes much of it, and nature is precisely what stands over the political sphere as its judge, especially of the way that a corrupt politics can so reduce the space wherein natural virtue can operate freely as to eliminate it entirely. Such an account of nature as a norm of virtue makes sense in context precisely in contrast with the style of an Augustinian political logic of sin, that since human nature is fallen secular government is bound to be bad and there is nothing else to be done about it but to seek a kingdom elsewhere than in the city of man. In short, Marco Lombardi's point is in resistance to that *Augustinian* account of "original" sin. Dante's point is entirely missed if on that account it is taken to entail a denial of the general doctrine as such.

Dante is not alone even in his own time in rejecting such theologies of original sin. Duns Scotus had resisted also the broadly Augustinian–Anselmian proposition that the Incarnation was primarily a response to Adam's fall, preferring to say that it was willed by a perfect love from all eternity unconditionally, the contingent event of the fall that will in due course afflict us all notwithstanding. For Scotus it is not sin that is the primary event, salvation being the secondary response to it, but the other way round; we were forgiven *before* we sinned, the only question being how, having sinned, we will be induced to return to the place of that forgiveness.[30] And it was precisely that bad theology of sin's primordial ultimacy, that conniving doctrinal upstart that parades sin itself as the original, that was drowned in Dante's name in the waters of Lethe, thereupon reducing sin's "originality" to the standing of a tragic afterthought within history that masks, but cannot ultimately cancel, the primordial innocence. It is true, though, that to this day the assumption of sin's prior claim to originality has many a theology trailing obsessively in its tow as the theological and personal ultimately determining fact.

It is sin's tow, dragging Dante back into Hell's clutches, that provokes Beatrice to anger. For it is now essential

---

[30] See J. P. H. Clark, "Time and Eternity in Julian of Norwich," *Downside Review*, 109, no. 377, p. 272.

that he leave Purgatory and all its corresponding burden of guilt entirely behind. He must not stay there his mediocrity unchallenged, for to do so would instantly convert Purgatory back into Hell. He had carried with him the traces of Hell into Purgatory, and that mentality will cling to him for so long as he is not rid of all the apparatus of the purgatorial, even, and perhaps especially, of that form of self-accusation which presupposes that it was his judgment of sin or innocence that counted anyway. For that is the subtlest of all the devices of resistance to conversion, the feeling that imagines a better eschatological outcome will be guaranteed if one can get a bit of self-recrimination in first, just to show how enthusiastically submerged one is in the humiliated spirit of repentance.

It is for this reason that Beatrice must disable Dante's agency as such, render him helpless, for no longer does he have anything of himself to contribute to his conversion, and anything he does have keeps getting in the way, it being precisely what he thinks he can contribute to it that is the obstacle. For it is in thinking so that he is still far from being rid of those remnants of vulnerability to sin embodied in those damned and damning *fomes peccati*. That is why he must be humiliatingly reduced to the condition of a whimpering baby, and then drowned.

The Priority of Grace

Dante, then, is redeemed, but not because he has purged himself of sin. He has not *won* forgiveness. That is Pelagian heresy and is itself a response shaped by those pressures of the *fomes peccati*. Dante is indeed called upon to "forget" his sins, to get past the fateful memory of sin, the memory that blights all sense of selfhood and of relationship, and somehow to retrace his steps back to the place of original innocence, to the condition of human affairs before ever there was sin, back, therefore, to the Earthly Paradise. And therein is paradox. For Dante's Earthly Paradise is a strange place. It would seem to restore the original condition in the Garden of Eden in which human beings were created, a condition wholly innocent that existed before ever there was the sin by which humanity lost its birthright. But how is that possible? You cannot just pick up where you left off, for, innocence lost, "experience" can never regain it, as the Romantic poets and philosophers, typified by William Blake, said. After innocence there is only experience, and the experience is blighted by the innocence lost in which it originates.

Therefore, Dante's being thrust into Lethe's waters, his baptism, must be an act of forgetting, and the means of forgetting something that continually presses on memory must needs be entirely passive. It takes a trauma, a violent act, to be caused to forget it, for it is in the nature of the case that we can't get ourselves to forget, the effort to forget itself serving only to remind us, as the effort not to notice how often speakers casually say "you know …" at the end of sentences has their listeners obsessively counting how often they say it. Dante's agency must be disabled at its roots in memory, he must learn that his repentance is the act whereby he connects with the deeper truth that forgiveness comes first, causing repentance, and is not the happy outcome won by it. For repentance is itself a gift of grace, and it comes first in the drowning that is baptism. As Jesus had said, the Father sees his prodigal son from afar and had forgiven him before ever he begins to confess. That is why Dante's being drowned comes as such a shock to him, for it is not the natural outcome entailed in the purgatorial journey that had preceded it; nonetheless *when* it happens, he can rewrite all that precedes it as now intelligible in the light of those new terms. As Folco shows, it is not the sin itself that is forgotten, the forgetting is not simple oblivion – in that sense Blake is right. It is the oppressive weight of sin's guilt that is lifted. For that, the "sin of the world," is what has been "taken away."

From the moment of Dante's drowning his narrative is shown to be, and to have been, entirely a story of grace, the thing not won but simply given, the gift whereby the apparent lines of causation are reversed. For as we saw Aquinas to say, the free acceptance of grace is not itself a grace-free act of will, earning it; rather, Dante's free acceptance of forgiveness is work that the grace of forgiveness *itself* brings about, at once most intimately his and entirely beyond his power to acquire for himself. What alone he can do for himself is refuse to be forgiven.[31] Grace is entirely gift, not in any way won, the gift itself causing the freedom of its reception, and it is in that fact that is the mystery of its

---

[31] The last thing anyone ought to be asked to do is forgive themselves, as if the duty to do so entailed they are capable of it. That is a terrible imposition, for the impossibility of forgiving yourself causes the guilt to live on unchallenged – indeed is more likely doubled, adding a supposititious failure of self-forgiveness to the real failures for which forgiveness is needed. Unsurprisingly, most people when so called upon by their friends and their psychiatrists alike know of its impossibility all too well. That's the reason why our obligation is to give forgiveness to *one another*, and correspondingly to receive it from them.

essentially sacramental character. For the gift of grace is simply given *by* an eternal will but concretely *within* a personal narrative of free choice, a necessity on the Creator's side revealed in the contingency of the is-but-might-not-have-been on the creature's part. Such, we saw, was Augustine's experience of his own conversion. It was by grace that Dante was caused to forget his guilt and remember God.

And so it is that Dante now understands how his narrative, from his setting out on the dark mountainside in *Inferno* until his arrival at the end of *Purgatorio*, was never a story of two halves, as if the work achieved by Dante's secular will seeking repentance in Purgatory was the condition of the second which, by contrast, witnessed to the work of grace taking him on to a new phase in Paradise. For at this point in Purgatory he comes to see that while he told the story of his journey thus far as if it had been a work of his free choice alone, he is now able to read back the narrative as having led to the realization that *all of it* was the work of grace, a grace that all along was given in the very first lines of the *Comedy* in Hell. From the outset Dante makes plain that the initiative for his journey through Hell and Purgatory came from Paradise, wherein, at the initiative of the Virgin Mary, Beatrice and St. Lucy plot to convert Dante. There were not two phases, a secular work of moral reform in which the agency was that of a natural human will, and a sacred, in which all is the work of grace. Still less was it the case that the first was a condition of the second. The whole narrative from the beginning in Hell to the exit from Purgatory was the work of grace; but just because of that, at the same time it was the work of Dante's freedom.

For the grace, the work of God, causes the freedom through which alone it works.

And so it is that, as before Hell had faded away into Purgatory, so now Purgatory fades away and turns into the Earthly Paradise, the place that is at once where human freedom is finally and fully obtained and the place where all is grace, the paradox of the conjunction resolved in a causal mutuality, the one possible only because of the other.

PART III
PARADISE

6

Paradise and *Paideia*

On Poetry, Ecstasy, and How to Get Language to Fail

For all that Dante has little use for the word "mystical," no literary work has earned a better right to that name than has the *Comedy*'s third cantica. That being so, questions about Dante's understanding of the mystical arise in a distinctively medieval way, for the sense in which *Paradiso* takes Dante beyond the second cantica's purgatorial and ascetical character into a mystical path is one indebted to a complex medieval inheritance of theological traditions; and those traditions carry with them resonances that quite markedly differ from those of the anthropologically and comparativist-inspired notions of the mystical common in our times since, among others, William James.[1]

Even in Dante's time and within his Western Christian culture there were more ways than one of understanding the nature of the mystical, though the differences are more in style, imagery, and emphasis than in substance, for all of them share one thing in common as to the word's core meaning: The "mystical" is nothing special, exceptional,

---

[1] *The Varieties of Religious Experience*, Penguin: Harmondsworth, 1982. In general, the trouble with comparativist notions of the mystical is that in the effort required to identify some transcultural common conception of the mystical you get as a result what belongs properly to the culture of none of them.

the achievement of but a few. It is not an achievement at all. The "mystical" names a place where grace takes you as a matter of course, it's where grace will have you go unless you decline to go there. The mystical is that within earthly temporal existence in which Heaven's reality is in some way present, in some sort knowable, in some degree capable of being experienced, so that Heaven's native knowledge, Heaven's love, Heaven's eternal life, Heaven's soul redeemed, Heaven's body raised to glory, Heaven's happiness won, and above all Heaven's community in a shared vision of God, are all experienced on earth, as best they may be in time, in contingency, and in a manner hidden and secret (for the etymology of our word "mystical" is that of the Greek word *muein*, "to hide"). And these are discoverable, if only in suggestion, in a wisp and in a trace of heaven, "in ordinary," as George Herbert said.[2] In Heaven itself the character all these have of the mystical disappears, for there they are no longer hidden. They *are* Heaven's ordinary, Heaven's vernacular, Heaven's everyday.

Such, in Dante's times, is the mystical's common core. Of its nature no human language, bound into time and history, can fully bear the weight placed upon it by the pressure of the mystical, and so its natural expression is in broken and only half-articulate forms of speech; and the brokenness of the language of the mystical is exactly appropriate, for its halting, hesitant character itself achieves an expression of language's failure to measure up to its objects. And a pretentious claim to a full

---

[2] George Herbert, "Prayer I," in *George Herbert, The Complete Poetry*, ed. John Drury and Victoria Moul, Harmondsworth: Penguin Classics, 2015, pp. 48–49.

comprehension would betray the mystical. In that spirit the Pseudo-Denys speaks of the "mystic scripture" that is indeed a word, but one spoken in "a hidden silence";[3] it is indeed a kind of knowledge, but a "knowing unknowing";[4] and John of the Cross who talks about this at length is at his best not when he is "saying" it in his fully articulated mystical theology but when he "shows" it within his poetry, as when in the *Spiritual Canticle* he speaks of the experience of God's darkness as being "un no sé qué quedan balbuciendo," "an I-know-not-what that leaves you babbling,"[5] where the language descriptive of this mystical stuttering itself stutters.

This "mystical" is, then, not the simple absence of knowledge, ignorance. On the contrary, the language breaks down because the reality that it seeks to convey is too full, is more than it can bear, and that is why it is an ignorance of the kind that is "learned" – Nicholas of Cusa called it a *docta ignorantia* – acquired at great cost, an ignorance achieved only by means of that profound conversion that Dante in Purgatory learns from Beatrice is called for there. And the expression of that mystical brokenness takes great poetry, as that of Hildegard of Bingen, of Hadewijch of Brabant, of John of the Cross, of Gerard Manley Hopkins; and so it takes Dante's poetry, that is, *Paradiso*. All take their cue from the biblical prophecies of

---

[3] Pseudo-Dionysius, *Mystical Theology*, 1 997B, in *Complete Works of the Pseudo-Dionysius*, trans. Colm Luibheid, New York, Paulist Press, 1987, p. 135.
[4] Ibid., 1, 1001A, p. 137.
[5] John of the Cross, *Spiritual Canticle*, verse 7, my translation: Spanish text in *Collected Works of St John of the Cross*, trans. Kieran Kavanaugh, Washington, DC: Institute of Carmelite Studies, 1991, p. 45.

Israel, and witness to the breakdown of language at the point where it is called upon to bear the weight of the mystical, because, by the standard of that which it seeks to express its inadequacy is shown in a kind of baby-talk, as Dante had said;[6] it's like "the bah, bah, bah," of Jeremiah, who, knowing that he is but a child in these things, is on that account called to be among the greatest of the prophets.[7]

Within the Christian mystical traditions, this intersection of the heavenly with the mundane ordinary is itself the common Christian ordinary, its everyday. It is not some special, esoteric achievement, though its ordinary expression takes more than one form. For the Pseudo-Denys, one of the principal authorities in the Middle Ages as to the standing of mystical language, the primary meaning of the word "mystical" is in reference to the liturgy, as in his own way it is for Aquinas, whose heaven is experienced this side of death as a *panis angelicus, fit panis hominum*,[8] the bread of heaven that has become the true food of humankind, given in the *sacramentum* – a word which, he said, derived its sense from the Latin *sanctum secretum*, the "holy hiddenness,"[9] that the sacraments embody. For they "contain" – they both signify and effect – in the everyday elements of water, wine, oil, in eating and washing, and in the bond of sex, the entire universe of salvation history, extended in that great arc that extends from the creation of the world out of nothing to

---

[6] *Inferno* 32.9.   [7] Jeremiah 1:6.
[8] Thomas Aquinas, the penultimate stanza of the hymn *Sacris Solemniis* composed for the office of the feast of Corpus Christi.
[9] *ST* 3a, q60, a1 *corp*.

the Kingdom of Heaven in which all is resolved. For him it is this *sacramentum* that is the *mysterium fidei*.

For the Pseudo-Denys the mystical, its "heaven in ordinary," is the holy secret that is the Church itself, expressed in the liturgical rhythms that move from moments of penitence through the demotic liturgy of the Word in the reading of Scripture where it is expressed openly to all, even to the uninitiated, from there on to the secret *epiclesis* uttered in the silence hidden behind the liturgical screens, which draws the materiality of bread and wine into a oneness of the Church with God that is achieved in its Eucharistic routine. Whether in the Pseudo-Denys or in Aquinas, the mystical is the community's everyday worship, its habit, its matter of course. Mystical is what the Church is and it is what the Church does, all the time.

By contrast with this strongly communal grounding of the mystical of the Pseudo-Denys and Aquinas the more common deployment of the language of the mystical in the Western theological traditions of the high Middle Ages is focused upon the progress of the individual soul in its journey to God, though in mapping that journey it commonly borrows from the Pseudo-Denys the language of the threefold way of the purgative, illuminative, and the unitive,[10] these marking stages on the "journey of the soul into God," as Bonaventure in the thirteenth century put it.[11] Bernard of Clairvaux spoke of the mystical

---

[10] Pseudo-Dionysius, *Celestial Hierarchy*, 3, 165B, in *Complete Works*, trans. Luibheid, pp. 154–155.

[11] Though this is not an exclusively late medieval, or even an exclusively Latin, turn. Plotinus, who, though no Christian himself, was at least indirectly of much influence on Augustine, spoke of the mystical journey as a "flight of the unknown to the unknown," see *Enneads* VI, 9.

in terms less formally epistemological than those of the Pseudo-Denys, in language more vivid, distinctively affective, and experiential – *hodie legimus in libro experientiae*,[12] he says to his fellow monks in Clairvaux, "today we read in the book of experience." And that book's imagery is that of a passionate love, drawing openly and without apology on the erotic language of the Song of Songs, the scriptural *fons et origo* of the Western Christian mystical traditions of the later Middle Ages. Bernard too has his three "stages" of mystical ascent, but his are three kisses that are ranked on an ascending scale of ever closer and more delicate intimacy, the kiss of the feet, the kiss of the hands, and the kiss of the mouth.[13] It is the biblical Song of Songs that tells him to do this: "Oh that he would kiss me with the kiss of his mouth!"[14] pleads the Bride in its opening verse, "for your breasts (as in Jerome's faulty Latin translation of the Septuagint) are better than wine."[15] "Feed me with apples, sustain me with raisins, *quia amore langueo*, for I am sick with love,"[16] she cries, and, dominating all, are the shifting moods of a love-sickness that, whether in the lovers' presence to one another, a *dilectio*, a delight, or in their separation and absence from one another, a *desiderium*, a longing, the language of the love-tryst transforms into an

---

[12] Bernard of Clairvaux, *Sermons on the Song of Songs*, vol. 1, trans. Killian Walsh OCSO, Kalamazoo, MI: Cistercian Publications, 1977, p. 16.
[13] Bernard of Clairvaux, *Sermons on the Song*, Sermon 3, pp. 16ff.
[14] Song of Songs 1:1.
[15] Thus, in the Vulgate Latin: *Osculatur me osculo oris sui, quia meliora sunt ubera tua quam vino* mistranslates the Hebrew for "loves" as "breasts" causing all sorts of tortured interpretive strategies for the medieval commentators in search of an explanation of how the Bridegroom can be in possession of a woman's breasts.
[16] *[Q]uia amore langueo…*, Song of Songs 2:5.

emotionally earthier and more individualistic emphasis the Dionysian liturgical dynamic of presence and absence, the emotional vicissitudes of lovers replacing the Dionysian high grammatical discourse of affirmation and negation.

These two general models, those of the Pseudo-Denys and of Bernard of Clairvaux, dominate the mystical theologies of the high to later Middle Ages of the Western Church, and though they share much in common formally they differ dramatically in feel. Bernard of Clairvaux is the mystical poet as lover in the *schola caritatis*, whose distinctive speech, he says, is that of the marriage bed,[17] its imagery being perfectly attuned to the life of the contemplative Cistercian monk, student in the school of love.[18] He even thinks that pregnancy is a source of the most appropriate imagery of the monk at prayer.[19] And though there is no evidence of Pseudo-Denys's influence directly on Bernard,[20] they do share a common construal of Christian love as a form of *eros*, albeit that in the Pseudo-Denys it is the Church's liturgy that embodies and expresses this desire, while in Bernard it is the Cistercian monk who in his prayer, casting himself as mystical bride, pants with longing for Christ the Bridegroom.

---

[17] Bernard of Clairvaux, *Sermons on the Song*, Sermon 1, pp. 1–7.
[18] As the Cistercian monks liked to think of their communities. See Jean Leclerq, *The Love of Learning and the Desire for God*, trans. Catharine Misrahi, London: SPCK, 1978, pp. 7–8.
[19] Bernard of Clairvaux, *Sermons on the Song*, Sermon 1, p. 5.
[20] Even Étienne Gilson, keen to find in Bernard traces of some Neoplatonic influence (see his *Mystical Theology of St Bernard*, Kalamazoo, MI: Cistercian Publications, 1990) admits that the influence of the Pseudo-Denys is indirect and secondhand, mediated, he speculates (though without evidence) through the Latin translation of Maximus the Confessor.

A third style, that of the Franciscan Bonaventure, to which Dante's own mystical theology – his *Paradiso* – is perhaps closer, is in essence a modification of Bernard's three-stage mystical ascent to God. Especially in his emphasis on the word *via*, Bonaventure's account of the "threefold way" of the *itinerarium mentis in Deum* pays attention less to signposts that point along the route of a journey's way, less therefore to the map of it, and more, like Dante's, to the journey itself as experienced, to the *tale* of the traveler's journey, its journal.

Of course, Bonaventure's journey to God does have a map; he describes it, and from his account you can discern routes, it shows where the journey begins, in the externality of the carnal *imagines* drawn from the material world, and where it will end, the journey completed in a mystical union with God. And if it is true that these external images all lead to God their source, some do so only as it were from a distance, like the fingerpost that indeed points out the direction to follow but of itself shares nothing of the reality it points to. Such, for example, is the imagery of the Psalms, which speak as readily of God as a rock as it does of a gentle breeze, though, of course, God is neither, the negation being implied. Other metaphors already contain in some way the reality itself that they point to, they make present here and now what they signify,[21] for they contain "likenesses"[22] of God

---

[21] God is there in the first case *through* the image (*per imaginem*), in the second is contained *in* the image (*in imagine*): See *Itinerarium Mentis in Deum*, intro., trans., and commentary, Philotheus Boehner OFM, New York: the Franciscan Institute, 1990, chapters 1 and 2 respectively.

[22] "God made man according to his own image and likeness," *ad imaginem et similitudinem*, Vulgate Genesis 1:27.

that draw the soul back into its most intimate powers, of intellect, memory, and will, where, by grace the soul not only images the Trinity, for it also begins to share the Trinitarian life itself. Unlike the "images" that point to God from a distance, God is there by grace *in* the "likenesses" and not just as indicating that which lies *beyond* them. Finally, the soul travels onward into a union with God that lies far beyond all image, every metaphor, all likeness, every concept, wherein one can truly say that for Bonaventure, as for Dante, the will is moved by that same love that moves the sun and other stars. For present here is all creation and all grace, the creature fulfilled by the gift of a share in the divine life itself, and therein its oneness with God is simply beyond all speech.

Such is the map of the soul's journey into God. But more closely drawing Dante and Bonaventure together than do such similarities of spiritual topography – as it were, the geography of the land traveled – is the driving energy of the traveling itself. Those three stages are related not principally in terms of discrete staging posts that you might pass through, one by one, leaving each behind as you move on to the next, as when tracing a route with your finger on a map. For the principal meaning of *itinerarium* denotes the travelers' *experience* of the journeying, the traveling itself, not just descriptions of the journey's route. And in that primary sense, the experience of the journey is cumulative, in that as you pass on from one staging post to the next you carry forward with you as you go the experience of the journey before, and so it goes on thereafter in a continuous, progressive, new accumulation. In short, as Bonaventure says, *memory* does its work of continuous retelling as it gathers up the past into each new present and experiences it all anew it as it does so,[23] a retelling that is thus a constant reinterpretation, not as sentimental nostalgia but as an enrichment of the past as the journey proceeds beyond it. This is the storytelling of lovers who carry the memories of their past love-story, not as if stuck in them in their pastness but as active within their present relationship, their recollection of a past love being itself renewed in that present love.

Thus, Bonaventure says, you carry the sensual image of God with you into conceptual likeness, and likeness into the intimacy of transforming union, therein achieving a sort of identity with God, so that what is gained from the earlier is drawn, transformed, into the later, the lower into the higher, leaving the confining shell of the lower behind but retaining its kernel and thereby drawing it into a new life. And that energy of a narrative that continuously rereads itself, shedding its limitations as it continues on the map's course and acquiring a new life as it does so, shows itself not in the abolition of the images of previous stages but in their renewal in the higher setting of the likenesses. That is why in the last chapter of his *Itinerarium* Bonaventure can do exactly what Augustine does in his *Confessions*, book 10, paradoxically using the grossness of the sensual as image of that spiritual reality that utterly transcends it. "Late have I loved you," Augustine exclaims, "beauty so old and so new: late have I loved you." His love has been "late" because he had been held back from the God "within," he says, and he had sought the God only "without" and "in my unlovely state

---

[23] *Itinerarium* IV, 7.

I plunged into those lovely, created things which you made." And so, seeking God in the wrong place, he found only idols, false images, in his sensual self. Yet, when he wishes to speak of the true God that, upon his conversion, he had found within himself, it is precisely the language of outer imagination derived from each of the five bodily senses that provides him with the vocabulary in which to describe this renewed inwardness: In this way is the higher spiritual grounded in the lower sensual and the sensual elevated to the spiritual. Therefore, Augustine says,

> [y]ou called and cried out and shattered my deafness. You were radiant and resplendent, you put flight to my blindness. You were fragrant, and I drew in my breath and now pant after you. I tasted you, and I feel but hunger and thirst for you. You touched me, and I am set on fire to attain the peace that is yours.[24]

Just so, in his own way, Bonaventure in the final chapter of his *Itinerarium* concludes:

> If you wish to know how these things may come about, ask grace, not learning; desire, not understanding; the groaning of prayer, not diligence in reading; the Bridegroom, not the teacher; God, not man; darkness, not clarity; not light, but the fire that wholly inflames and carries one into God through life-transforming anointings and consuming affections.[25]

Thus is the sensual retrieved from its limitations; and, with nothing sensual left behind, all of it is saved as true likeness, containing within itself a world of meaning far

---

[24] *Confessions* 10: 27. [25] *Itinerarium* VII, 6, p. 101.

above the sensual. It is a strategy, as it were, of cumulative reinterpretation, consciously embedded within the hierarchical traditions of mystical theology for which, as the mind ascends from lower to higher, it does not cancel what it transcends but draws it up with it as it goes beyond.

Nor is this strategy, whereby the lower grounds the higher and the higher transforms the lower it is grounded in, unique to Bonaventure or to his broadly affirmative theological style. It is the strategy also of the very different, because epistemologically more negative, style of the anonymous author of the *Cloud of Unknowing*, who, noting how many spiritual writers urge the novice contemplative to seek God "within themselves," says that speaking for himself he does not advise it. For, he says, young inexperienced monks are all too easily misled by such emphatically materialistic images, taking in a crudely literal sense what in truth is but a helpful metaphor designed to take the mind beyond the material. In consequence they find themselves dragging the images of "interiority" down into a materialistic parody and, in an effort to achieve a spiritual inwardness, the novice contemplative screws up his face and stares with his eyes as if he were "a silly sheep that had been banged on the head," straining to translate into terms of performable mental and physical acts that which is inherently an achievement of grace, a gift of inwardness that is no one's to give but God's.[26] In such deformed spiritual practices, he says, is a reversal of the

---

[26] See *Cloud of Unknowing*, in *The Cloud of Unknowing and Other Works*, trans. and intro. A. C. Spearing, Harmondsworth: Penguin Books, 2001, chapters 51–53.

true mystical journey, pulling the free mystical spirit back down into the limitations of the carnal and the sensual.

Well, then, if not "within," "where should I be?" asks the novice contemplative, "since on your account you would seem to want me to be nowhere at all, neither within nor without, neither above nor below." "Exactly so," replies the *Cloud* Author, because he knows that he must get the aspirant contemplative to drop the idea altogether that there might be *better* metaphors for the mystical than those of inwardness – a metaphor's being better than others, or even being the best of all, doesn't get you past the common limitations of the metaphorical itself to some higher nonmetaphorical language. For there is no such higher language. Metaphors are all we have,[27] and though they stretch toward the mystical and truly speak it they cannot fully encompass what they speak of. Therefore, he says, as to the question where God is to be found, it is right to say that God is not as enclosed "within"; but since God is not to be found "without" either it would have been better to have said that God is to be found only in a "nowhere" were it not that even "nowhere" fails, for this "nowhere" is also

---

[27] In a general sense. For some purposes it is important to distinguish between metaphors and analogies. Metaphors extend the reach of language by way of a negation of literalness: My tiresome droning in the lecture hall may be described as "boring" because it is a blunt drill slowly and painfully making a hole in my students' heads, but thankfully it is literally false so to say. But when, rarely, a lecture is said to be a good one, and the pint enjoyed in the pub after it even better, the goodness of both are *literally* asserted, neither being a metaphor for the other. And even though there are no good-making descriptions shared by the lecture and the pint there is no equivocation in saying of both that they are "good." But in the general sense in which a variety of modes of speech are available to stretch language out beyond the immediate, all may be loosely described as "metaphorical."

an "everywhere." But even that doesn't get you beyond the metaphorical, for "everywhere" fails just as much. You can throw every possible metaphor at the mystical – and so you should, he says – but even though every one of those metaphors falls short in relation to every other in a general congregation of failures, the conjunction of them all is as necessary as it is deficient. For there is no other language. The *Cloud* Author's lesson, so different in rhetorical feel from Augustine's or Bonaventure's, yet no different in substance, is that we cannot directly name the mystical, for the mystical has no sui generis language, no vocabulary of its own, and it is only through the many-sided proliferation of our carnal language, through a self-correcting profligacy of image – not, therefore, through its attenuation – that we can speak of it at all.[28] In short, the natural language of the mystical is poetry, the language of the carnal bent to the expression of that which lies far beyond it.

It is the same tradition of a mystical epistemology, that constantly self-corrects and qualifies in a strategy of successive reinterpretation, every new landscape experienced reinterpreting the journey already traveled, that governs Dante's narrative as he progresses through the three cantiche of the *Comedy*. As it has seemed necessary to insist, Hell's pains and Purgatory's do differ ultimately; Ugolino's humiliating despair in *Inferno* 32–33 and Dante's hope-transforming humiliation at the hands of Beatrice in *Purgatorio* 30–31, contrast not just in their durations but in the very texture of their pains, the one but humiliating, the other teaching humility. Nonetheless, from the standpoint of Dante's journey, Purgatory is in a way Hell

[28] *Cloud*, chapter 68.

redeemed: Purgatory is what Hell becomes when you travel *through* it and won't stay stuck in it. Hell and Purgatory share a common scope that is set by sin; but they are distinguished precisely by their contrasting responses to sin's reality, the one by entrapment in it, the other by the redeeming liberation from it, so that Dante's journey, which takes him on a redemptive course through Hell into Purgatory, enables him to reread Hell not on its own terms, as those forever condemned there must, but on Purgatory's terms. And that, we saw, *wholly* transforms what Hell is for him. That is why the journey from the one to the other has made all the difference between the endless punishment that has reduced Ugolino to his dumb and sullen silence, to an end of all speech in Hell, and a purgative *paideia*, a hard learning, which leaves Dante at the end of Purgatory with eternal happiness on the tip of his tongue. It is in this narrow but significant sense in which you can see Hell from the standpoint of redemption, as indeed Dante does in Paradise.[29] As thus seen, Hell retrieved, reinterpreted, is Purgatory.[30]

[29] In *Paradiso* 28, Dante sees Ulysses' wild escapade for what it is, a parable of intellect that, striving for a transcendence of its own making, comes only to disaster, for any transcendence that is ours to achieve is a "proud ambition" that, as Macbeth says, "o'er leaps itself and falls on t'other" side (Act 1, scene 7, 27–28). Much of the theological work done by *Paradiso* is devoted to the discovery of how exactly a Ulyssian goal of transcendence, Ulysses' pursuit of which lands him in Hell, differs from Dante's journey that discovers the truly human to lie beyond the human, to do which is *transhumanar*, an achievement that is perfected only in the human nature of Christ. See Chapter 7.

[30] This requirement to read *Inferno* through *Purgatorio* does not in itself sustain the argument, to whose validity I am partial, that, for Dante, there is no Hell, but only Purgatory, nor any Purgatory, but only Heaven. For *Inferno* describes what Hell must be for those for whom there is no Purgatory and who settle for the world of their sin's making.

Therefore, in the same way that Hell becomes Purgatory for Dante, so his journey through Purgatory is a *paideia*, a place of learning by means of suffering, whose fulfilment is in Paradise. For all that Dante's Purgatory is so painful a struggle, at no point on the way from the foot of the mountain to its summit is Dante more than a hair's breadth away from Paradise. Purgatory is Paradise in anticipation; in Purgatory Paradise is present within Dante's every desire, even though those desires are at first almost invisible to himself, so that it will take that arduous journey for him to have the broken connections remade between his conscious self and the deepest truth of those desires. All those desires – those of the five powers of his sensual self, those of his higher powers of intellect, memory, and will, and the grounding of all of them in the God who lies so deeply within him as to defeat all powers of description whatsoever – all of these are there waiting to be elicited; they are Dante's true desires awaiting their paradisal retrieval. And it is that pressure that requires of him the poetry that is the *Comedy*.

A Paradisal Politics

Dante's version of the *triplex via* is thus different in imagery from that of Denys the Areopagite and of Bernard of Clairvaux, and is nearer, if not in every detail, to the inner energies of Bonaventure's theology. Nonetheless, if Dante's narrative does indeed tell of a map of the soul in its subjective structure and if, more importantly, like Bonaventure's, it tells of a soul's journey across the inner world thus mapped, there is a distinctively Dantean element in his journey's tale that shifts the balance away from exclusive attention to the subjective transformation of the individual soul that is the common element in the theological models of Bernard and Bonaventure.[31] Three times Dante reminds us in the last words of each cantica that his journey has a cosmological dimension, ultimately defined by "the love that moves the sun and other stars." Dante's traversing the map of the soul in its journey into God can be understood only insofar as the soul's journey within the self shares in "microcosm" the shape and dynamic of the entire universe, its moral, political, and cosmological "macrocosm."[32] As Christian Moevs says, Dante's "world" is essentially a moral order, its shape is that of an ethical and spiritual demand.[33] It is here that Dante shares with Plato the further insight that for every form of social order there is a corresponding moral type that individuates it in a typical embodiment,[34] an aristocratic persona, a democratic persona, an oligarchic, and so forth. As with Plato, so with Dante, and Moevs's point will be sorely misunderstood if the moral and political orders are not set within an ultimate

---

[31] Not, I think, in the Pseudo-Denys. I am persuaded by Andrew Louth and others that in the Western theological uptake of the Pseudo-Denys from the twelfth century until the end of the fifteenth his emphasis on the mystical journey's ecclesial and sacramental character and shape is noticeably absent and a more individualistic uptake of his theology and of the *itinerarium mentis in Deum* takes its place.

[32] See *Itinerarium* VI, 7.

[33] "A grasp of the metaphysical underpinnings of the *Comedy* ... is the basis for understanding the *Comedy*'s purposes and poetics in a way ... consonant with Dante's own understanding." Christian Moevs, *The Metaphysics of Dante's* Comedy, Oxford: Oxford University Press, 2005, p. 8.

[34] See *Republic* VIII, 544d: "Are you aware ... that there must be as many types of character among men as there are forms of government?"

cosmological and metaphysical grounding.[35] This close relation between the moral and metaphysical is classical in one way and medieval in another, and in either case so strikingly different from conceptions of the moral of our times as to amount to their reversal. For Dante the ethical is determined by the cosmological, the imperative of how to live is entailed by the shape of the created universe itself. For many today in our individualistic ways, it is, by contrast, our moral choices that determine how we conceive of the cosmos.

This is the reason why it is so important to understand Dante's Hell, Purgatory, and Paradise as places wherein are *regimes*: "place" and "regime" cannot be disengaged from the cosmologies that entail them into the standing of fictional analogies serving practical purposes of individuals alone, as it is our tendency to do. For Dante the call of the moral imperative comes from no private will that evaluatively construes a morality out of individual choices of how to live with personal consistency and coherence. For Dante the moral call is made from the cosmological foundation of Hell, Purgatory, and Paradise, and if, when reading Dante, you don't believe in them as real places you are going to have to put up with them at least as hypotheses entertained for the sake of a sound understanding of the governing shape of the story's ethical demand. What you may not do is so read the *Comedy* as if you might happily drop the cosmology and retain a free-floating ethic independently of its foundation. For though you might

---

[35] See Vittorio Montemaggi, *Reading Dante's* Commedia *as Theology, Divinity Realised as Human Encounter*, Oxford: Oxford University Press, 2016, Prologue, pp. 1–30.

want to do so Dante, at least, resists. Dante asks you to imagine the world implied by your value-choices and take responsibility for that world.

Dante therefore entertains no scruple in the way that many post-Kantian philosophies of our times do on a general principle that the "is" of cosmological fact can generate no entailments of moral force upon the human will, the way things are in the cosmos carrying no moral obligations with it. Far from it. Again and again, Dante shows that it is not private will that settles moral questions. Rather, moral demand is already there within the understanding of the universe, entailed in how things really are, and in telling of the illusions of a false consciousness by which the world misreads itself ethically. What, for Dante, gets you to Hell is precisely your desire for just that world which is implied in your debased ethic; you can't choose the ethic without choosing the corresponding world.[36] And we might well put the point more strongly still, for it is not even as if there is for him some device of *inference* that crosses the gap between the way you believe things are and the way things ought to be, because there is no such gap to be negotiated in the first place, no "therefore" needed to get you from the fact to the moral ought, for the values are embedded in the cosmological fact. For Dante it is only a false will that claims for itself a moral autonomy over and against the claims of the facts, as if "facts" are in their conception understood as in themselves morally neutral,

---

[36] Of course, you can *wish* that your ethical commitments entailed no unhappy cosmology, but within the circles of bad faith even contradictions are possible wishes.

becoming value-laden only when a moral agent deems them to be so. Dante knows nothing of our modernist denials of any possible inference from facts to values. Everything is the other way round: The universe makes moral demands because in the world's shape is discovered the divine will for creatures. That is why there are no entailments, valid or invalid, from the cosmological to the moral when separately understood. They are not needed, for the shape of the one *just is* where the shape of the other is to be found.

Such seems to be Moevs's point. For Dante, not to understand the cosmos as in itself moral demand is not to understand the cosmos at all. And if the three worlds of Hell, Purgatory, and Paradise have moral force upon lives, it is because for Dante the shape of a life is already given in the shape of each community precisely because the mind and will of God for all is shown therein. All obligation is in the world's createdness, and if the world is a book, as Hugh of St. Victor had said early in the twelfth century,[37] then its text reveals its author's mind and will – its author's mind in its structure and organization, and its author's will in the imperatives the structure embodies. Dante's universe is *itself* a judge of human right and wrong. And we may add that if for Dante, as it was for Bonaventure, the universe is a book, it may contain much dull prose in the tedious scientific prefaces introducing it, but in the end the book itself is a book of poetry, reaching out toward the hidden secret that sustains it, wherein the "love that moves the sun and the

---

[37] Hugh of St. Victor, *De Sacramentis*, 1.16.12, *Patrologia Latina*, 176. 270. C–D.

other stars" is the same love that moves Dante's will. For in the same way that you cannot separate the ethic from the cosmology you cannot separate the cosmology from the mystical nor the mystical from the poetry; for poetry is the best that can be done by way of giving expression to both.

In this way is moral judgment embedded in the cosmic fact: Hell's cosmos is the embodiment of God's judgment of sin, and so Hell's shape as a society shows you what are sin's politics. If sin had an agency, and devised its corresponding politics, Hell would describe it. It is the politics of a place without a future, a fantasyland in which you endlessly sink down into an ultimate inertia represented by Satan's frozen silence from which nothing new is ever to come. Purgatory's mountain reimagines the political in terms of a community of the repentant and so of hope, for it is there that together with others you arduously climb back into your humanity. Heaven describes the politics of salvation; it is the politics of a community that is shaped like the petals of a rose.[38] Each tells you what the real politics are, respectively of a community that has utterly failed, of a community that waits in hope's certainty of redemption, and of the community fulfilled. All three exist. All three have a politics. All three have a world, whether real or fantastic, and each has a "here." "Here" it says on Hell's gate, "abandon hope," for within there is no future at all.[39] "Here" in Purgatory, even the unbaptized pagan Statius is saved.[40] "Here in heaven," says Folco, "we do not remember our guilt." "Here," he says, "we smile."[41] Each

---

[38] *Paradiso* 31.1–21.   [39] *Inferno* 5.   [40] *Purgatorio* 21.   [41] *Paradiso* 9.

condition of soul is a place, and each place a world. To think of Dante's world as no more than a moral metaphor is to upturn everything distinctive of his mysticism, which is rooted in, expresses itself by means of, finds its fulfilment in, the community of all the saved in Paradise. Paradise, its politics, its ethic, its vision of an ultimate community, *that* is Dante's mystical. All else is on the way to it, a glimpse of an eternal light edged on the horizon of the dark temporal.

Paradise as Mystical Community

And so it is that at last Dante's journey brings him to the point of entry into the "mystical," the paradisal; and whereas on his journey through Purgatory he could know of Paradise only as set at a distance from him, as something new sought, now when he enters Paradise it is a homecoming. "*Here* I belong. I have always belonged here, from here I came, and I am but returning home." This is what would have been had we not sinned, or rather, once the illusions of a sinful self are finally dispelled in Purgatory, that is what we see as always having been the reality. That's the meaning of the Earthly Paradise, and its mysterious kaleidoscope of images.

For though Dante has not been there before,[42] he is able to recognize it upon arrival, it is familiar, because, although until now it has belonged to a future at a distance

---

[42] Unlike Origen who, influenced by Plato, thought that before our birth in a mortal body we already existed as complete souls in Paradise, for which birth in a body was a kind of humiliating catastrophe. Still, remnants of the idea that we belong where our origins are and that, after death, we return to that place in God from which we first came, remain long after Origen's version of it has been formally abandoned.

and as a place not yet attained, upon arrival he *remembers* it. *Paradiso* therefore tells of Dante's entry not just into a new episode of the same story that had preceded it, nor into a different story, but as into a quite different sense of the word "story" itself. For just as the narrative of Dante's journey through Hell's circles reads quite differently when, upon descending Satan's inert limbs, Dante and Virgil discover that they are in truth making their way to the foot of Mount Purgatory, so *Paradiso* looks back upon *Purgatorio* and sheds an entirely new light on it when it is seen from that heavenly vantage point. You do not fully understand Purgatory until you find the meaning of it in Paradise. In fact, Purgatory has no meaning at all except on those celestial terms.

It is perhaps because of expecting *Paradiso* to be but the next episode of a narrative taking Dante on from where *Purgatorio* left off, that some find *Paradiso* to be lacking in a *Purgatorio*'s drama – as if the journey through Paradise ought to have had its own equivalently dramatic critical moments. It is true that nothing happens in Paradise that has the immediate dramatic power of Dante's conversion in Purgatory, for in the sense that Paradise completes the meaning of Purgatory, Paradise is self-complete, it is the end of all possible story, there being nowhere else for stories to go. Thus, the finality of Paradise is nothing like the finality of Hell, where nothing new can happen and there is only an endless repetition – therein is its true horror, for *Inferno* is more like an unending incompleteness, its endless repetitions forever resolving nothing. For if in Dante's Paradise there is nowhere else to go, there is also endless renewal. Nothing at all just stops there.

Why should it? As Dante will have it, *within* Paradise itself there is change, and if Dante's journey through Paradise lacks new dramas of an equivalently challenging kind to those of Purgatory it is the expectation of them that is mistaken. Dante's last true *conversion* was achieved once and for all in his encounter with Beatrice at the end of *Purgatorio*, so that in Dante's entry into the mystical realms of Paradise there are no further crises of conversion to match that which caught Dante unawares upon his arrival at the summit of Mount Purgatory; but neither is his entry into Paradise but an extension of the narrative seamlessly succeeding that of *Purgatorio*, as if Dante has nothing new to learn in Paradise. Indeed in Paradise Peter, James, and John submit Dante to a searching examination of his readiness with the gifts of faith, hope, and charity, and in that testing of the theological virtues they are genuinely demanding to know whether Dante has even now learned what is needed.[43] For these three, faith, hope, and charity, St. Paul had said, "remain" when all else having relevance only to a life before death is in Paradise left behind, and Dante has no place there unless they are to be found in him fully realized. Therefore, he submits to the test, for there is nothing he can carry into Paradise but these virtues, Purgatory having stripped him of all other baggage. He passes the tests, but even then, Dante still has it all to learn, the theological virtues acquired are not the end of the matter. For as to those virtues themselves there is not and cannot be an end to the matter. They are called "theological virtues," the medieval theologians said, because they are constitutive

---

[43] Peter in *Paradiso* 24; James in *Paradiso* 25; John in *Paradiso* 26.

of, not dependent on, the eternal, and their acquisition ends nothing, but rather begins everything.

That is why it would seem wrong to suppose that there can be no learning in Heaven. Hell, not Heaven, is where there is no learning because there is nothing new there to learn and neither the will nor the capacity for it. Hell is endlessly boring, and its boredom can only get worse and worse. And the difference between Purgatory and Heaven is that in Purgatory Dante must relearn *how* to learn in the way learning is going to be required of him in Heaven, for if there is no learning in Hell, and a painful relearning in Purgatory, in Heaven the learning is a joy, being like the continuing joy of the scholar upon discovering a new source that sheds a fresh light transforming what they already knew. It is true, then, that there are no existential crises in Heaven. But as Dante discovers, there is no end to Heaven's *paideia*, and not just for him who is passing through, but inherently, for it is what Heaven is like.

And in this way the story of Dante in Paradise tells of something more surprising than anything to be found in the preceding cantiche. Hell and Heaven are both places from which there is no exit, the judgment of death that places a person in one or the other is irreversible. Dante, however, not being dead, can pass through them both and premortem discover at once his true self and the truth of his world. Not that at any point on the journey is it easy or Dante ready for it, and Virgil drags him all unwilling into Hell insisting that he take the journey because there is that of Hell in him that he *must* pass through, and much to be learned of Hell's world that only the experience of traveling throughout its extent can teach him. Reluctantly he obeys Virgil's summons and there in Hell's people's refusal to learn *he* learns what are the consequences of their doing so. But Heaven is different. For not only does Dante have to be educated by Heaven as one passing into it, also, when there, he discovers that Heaven is of itself a place where forever there is learning, and that whereas those in Hell are forever unteachable those in Heaven are endlessly taught.

For the Paradise Dante now enters has a twofold character, two dimensions that might not seem to fit with one another. For the one part, there is the final act of the *Comedy* wherein *Paradiso* 33 tells of a transition more absolute than any that Dante has at any point previously encountered. For the final act of Dante's *paideia* is not just the end of Dante's poem, it is the apotheosis of all narrative, of language as such, and therefore of poetry itself. For the true word of Paradise – as it were, Heaven's vernacular – is uttered only upon the cessation of all earthly speech, Heaven's speech being silence on earth, even if on earth it is not mere aphasia, the silence of having nothing to say, for it is more like the silence *within* speech when at its ultimate stretch. And it is from that point of view that *Paradiso* is best understood not as a continuation of the narrative of the two cantiche that precede it but more in the way in which it is only at a journey's end that you get to understand the final meaning of the itinerary that got you there. For among the many other things that can be said about the *Comedy*'s narrative is that it is a story about stories as such, about what a story can do and what it can't. It is like book 10 of Augustine's *Confessions*, wherein the drama of his conversion told in the previous nine books is completed with a résumé, a formal account of their narrative's meaning made explicit. In Dante, that final canto tells you that the preceding ninety-nine have been a comedy about the limits of comedy, about what all comedy must be, a tale of conclusive redemption, an end. Therein is a final, unconditional, resolution of all poetry, for there is none but only Heaven's.

In that one aspect of Heaven, it is the place where everything is conclusively settled in an all-consuming vision. It is all-consuming because the whole narrative, all 14,000 lines of it, are contained in a single, final, momentary, glance. That, for the one part. For the other, Heaven is a place of *paideia*, of learning, the narrative the telling of which requires *Paradiso*'s thirty-two cantos that precede the last. And it might seem as if the first excludes the second, that because in the whole stretch of *Paradiso*'s narrative up to that final canto Dante is still learning what it takes to be worthy of that final vision, he cannot at the same time be said to share in heaven's finality; and, that being so, it follows that it is only after the celestial pedagogy ends that its purpose is achieved once and for all. In short, it might seem that Dante enters Paradise only in that final, consuming, vision of the Trinity in Christ in canto 33 with which the *Comedy* ends.

But that doesn't seem right. It does not seem to be Dante's own intent. For it is hard to make sense of a notion of an eternal vision of God that is not itself an endless journey, a journey forever "further up and further in," as C. S. Lewis has it, "for this is my real country! I belong here."[44] And there seems to be no reason to take

---

[44] *The Last Battle*, New York: Collier Books, 1980, chapter 15.

the narrative sequence of *Paradiso* as successive either in the way in which there is succession in Purgatory, or as purposeless repetition in Hell's way, but rather in Bonaventure's way of understanding the threefold journey into God, as from one point of view to be seen as a sequence of phases leading to a culmination, and from another to be seen in terms of its completion containing all its phases simultaneously. Thus do both process and simultaneity belong together in one complex whole, a journey forever further up and further in and at no point less than all the way there, the learning and the vision one and the same, the process raveled up in its fulfilment. We will see more of this in Chapter 7.

Three Silences

Each phase of the *Comedy*'s trajectory is defined by its distinctive, typifying, configuration of knowledge and practice. If in the shape of Dante's journey through Hell and Purgatory to Heaven is his version of the mystical threefold way, then from the point of view of the poet there correspond what one might call three corresponding trials of language as such, three distinct ways in which human speech, even the speech of the poet, fails, and so three species of silence. It is true that the silence of *Paradiso* puts an end even to poetry, but Heaven's silence is the culminating apophasis in a succession of silences distinctive to the preceding two cantiche, and Dante tells us how the three pressures differently shape the poetics of each cantica in turn, in such ways that, whatever the demands they may place upon the poet's resources, Dante can hope to write of them.

From this second-order point of view, that is, from the standpoint of the constraints that the social context of description places on its distinctive language, *Inferno*'s drama, Dante says, lies in an open and sharp contrast between his telling of what he witnesses in Hell as one passing through it and Hell's own vernacular as the speech of those sunk forever in its own unchangeably infernal conditions. Hell's infernal vernacular is but a wretchedly empty chatter – it is pitiable to hear, for the stories of grown men and women, some once fine poets, have, as Courtney Palmbush has put it, the obsessive tedium that other people's home videos impose upon all but their psychiatrists. In consequence it is impossible for Dante to respond to them in kind, because Hell so drags their narratives down that they fall to the level at which, Dante says, there can be no poetry at all therein, a level so low as to tax the limits also of his poetic powers to describe it,[45] though he himself is not one condemned. The hells of the condemned are indeed terrible. But there is no true tragedy in the tales they tell, and though Dante does his best to give voice to the pathos of Francesca da Rimini and Paolo – he faints at the impossibility of responding as sympathetically as he would wish[46] – theirs is not the voice of tragedy, for tragedy is a drama of death's learning and discovery and Francesca and Paolo in Hell have learned absolutely nothing. Hell's outcome is always unchangeably the same, always that Sartrean *Huis clos*. And if that is so with Francesca and Paolo, all the more is it true of the bragging and unteachable Ulysses, yet truer still of Ugolino's pathetic

---

[45] In conversation with her at breakfast.   [46] *Inferno* 5.1–5.

aphasia, which in degree of horror falls just short of Satan's own ultimate silence, whose mouth has neither words to utter nor food to chew on. For so full of a cannibalistic parody of the Eucharist's perfect integration of bread and word is his silence that he can but masticate on his own progeny, Brutus, Cassius, and Judas. Therefore, his silence's emptiness stands at the opposed end of the scale of articulateness to that of Paradise, wherein Dante meets with the *apotheosis* of all speech in silence's ultimate fullness of meaning.

This was the reason why it is *Dante's* experience in Hell wherein is the drama of the first cantica. It lies in the tension between the dreary repetitiveness of Hell's people, whose narratives can for us evoke little more than an ugly, almost prurient, fascination, and the poet's own vernacular, that is, *la lingua che chiamo mamma o babbo*,[47] the dependent speech of children who, scared by lonely nightmares, call out for their mothers in the night. For Dante, poetry seemed just about possible in the recounting of the story of Francesca and Paolo – conceivably the reason he faints at Francesca's telling of the events that lead to her fate in Hell is that they touch all too closely upon his own life's experience. For as she had lustfully betrayed her husband, so Dante had been poetically and personally unfaithful to Beatrice. But as Dante descends deeper into Hell, its own vernacular, the language of interaction therein, is increasingly weighed down by pressures more primitive than any that poetry in its lowest capacity can reach to, and when Dante stands on the edge of the final abyss of meaninglessness that he has been forced to witness, he protests

[47] *Inferno* 32.9.

that he has wrung his poetic resources dry and he has no language hellish enough to match its depravity.

> If I had rhymes that rawly rasped and cackled
> (and chimed in keeping with that cacky hole
> at which, point down, all other rock rings peak),
> I might then squeeze the juices of my thought
> more fully out of me. But since I don't,
> not without dread, I bring myself to speak.
> It's not (no kidding) any sort of joke
> To form in words the universal bum,
> No task for tongues still whimpering "Mum!"
> and "Dad!"
> The Muses, though, may raise my verse …
> so fact and word may not too far diverge.[48]

Therefore, Dante can but gesture to that infernal language, report *on* its hellishness, but *from* the personal experience of it only insofar as in Hell there is an image of an abyss of meaninglessness discoverable in himself too. But whether in Hell's regime or in himself, there is no inner, personal, depth to the language in which Hell's inhabitants tell of their condition; there is nothing to tell, and therefore their reports are startlingly matter of fact, terrifyingly bland, lacking any hint of repentance; perhaps for that reason Dante is himself scared that in reporting on their pain in a manner so objective and detached he is indirectly admitting to a hell of his own as he describes theirs. They do not despair because their condition is eternal; their condition is eternal because they despair, all redeeming conscience having disappeared without a flicker of remorse. Such self-knowledge as they retain is

---

[48] *Inferno* 32.1–9.

emotionally and morally paralyzing in the way that we saw was imagined by Chaucer's Pardoner, who falsified by way of a cynical, empty, parody of truth-telling. What the condemned tell of their guilty deeds is true enough, but only in the way that persons trapped within the circles of their own mendacity have become indifferent to the consequences of such truth as they acknowledge; theirs is a truth that is empty because wholly transparent, but only to itself, for it is all self-reference without content, and it entraps the soul in the guilt it acknowledges. That is why there is no way out of it. Souls in Hell have closed Hell's gates permanently upon themselves.

Hence Dante's doubt whether in describing their Hell he might be personally submitting to Hell's own power is in fact groundless. That the question arises for him at all answers itself. Dante can reflect truthfully on what he sees there in a way that Hell's inhabitants cannot, and that is because his experience in Hell is in fact purgatorial. For that same reason Dante can find a way out of Hell and there is no way out for them, because there is no such second-order reflective language within Hell itself available to its inhabitants, whereas Dante in Hell is hovering in that uneasy space created by the constructive fantasy of *Inferno*, the poetic device that enables him to say that he is at once a visitor there and by way of that fantasy is engaged in a journey of self-discovery for real. In contrast, because Hell's people are incapable of such reflection as would in repentance lift them above their sinful condition they are entirely and eternally sunk in it.

Therein is a crisis of experience for Dante the poet, presenting an ultimate dilemma. He confesses that all words fail of Hell's depravity; but the reason for that failure is not because being only a visitor he cannot experience Hell as fully and intimately as do those eternally condemned; on the contrary, Dante is able to speak of Hell truthfully precisely because he is *not* there as one condemned, and it is the words of the condemned, who are at no reflective distance from their plight, that fail ultimately, for Hell is a sort of equivalent, linguistic and theological, of the astronomers' black hole that sucks all language and perception and experience into its emptiness, and there devours it forever. In that way Hell corrupts everything. It is emptiness as a way of life. It has its own corrupted apophatic, the inverse of the mystical, for whereas the mystical is too full of meaning for creaturely language to contain it, Hell's emptiness is too complete for any language, even the poet's, to give expression to the degree of its failure.[49] And, confronted with the impossibility of an adequately infernal poetic, Dante can do no more than complain about it and do his best, in hope that the Muses will raise his verse to the challenge.

There are tensions internal to the poetics of *Purgatorio* too, but they are quite different from those imposed on *Inferno*, like in manner as *Purgatorio*'s grammar is in its similarly being grounded in the social conditions of the place Dante is describing there. Here too he must learn the local vernacular, Purgatory's idiom being that of repentant sinners speaking in hope of the salvation which

---

[49] There are versions of a theological apophasis that in effect collapse the distinction between an infernal and a celestial failure of speech into one another, confusing the stupid with the mystical. Such, also in effect – and also in other cases intentional – would be to collapse the distinction between Heaven and Hell themselves. I discuss this further in Chapter 7, "The two eternities."

they have won but do not yet have the capacity to enjoy. In Purgatory *la lingua che chiamo mamma e babbo*, the idiom of Dante's poetry that had no place in Hell, is now exactly appropriate. Purgatory's vernacular is that of the infant's longing, the vernacular of dependence and of trust: *That's* how to talk in Purgatory, and, as we have seen, even so close to emerging from Purgatory Beatrice has sharply to rebuke Dante for still speaking in an alien, adult, hellish, tongue that has no place there. Here, in Purgatory, she had told him in perhaps her sternest rebuke, we learn how to smile, for smiles are Heaven's vernacular.[50]

For in Purgatory the speech that Dante finally learns is not at all the vernacular of the sinful humanity that is his *lingua franca* as a mundane author. Purgatory's is the vernacular that by means of its purgation in the waters of Lethe is truly rescued, retrieved from its condition of fallenness, and restored as the common tongue not of the misnamed "original" sin, but of the more truly original condition that was the Earthly Paradise. This vernacular is the true original speech of Adam and Eve, and, in a reversal of the Fall's history, in Purgatory their primal innocence is now recovered, but not, as Dante had speculated in his earlier *De vulgari eloquentia*, in some return to a mythical Hebrew *lingua franca* that had bound the human race together in a common vernacular before Babel dispersed it into separate incommunicable dialects.[51] Rather, now in the Earthly Paradise, there flourishes the theologically expressive diversity

---

[50] *Purgatorio* 30.75.
[51] *De vulgari eloquentia* I: 4, 2–6, ed. and trans. Steven Botterill, Cambridge: Cambridge University Press, 1996, p. 9.

of vernaculars, all of them having in common that they have become the speech of the Garden of Eden regained. We do not in our fallen condition have this language at our command except in the traces of it that remain in those ineradicable moments of what the Western theological tradition called *synderesis*, a primary will for the good, more primitive, and more properly human, than the operative will that can be led astray, and, in consequence of the Fall, more often than not is.[52] For within our fallen condition are the fragmented remnants of a holier will that have survived unscathed even within the devastation of the Fall's shipwreck of conscience, the primal will that Julian of Norwich was later in Dante's century to say had never consented to sin, and never can.[53] But because of Adam's fall these primary traces of conscience are but the broken fragments of that original condition lost, they are the residues of the vernacular of Eden's Garden, and in Purgatory Dante must learn to reconstruct that grammar and syntax, its poetry and its imagery, as his natural human language, his vernacular. Hence that complex, mysterious, succession of televisual images of *Purgatorio*'s final canto, mimicking the visions of the book of Revelation, that at once reach out to the

---

[52] This notion of *synderesis* as an ineradicable sense of distinction between good and bad actions, missing only in a psychopathic condition, seems to reflect a long tradition within the Christian West that parallels the distinction in the Eastern Christian traditions made by Maximus the Confessor between "natural" and "gnomic" wills – on which see Andrew Louth, *Maximus the Confessor*, London: Routledge, 1996.

[53] Julian of Norwich, *Revelations of Divine Love*, trans. Elizabeth Spearing, intro. and notes A. C. Spearing, Harmondsworth: Penguin Books, 1998, chapter 37, p. 93; but see also chapter 53, p. 128.

final meaning of Paradise but only as prophetic anticipation. For Dante cannot pass out of Purgatory until he has learned to speak this true human vernacular and in it write the poetry of *Paradiso*.

Therefore, whereas Hell's is a mindlessly grim vernacular – as a discourse internal to Hell's experience it is a sort of grunt language – Dante in Purgatory is challenged in a quite different way to relearn that characteristically human vernacular which he, along with every human, had lost in the chaos of the Fall. It was sin that had denied him the poetic voice, and he writes the *Comedy* so as to tell the tale of its recovery. So it is that the tension between Dante the poet and the experience that challenges his powers of description, requires for its resolution a second, remedial, silence, a silence that is the more acute and painful in that for the time being it suspends his poetical powers entirely. It is Beatrice herself, the muse, object, and agent of his poetry, who must first reduce him to helpless silence, to a level of absolute poetic inarticulateness, to a linguistic point zero, and to a drowning in Lethe's waters, before he can hope to recover the true voice of the poet, the voice that speaks not only of, but more fundamentally from out of, the innocence of the Earthly Paradise regained. It is here, then, that Dante learns how to write the *Comedy* itself, including even *Inferno*. For it is only because of Purgatory's transformations that Dante can so understand Hell as to make possible his writing of it in a way that its inhabitants themselves cannot. For it is in Purgatory that Dante has been baptized into that "justice and primal love" that on the one hand made Hell but on the other is wholly beyond the reach of those within it.

Three Silences

Upon exit from Purgatory Dante has yet to learn how to write of Heaven and from within it. For in Heaven alone are all Purgatory's hopes fully and finally met. Only here has Dante arrived at the place where the promise of *Vita nuova* is fulfilled wherein he will find that poetic self that is adequate to the love that Beatrice calls upon him to show her. In Heaven the earthly mystical which was hard-won in Purgatory and possible there in but an apophatic mode (for it as much registers speech's failure as its success) is resolved into a true vernacular, into a language no longer poised between the twin pressures of saying and unsaying by which the Pseudo-Denys had shown our premortem mystical discourses are shaped. For these paradoxes of the apophatic signal at once language's transcendent goal and its insufficiency to the speaking of it, and they define the language of poetry in its anticipation rather than in its fulfilment achieved. Dante's language *about* Paradise is not yet the language *of* Paradise, it is not Heaven's vernacular. Not we readers, then, not Dante-author, not anyone before death, is yet there in the place he describes, and so the paradisal truths exert a pressure on the powers of imagination, a pressure that shapes the poetics of *Paradiso* as provisional, faced with the inexpressible, until that final self-transcending experience of the *Comedy*'s end.

The theological model for the ecstasy with which *Paradiso*, and so the *Comedy*, ends is scriptural. Specifically, it recalls the apostle Paul's rapture as he tells of it in 2 Corinthians 12. There Paul says he "knows a man" who was once taken up into the "third heaven"; but whether when thus "taken up" he was in the body or not, "he does not know." In his commentary on these verses Aquinas emphasizes the theological problem about the body that St. Paul says he is unable to solve. Could his rapture into the third heaven have been in some way an anticipation of, by way of a real participation in, the body's final resurrection? Or should we not rather say that it anticipates but his death by way of a momentary suspension of his premortem embodiment, as if in a fleeting rehearsal for a final resolution? Paul "cannot say" which it is, and Aquinas, commenting on Paul's letter, doesn't try to outsmart him.[54] One way or another, in Dante's case as in St. Paul's, it is an eschatological moment, brief and exceptional, for quickly St. Paul snaps out of it back into an unambiguous premortem embodiment. But traces of that rapture, itself beyond all communicable experience, remain with him in their effect upon his mundane condition as the apostle to the Gentiles. Because of it St. Paul was able to write that second letter to the Corinthians and all else that he ever wrote, as if they were halting translations into a worldly vernacular of a celestial experience that is fully expressible only when, having died, he is raised again in the body. All St. Paul can say is that what he saw in that rapture was the whole point of his life, all the meaning of his conversion, the source of all his preaching, the cause of his sufferings and persecutions and the power of them, through grace, to redeem; therein he saw the

---

[54] See his *Commentary on II Corinthians*, in *Saint Thomas Aquinas and Peter of Tarantaise, Commentary on the Letters of St Paul to the Corinthians*, trans. F. R. Larcher, OP, B. Mortensen, and D. Keating, ed. J. Mortensen and E. Alarcón, Biblical Commentaries 38, Lander, WY: Aquinas Institute for the Study of Sacred Doctrine, 2012, chapter 12, lecture 1, pp. 587ff.

whole narrative of a life to be in some way contained in an instant, the earthly sequence contained in a timeless vision, life's long sequences compressed into an eternal "now," the exact antitype of Hell's black hole.

And that same moment of ecstasy with which Dante's *Paradiso* ends likewise contains the whole of the *Comedy* in an instant of incommunicable silence. And though it is with that ecstatic moment that the *Comedy* ends in the silence of Heaven, it is on account of that silence that Dante, like Paul, can write it at all. Now, "midway in life's journey" Dante can begin to write the first canto of *Inferno*. As T. S. Eliot said, it is "in my beginning" that "is my end."[55]

Whatever may be the epistemological standing of Dante's closing rapture, its meaning cannot be translated directly into any vernacular available to him. Herein is a third and final apophatic moment, the antitype of the false, unspeakable, speechlessness of Hell, or even the inadequacy of the purgatorial vernacular. All that Dante can say of it is that it is a moment of knowledge that is in perfect harmony with the love that moves the sun and the other stars – what Dante in *Vita nuova* called the *intelletto d'amore* has for Dante a theological resonance too,[56] recalling the phrase of William of St. Thierry, who, following in a Western tradition that originates in Gregory the Great, spoke of a love that is on its own terms an understanding – *amor ipse intellectus est*, Gregory had

---

[55] *East Coker*, I, line 1, n. 23, in T. S. Eliot, *Four Quartets*, Harcourt: New York: n.d.
[56] See *La vita nuova*, xix, ed. and trans. Mark Musa, Bloomington: Indiana University Press, 1973, p. 30.

said.⁵⁷ Here even *alta fantasia*, poetry, ceases, and the *Comedy* must end. But that is not because poetry is abolished, for herein is Dante's Bonaventuran point: High imagination got him there and what poetry gained for him stays with him, the whole of it, from the lost poet on the dark hillside to the poet lost again but this time in the vision of the Trinity shown "in our human form," the résumé of the whole narrative contained in that final moment of silence. For all Dante's knowledge and all his loves are now resumed in and are together constitutive of the end. Within this conjunction of intellect's vision and the ecstasy of will's love there is no tendency to prioritize the one over the other, no trace in Dante of that fourteenth-century tendency, first, of the fragmentation of knowledge broken away from the will, of vision from affect, their disjunction being so enforced that you are made to contest as to which gains the upper hand, as, in Dante's own time, did the Carthusian Hugh of Balma. Here, Dante says, resisting the polarizations, is both love's understanding and the vision that evokes an ultimate love, the *intelletto d'amore*.

That's what you can say *about* this final ecstasy: Dante's witness to it is akin to that which Herbert McCabe once described of young Rose, who for the first time was invited to join in the conversation of her parents and their adult friends in their local pub. There was joy and amazement for her in the invitation into the company of her parents in their adult world, though they drank the beer and she

---

⁵⁷ William of St. Thierry, *Golden Epistle*, III, paras. 249–251, trans. Theodore Berkeley, Kalamazoo, MI: Cistercian Publications, 1971, pp. 92–93. Gregory the Great, *Homily 27 on the Gospel*, PL 76: 1207.

only the lemonade; and while they shared the adult conversation it was so far above Rose's comprehension that if afterwards you had asked her what they spoke about she would have been able to report little of it. Still, she knew that at last she had grown up beyond her wildest dreams, that she now belonged to a new form of life in which she had it all to learn, and that, now and forever after, adult learning can begin. *Paradiso* describes the process by means of which finally Dante is in the place where he may learn the adult tongue, Celestial, the language wherein poetry is finally realized, and, in that realization, poetry passes over into that which infinitely exceeds it, abolished, as Hegel said, by its realization, an *aufhebung*, a "sublation." Poetry's realization therefore comes only at the end, in the third silence, that of Paradise. In only one way does the silence put an end to poetry; in another, poetry defines its essential nature in terms of silence, by way of the excess it points to but cannot itself ever fully express. It is at just that point that only poetry will do.

The silence in which the *Comedy* ends is, therefore, filled with a new meaning now fully realized in the beatific vision, the Trinity's self-utterance in the Word, the language that is the Trinity having become the new language of the redeemed. That final silence of *Paradiso* is neither filled by the affirmative word of the cataphatic nor emptied into the deficiency of an apophatic negation, for both the truth-bearing grip of the affirmative and the loosening of it of the negative belong to the language of a premortem life. But for all that there is no natural human capacity to see God "face to face" even in heaven – for even there that final vision is made possible by grace alone – still it will be experienced as a true homecoming, for the blessed will recognize it as the place to which they have always belonged, though they had been led astray along many a diverted path in the meantime. It was in God's eternal knowledge and will that they existed before they were created, and it is to that same place that they are to return, "home to his mother's house," as Milton put it, though the "return" was not for Dante as it was for Milton, "private"[58] but to the "mystic rose," to the Church triumphant, a flower in the bloom of a million petals. In consequence, Heaven's own *eloquentia vulgaris* that goes with that vision will then be no unrecognizable foreign language but will give truer expression to what in some way we had always known how to say – as when the naïve and simplistic early draft of a paper or essay may in an inchoate and stumbling way show signs of what you had in mind to say, though what you have written doesn't yet say it. As it is with that early draft of a life, embodied in *Vita nuova*, Dante may legitimately claim when eventually he does get it right that that is what from the start he had always meant to say, and rightly claim to have come home to a truth of his own that he hadn't realized till then that he already knew. That, Dante says, is how it will be in Paradise, a true memory at last restored.

[58] The concluding stanza of Milton's *Paradise Regained*, IV.

7
Paradise and the End of Poetry

~

In the opening verses of *Paradiso* 2 Dante gives notice to any of his readers who lack the intellectual and spiritual maturity required to understand it that they would be best advised to read no further. They should stay within sight of their "native shores," better not to set out "upon these open seas | lest losing me [they] end confused and lost."[1] Thereby Dante announces that he has entered entirely new territory, even for poets. Those not up to it would be able to understand the *Comedy*'s argument well enough so long as they had properly understood *Inferno* and *Purgatorio*, and they would be better off there, holding on to nurse for fear of finding something worse. Even those few who wish to satisfy the "perpetual thirst | to reach the deiform domain" that is Paradise,[2] and have the intellectual and spiritual maturity required, are warned that the new journey will make demands on them of a wholly different caliber from those of *Inferno* and *Purgatorio*.

Dante's advice to his readers to stick to *Inferno* and *Purgatorio*, if that is the best they can manage, clearly didn't mean that every reader might safely skip *Paradiso* as if to say that it does no work that is not done by the first two cantiche. Dante's journey within Paradise does indeed add wholly new dimensions of meaning to the *Comedy*'s narrative in a way that parallels Beatrice's challenge in

[1] *Paradiso* 2.4–6.   [2] *Paradiso* 2.19–20.

Purgatorio 30 that had caught him all unawares – and we with him – demanding of him work of repentance still to do that he had convinced himself he had already done. Now in Paradise, Dante warns his reader that the journey will not take him on a route simply continuous with that of *Purgatorio*. The challenge of the Earthly Paradise now met, he is faced with a true *ne plus ultra*: *Dante* has done all that Dante can do, his part in the journey is complete, and if, as we saw in Chapter 5, grace and free will are both fully engaged on equal terms in the Earthly Paradise, all action being not the less free for being grace's work, indeed, being made fully free only by means of it, now, in Paradise, what remains to be done cannot be done by Dante. *His* story is over; what remains now to happen is his discovery of that story's true meaning. For that does indeed take Dante into a whole new world of understanding, completed in a concluding vision, in the light of which alone all the narrative of the preceding *cantiche*, through Hell and Purgatory and within Paradise, can be finally understood.

It is not, therefore, that there is nothing left to be done in Heaven. Far from it, work remains to do that will once again require profound reassessments of the whole journey thus far, reassessments that will unmake Dante all over again. But the "work" needed is no longer penitential; it is now pedagogical, a work of learning that will lead Dante far beyond the imagination even of the poet who was humiliated by the crisis of the Earthly Paradise. That is why the first canto of *Paradiso* opens with a prefatory prayer, recalling the full meaning of what is now at stake: Dante can see God's "glory in his penetration of all creation" because it "shines back | Reflected more in one part, less elsewhere." That much Dante had always known. The trajectory that took him through creation had governed all Dante's progress through Hell and Purgatory, and on the way the interplay of grace and free will was foremost; but now all created agency falls short of what providence calls for, just as all Dante's knowledge falls short of understanding it. For,

> High in that sphere which takes from him most light
> I was – I was! – and saw things there that no one
> who descends knows how or ever can repeat.
>   For, drawing near to what it most desires,
> our intellect so sinks into the deep
> no memory can follow it that far.[3]

Nonetheless, there is a *Paradiso* to be written, and "[a]s much ... truly of that holy realm | as I could keep as treasure in my mind | will now become the substance of my song."[4] He must learn to convert the vision of the unknowable mystery of God into a song on earth.

Knowing and unknowing, what can be said and what is beyond speech, the poetics of that oxymoronic predicament, these are the songs that he now must sing, though their "substance," sung only in the final moment when the "high fantasy" that got him there has at last failed him, will be reflected in the meantime at best in but a trace left on the memory by that experience, like the impression still left on the waking mind by a dream whose images, so vivid when asleep, can no longer be recalled. It is a song that is too much for many to sing and they would be better off not trying to sing it, better

---

[3] Ibid., 1.1–9. [4] Ibid., 1.10–12.

staying closer their "native shores." And for all that the elaborate detail by means of which Dante takes us on his journey through the circles of Paradise might suggest otherwise, Dante is emphatic that all of it is but the tentative, experimental, halting language of the poet, who can do no more than fill the well of his verse with the few drops of meaning that have not slipped between his fingers unretained. In those prefatory words of *Paradiso*, placing in conjunction the openings of its first and second cantos, are contained the key both to the *Comedy*'s theological epistemology and to Dante's poetics: You need poetry and the poet's sense of the fleeting, tenuous grip of language on meaning, if you are to have any chance at all of retaining for theology even the little that is its own fleeting, tenuous grip on the mystery of Paradise.

Hell and Paradise

Such is how Dante envisages the epistemological standing of his final poem. Powerfully affirmative as is the robust imagery of *Paradiso*, tentativeness qualifies all of it. There is no inconsistency in this, no attempt on Dante's part surreptitiously to have it both ways, as though the rich affirmative complexity of *Paradiso*'s imagery necessarily stood in unreconciled contradiction with Dante's insistence that all of it ultimately fails of the celestial truths that it points to. The success of *Paradiso* as poetry not only survives any such self-defeating polarization of the poet's affirmation with the mystic's negation, it succeeds just because Dante's poetics will set at odds neither the grammatically affirmative against some general epistemological negation, nor the grammatically negative at odds with an epistemological affirmation. The failure of speech to which Dante witnesses at the opening of *Paradiso* applies to speech as such, whether grammatically affirmative or grammatically negative, as much to the negative image as to the affirmative, and Dante must witness to that theological failure precisely in the proliferation of affirmative imagery, not in its attenuation. In fact, to get the poetic feel of the epistemological failure called for, to serve it well in practice, you just have to keep writing until the poet's speech falls under its own weight of excess into an open acknowledgment of its failure. Such is Dante's *Paradiso*.

But there are two failures of speech, not one, Hell's as well as Heaven's. The distinction between the two is central to the theology of this cantica, one third of the total that is the *Comedy*. And it is quite crucial to the understanding of the dynamic of the story's whole sweep, for without it the journey's meaning is entirely lost in a cloud of theological confusion. Just because Dante will never be able to comprehend the full meaning of Heaven it doesn't follow that his theological epistemology allows for an ungoverned incoherence, as if it had no grammar; and Dante needs some account of how to give form and shape to the distinction on which the *Comedy*'s structure rests, namely that between Hell and Heaven themselves, the distinction, that is, between the two eternities, the two termini that bracket the peregrination that is the *Comedy*. For without a clear understanding of that difference all difference between Hell and Paradise themselves is lost and the whole narrative of the *Comedy* collapses entirely into meaninglessness.

It is for Dante as it was for Augustine: Once the whole story has been told from its beginning to its end, then it is that they need to reread all of it the other way round, back from the end to its beginning, Dante's decisive choice at the beginning to take the journey at all being finally understood in terms of the ecstatic moment with which the *Comedy* ends. But the question now is whether that very distinction between the end and the beginning can be made and defended, between Hell and Paradise and their defining eternities. For if Dante the theologian cannot secure that distinction, then the poet Dante's story cannot carry the weight of its own significance.

The Two Eternities

Given how crucial that distinction between the two eternities is, both to the narrative's meaning and so to the formal theology of the *Comedy*, it is necessary to confront a doubt that for some is explicit, for others manifested in an unformulated sense of unease, whether any such distinction can be sustained even in principle. It is a doubt that most of us in some degree share about the two eternities that bracket Dante's time-bound purgatorial journey as a whole: Namely, that eternity itself, in its very nature, is essentially infernal; that while a "moment" of paradisal ecstasy, suspending all time and change, could be bliss for the nonce, as it was for Dante at the end of *Paradiso* 33, its extension into eternity's endlessness would be another, wholly different, matter – indeed, to put the matter strongly, a wholly undesirable one. Would not that eternity itself make Paradise to be a place far from joyous and, on the contrary, a place of ultimate tedium and so of despair, in short, Hell?

Mark Twain is reported to have said that for himself he would choose Heaven for the climate but Hell for the company,[5] capturing the feeling that despite all the fine rhetoric about Heaven its eternity must make it to be a friendless, heartless, desolate, place, a place of but endless, and hopeless, repetition. Dante wrote *Paradiso* apparently in answer to that difficulty. As between the two everything is different, and Dante's poetry makes this difference so clear that no one could mistake the feel of the one for the feel for the other. But is not the difference a theological fantasy? How could any social world, or any true friendship, survive such endlessness? Must not Heaven's relentless and uninterrupted cheerfulness soon enough degenerate into a tedious despair? George Bernard Shaw entertained the thought, hard to resist,[6] that it is impossible to tell the difference between Heaven and Hell precisely on account of their both being eternal. For any eternity whatever would, it seems, be unendurable torture, however ecstatic a moment or two of it might be. Shaw's is a Nietzschean thought. Eternity, he believed, was conceivable only as invariant repetition, as an "eternal

---

[5] Suppose that Beethoven is in Hell, and Homer, and Shakespeare, and the Buddha, together with, as Dante has it, Mohammad, and then Dante himself too – and if we are to believe the decree of the Fourth Lateran Council of 1215 (as also particularists of our times) it's a general truth that it is more likely than not that they are – would there not be a reason to prefer Hell's company to that of an elite collection of tediously small-time sinners in Heaven?

[6] In his sub-Nietzschean *Man and Superman*, ed. Dan H. Laurence, Harmondsworth: Penguin Classics, 2004, Act 3, pp. 124–177.

recurrence" of all your past upon itself, reducing the best joy in principle to endless pain in the event. How could an eternity of Heaven be distinguished from Hell's?

Shaw does indeed touch on a raw theological nerve, his question being a challenge to any imagination of Paradise, including Dante's. Shaw's intuition seems right, that eternity, considered as endlessly extended time, whether Hell's or Heaven's indifferently, would yield despair as its result. Dante's account of Paradise carries conviction as a place of happiness only if he can relieve the thought that very conception of "eternal happiness" is an ultimately self-destructive oxymoron, only, that is, on condition that he can show that if Shaw is right about Hell he is wrong about Heaven, for the two "eternities" are not the same. Otherwise, we are left with the dispiriting conclusion that Dante can make sense only of Hell. And if that were so, would not death's total annihilation be preferable in the long run when compared with the alternative of a finite life that goes on endlessly because we are *never* going to be finally dead. For then the one desire that would forever be aroused in Hell would be the one desire that Hell's endlessness forever frustrates – the desire finally to cease to exist, the desire of those, Dante's apathetic, who, imprisoned in proto-Hell, "have no hope that death will ever come."[7]

Therefore, the point of Dante's *Paradiso*, and the reason why its presence within the *Comedy* is essential, is that it meets a need, on which the very meaning of the poem depends, of showing, not just in a formal theological way, but also in a third convincing narrative, one that describes Dante's

---

[7] *Inferno* 3.46.

journey therein, in what way exactly the Shaw-instinct is wrong, and that the oxymoron, if any, is benign. Dante must so tell the story of *Paradiso* as to sustain the theological conviction that the distinction between the two lies in Hell's meaning being the inverse of Heaven's, and that between Heaven and Hell there is a sort of ultimate, cosmic, irony, a *contrapasso* on the scale of Hell as a whole. Any successful defense of heaven's eternity against the charge of its reducibility to Hell's endless "same again" therefore requires a new narrative, a narrative describing what it takes to learn of this distinction. The composition of such a narrative would, on this account, be far from optional. It would be essential to the coherence of the *Comedy* as a whole.

It is in the light of this theological need that *Paradiso* opens with so powerful a statement of its underlying apophaticism. We know Hell all too well, its horrors are all too familiar. Hell is home territory; Heaven is mind-bogglingly foreign – and yet it reminds us of something promised. In fact the strategy of the *Comedy* works only by showing that Shaw is perceptively right about Hell's endlessness and entirely wrong in having reduced Dante's Heaven's eternity to Hell's. Nietzsche is right, time endlessly extruded entails an endless cycle of repetition, and an endless cycle of repetition reduces every distinctiveness, every uniqueness, to an undifferentiated night in which, as Schelling put it, "all cows are black," the transcendent beauty of Beethoven's Archduke Trio reduced to the tawdry and worthless mediocrity of Sinatra's having it "his way." When listening to Sinatra your eye is in desperation on the clock, hoping that an end to it will come quickly. It is when listening to the Archduke Trio that the clock is internal to the music; it is then that, all other time suspended, music's time touches upon eternity. And in that distinction lies a clue: It is the confusion of eternity with endless time that reduces Heaven and Hell to this indistinguishable sameness. It is not just that Hell is endless. It is that endlessness itself *is* Hell.

Therein is Shaw's theological error, for, as Aquinas says, eternity is nothing to do with any kind of duration, short, long, or endless.[8] All time, even if endless is, in as much as it is successive duration, finite, a creature. It was for that reason that Aquinas could see no problem with the *logic* of the contemporary Aristotelian philosophers in the University of Paris – among whom was Siger of Brabant, now in Paradise along with Aquinas – who held that the world has always existed without beginning in time. For, Aquinas said, that the world has always existed is not true as to fact, but it is perfectly possible. Either way, however, its duration would still be measured by clocks. Aquinas denied only that the world was *demonstrably* either with or without beginning in time, believing rather that the book of Genesis had authoritatively settled the philosophically open question in favor of the former.[9] Crucially, Aquinas objected to the confusion of

---

[8] *Summa theologia*e, 1a q10 a1. For the distinction between eternity and endless time, q10 a 4.

[9] He thought they were wrong about this because Scripture denied it, but that had Scripture not told us to the contrary we might well have believed with Aristotle that the world is endlessly old, without beginning in time. Such belief, he thought, would have no consequences one way or the other for a doctrine of creation out of nothing. See Aquinas's *De aeternitate mundi contra murmurantes* (*On the Eternity of the World Against the Rumormongers*), in *Thomas Aquinas, Selected Writings*, ed. and trans. Ralph McInerny, Harmondsworth: Penguin Classics, 1998, pp. 710–717.

time, even time without beginning or end, with God's eternity. For, whether the world has existed for infinitely extended duration or only in a fixed and measurable time, one way or the other it would still be a finite world, at every point dependent for its existence on the creative activity of God, by way of an eternal uncreated act that brings about the time-bound creature.

For human beings to live too long is, as it was for Makropulos in Janáček's opera, unendurable, and they will long for death. For endless time is Hell. And after death only some share in God's eternity would not be Hell, an eternity that is not endless succession but a *nunc stans*, as Boethius called it, a "*forever* now," not time's succession, but an immediacy with no beginning or end and with no duration in between. Boethius said that *nunc fluens facit tempus, nunc stans facit aeternitatem*, "a 'now' that flows forward makes for time, a 'now' stopped makes for eternity."[10] Successive time, "labour time," is fine for the accumulation of capital, as Marx said. He added that it is when making love that time stops still and bears some relation to eternity.[11]

It is not bare immortality that answers to ultimate human desire, and it is here again that Scotus seems to get the logic right when he said that we naturally desire an eternity that no nature could possibly provide, nor any human intellect properly understand. For eternity is God's alone who is above all time, whether human or

---

[10] Boethius, *On the Trinity*, 4.
[11] *Economic and Philosophical MSS (1844)*, in *Karl Marx: Early Writings*, trans. and ed. T. B. Bottomore, New York: McGraw-Hill, 1963, pp. 165–167.

angelic.¹² It is true that the distinction between eternity and endlessness is hard for us to make out. Nonetheless, it is the key to the distinction between Heaven and Hell; and the only thing to do is to stop trying to make it out, for it is necessarily beyond our sequential, and so time-bound, forms of comprehension, as Kant observed. And if we do try to understand it we will only get it wrong. Eternity is not a name that by right of nature creatures share with God, though we naturally desire it. The eternity that is God's by nature we share as grace, as gift: *That* is what Heaven is, the answer to a natural desire that only God can reveal to us and only grace can satisfy. What alone human beings can know of and by nature make a claim to, is immortality, endless survival, and that is just on account of our having naturally immortal souls.¹³

The logic of Shaw's argument, then, seems sound as to how things would be were the mere fact of personal survival of death to be all that is in question. On those terms there would be nothing after death but Hell, just that remorseless, endless, Nietzschean repetition – and Dante describes the pagan Virgil as understanding Hell well enough in some such terms, indebted as his *Inferno* is to book 6 of Virgil's *Aeneid*, wherein the souls on the banks of the Styx "reach out in longing for the other shore" – *tendebantque manus ripae ulterioris amore*.¹⁴ But because Virgil

---

¹² See Herbert McCabe, "Eternity," in *Cambridge Companion to the Summa Theologiae*, ed. Philip McCosker and Denys Turner, Cambridge: Cambridge University Press, 2016, pp. 102–116.

¹³ It remains, of course, a matter of argument between theologians in Dante's time whether a surviving human soul without its body is (as Bonaventure thought) or is not (as Aquinas thought) sufficient for the survival of individual persons. See Chapter 2.

¹⁴ Virgil, *Aeneid*, VI.

has no conception of eternity, but only of time's endlessness, Dante's heaven is quite beyond his comprehension;[15] and that is why Virgil must disappear from the narrative of the *Comedy* just at the point where Heaven is finally in prospect for Dante. For Virgil has no conception of Heaven's eternity. And Dante's Hell follows Virgil's in that for both Hell is immortality as being, precisely in as much as it is endless, nothing but punishment. Nor has Shaw any better understanding of it. The difference between Virgil and Shaw is that Virgil, realizing that there is more to eternity than he understands, knows that he must therefore fall silent, while Shaw, believing that he does understand, writes a bad play, getting it wrong.

Dante himself, however, does seem to grasp the implication of a doctrine of the soul's immortality as a purely natural condition, namely that were immortality all that there is to it then the Virgil of the *Aeneid* would have been right, and would have had Shaw with him, in concluding that upon death Hell is all there could be for human beings to count on. And Dante's conception of Hell seems close to Virgil's Hades, as the drearily endless outcome of the natural course of the soul's bare immortality. For Dante supposes that if you have rejected grace then in Hell you are stuck with what you have naturally got and no more – for Hell just is your being stuck with it. But Heaven's eternity has nothing in common with Hell's endlessness thus understood. Heaven is eternal life, and that is a supernatural gift, pure grace, the wholly unmerited gift of a share in God's own eternal life. For if immortality is ours by right, nothing but a gift could make eternal

[15] See Chapter 3.

life ours. And it is on such terms that Dante's *Paradiso* can be distinguished – in principle at least – from Hell, though the meaning of that distinction must be beyond Dante's comprehension. For Dante can only narrate in a time-bound succession that *nunc stans* of Boethius which is beyond all time.

Silence Imagined

It is for such reasons that Dante opens the *Paradiso* with so radically an apophatic statement of heaven's incomprehensibility. What differentiates *Paradiso*'s eternity from Hell's interminability is at once decisive and also beyond our understanding, a difference that on the one hand we cannot grasp but on the other makes all the difference in the world to what we *do* grasp. For Hell's interminability is both readily comprehensible and without doubt insufferable, whereas Heaven's eternity is neither. That said, if Dante is to write a *Paradiso* at all, he needs some imagery, metaphors – more, whole worlds of meaning – that will bear the weight systematically of that crucial distinction between Hell and Heaven, and the point of Purgatory is to be the place wherein the logic of that distinction is learned as a discipline of the soul: As in Chapter 4 we saw Robin Kirkpatrick say, the distinction Beatrice makes Dante learn in Purgatory is that between a grim and joyless achievement of will and the discovery of how to let go of finite agency and give way to the gift of true happiness.[16] Moreover, in Chapter 6, we saw that in Dante's mind nothing differentiates the postmortem outcomes

[16] Chapter 4, "Beatrice's challenge."

of Hell, Purgatory, and Heaven from one another more radically than the silences with which each cantica ends, each distinctive of a stage in the trajectory of his learning, personal and theological.[17] Those silences form a sequence, beginning from Hell's sullen dumb to which all the chatter of the condemned finally leads, Satan's mouth being stuffed too full of the indigestible gristle of Brutus, Cassius, and Judas to allow for any speech, through the repentant silence to which Beatrice reduces the poetical Dante in Purgatory, and on to that final ecstatic silence of *Paradiso* in which the meaning of the *Comedy*'s whole journey is finally disclosed. Now, though, we see that those three silences are in their distinctive ways modes of utterance – it is there that there is paradox, for the silences are themselves words, things said, audible only in their various relationships with sound. And the poetics of *Paradiso* is dominated by the *imagination* of those silences, above all by the imagination of the final silence of heaven.

That silence, the silence of the mystical – the final silence with which Dante completes the significance of the *Comedy*'s preceding 14,000 lines of poetry, standing in absolute contrast with Satan's – is the silence into which speech must fall, a silence the more complete the nearer it reaches to God. And this final silence of the mystical has its own work to do, it exerts a pressure of its own on our premortem human language, whether verbal or otherwise. Therefore, nothing that describes the silence of the mystical entails that the mystical has no language of its own, a characteristic communication embodied, and it is in recognition of this that, in a defining paradox, Michael

[17] Chapter 6, "Three silences."

Sells wrote of "the mystical languages of *un*saying."[18] Nor is it surprising that poetry should be mysticism's natural language. For poetry is exactly what you write when otherwise lost for words. Then it is that Shakespeare says, "words fail me!" and he writes Sonnet 30 about the "sessions of sweet silent thought"; and Dante, in awe of poetry's inadequacy says in those opening words of *Paradiso*, there defining the general character of the new stresses that the third cantica's poetry is going to have to bear, "to go beyond the human" – *trasumanar* is his word – "cannot be put into words"[19] – though, unperturbed, he writes the *Comedy* through to the very end, putting into words that very poetic transcendence of speech.

Of course, that the mystical needs poetry does not entail that all poetry is mystical – when jaded by too much theology I amuse myself (but alas no one else) composing in plain doggerel distinctly unmystical limericks in praise of my friends on their birthdays. But the converse is not so far from a general historical truth. For the mystical has always had to call upon poetry in some form or other, beginning from one of Jewish and Christian mysticism's originating texts in the Song of Songs, on through the long sequence of commentaries on Scripture's "mystical senses" in the patristic and medieval traditions, in the poetry of Mechtild of Magdeburg and the stanzas of John of the Cross's *Spiritual Canticle*, through the sonnets of John Donne and of George Herbert, and, nearer to our own times, in Hopkins's "terrible sonnets" or T. S. Eliot's *Four Quartets*, especially *Little*

---

[18] Michael Sells, *Mystical Languages of Unsaying*, Chicago: University of Chicago Press, 1994, emphasis added.
[19] *Trasumanar significar per verba non si poria*: *Paradiso* 1.70–71.

Gidding. But none of these poetical forays into the earthly language that is called upon in response to the experience of the mystical compares with the systematic challenge set for a poetics by Dante's journey into Paradise.

Dante, then, is faced with a challenge to explain how in any way at all the language of human terrestrial experience can match heaven's reality. But as if that were not challenge enough, he is beset at the very outset of *Paradiso* by the prior question of how he can engage in any conversation at all *in* Paradise with those who, unlike him who is but passing through, are there eternally experiencing the immediate presence of God. Dante visiting Paradise, and the blessed at home there, don't possess a common language, and while the vernacular of the blessed is a celestial demotic, Dante's is still *la lingua che chiami mama o babbo*. Granted, then, that in Paradise there is no conversion crisis of the sort that Purgatory required of Dante to undergo, the paradoxical character of Dante's journey there is not for all that eased; it is intensified. For even if he has not yet died and therefore has but little command over the paradisal *lingua franca*, Dante is no more but an observer passing through heaven on tour, like a traveler without French making his way through the sights of Paris, than he was but a tourist in Hell or Purgatory. Above all, the celestial journey leading up to its final moment is not to be understood as if it were for him no more than a further episode of Purgatory's repentance. That said, it is as much a *paideia*, a journey of learning, as were the infernal and the purgatorial journeys. In fact, it is in the very nature of Paradise itself that it is a place of learning, and Dante's learning has a *cursus* that is still an *itinerarium mentis in Deum*.

Paradise and the End of Poetry

For the new pressure that *Paradiso* brings to bear upon the language of poetry derives from the fact that Dante's account of his journey there tells the tale of one not yet dead meeting with those who, being dead and raised to glory, are themselves enjoying the beatific vision, a condition whose excess reaches far beyond all human experience, beyond even that which Dante had faced in *Purgatorio* where he had had to learn the vernacular of the Earthly Paradise. That is why after those very first words of *Paradiso* that describe how, now in Paradise, now "drawing near to what it most desires | our intellect so sinks into the deep | no memory can follow it that far,"[20] he adds: *Trasumanar significar per verba | non si poria*, "we cannot give meaning to what surpasses the human."[21]

Dante had had to be taught that his purgatorial conversion was not so small a matter as that of his achieving the moral qualifications of a Socrates only, and that more disturbingly radical than a moral-ascetical conversion was an epistemological, an "Abrahamic" conversion of faith, that intensified and transformed all the narrative that preceded it. Now in Paradise not even Abraham's faith is going to be enough for Dante, for the celestial vernacular is no longer that of faith perceived "in a glass darkly," as St. Paul had said,[22] but that of the vision of things, once hoped for in faith's faltering language, now fully granted. Dante before death is going to meet with Heaven's people, and if *they* converse with him, and if he can understand them when they do, that is only because they speak to him in translation out of their own celestial

---

[20] *Paradiso* 1.7–9. [21] Ibid., 1.70–71. [22] 1 Corinthians 13:12.

vernacular into his poetic mundane; at least that is so until the *Comedy*'s very last word, when Dante finally, and in a mere flash, at last sees, learns Heaven's speech, and utters but one word in it, a true Word in plain Celestial untranslated; and, his will then moved by the same love that moves the sun and other stars, he sees God the Trinity made known in the humanity of Christ in direct unmediated vision – upon which there is not, and cannot be, any more to be said.

It is only in that brief moment – it's the theologian's equivalent of the physicist's "singularity," an incalculable event of origination, at once inexplicable in any terms that precede it and also explaining all that follows, a timeless origin of time, an unnarratable origin of all narration – that Dante-poet is taken beyond the terrestrial apophatic, beyond that "knowing unknowing" of the Pseudo-Denys's *Mystical Theology*, beyond the *docta ignorantia* of Nicholas of Cusa, beyond the "dark nights" of John of the Cross, beyond all those limits that are imposed upon him in consequence of his not being dead, into the immediacy of vision, a seeing of God by way of a grace-given participation in God's perfect self-knowledge. Only then are the tensions of the apophatic finally resolved. Here at last what is silence for Dante is not silence in itself, for it is the true speech of heaven that in that brief moment with which the *Comedy* ends he has at last understood. But that moment cannot be sustained, for Dante, not yet dead, has no constant ear for it, nor any way of taking hold of it for himself, and in fidelity to that vision he must in awe fall silent, and his journey at last completed, he may now *begin* to write the *Comedy*.

That is why the *Comedy*'s last word is not *stelle*, but rather the silence into which thereafter the poem finally falls, like the amazed silence that falls briefly after the last note of the music; and though soon enough after the music's end we return to the street and the noise of its traffic, we bring that silence with us and on account of it can attempt to write of it all, an attempt that, in Dante's case, he calls the "Comedy." The *Comedy*'s 14,000 verses are the articulation of that final silence, an eternity recollected and narrated in time.

Poetry's End

Until that final moment Dante's journey through Paradise is still for him a *paideia*, an induction into the heavenly citizenship. But its learning is no longer purgatorial, no longer acquired through suffering, repentance, and penance; it is a place not of the hard ascetical slog up a steep mountainside but of the joy of illumination, a place of induction into an ever-intensifying new level of experience. For everything in Heaven is celestial. Therefore, if Dante has everything to learn, then both the pedagogical style and the syllabus of learning are heavenly too. But Dante does not set learning and contemplation, *paideia* and vision, at odds with one another, as the Western Christian theological tradition – in this following Gregory the Great – had tended to do. Denys the Carthusian, writing a century and a half after Dante, took note of Gregory the Great's opinion that the active life of teaching and preaching and of ministration to the poor, the sick, and the prisoner, is a labor that begins and ends in this life pre-mortem, and is typified by the complaining Martha who, in Luke's account,[23] slaves away in the kitchen; whereas the contemplative life, typified by Mary who does nothing to help out her sister with the chores and sits still at the feet of Jesus listening to him, begins in this life but never ends even in the next.[24] For that reason, Gregory says, Jesus commends Mary for having "chosen the better part" because hers is properly contemplative, and contemplation is, as Aristotle said, absolutely the best thing to be doing,[25] in itself a higher thing than any active work.[26] And, Gregory adds, contemplation is what the saints in heaven do, there being in Heaven no call for the active works that are called for this side of death. But Denys the Carthusian dissents, maintaining that even on Gregory's criterion teaching and learning belong in Heaven, for his namesake, Denys the Areopagite, had said in his *Celestial Hierarchy* that the higher angels instruct the lower angels in the business of celestial contemplation:[27] So will not the human blessed be learning there too? asks the Carthusian.

How the question at issue between Denys the Carthusian and Gregory the Great is resolved has significant consequences for how we are to read Dante's

---

[23] Luke 18:38–42.
[24] Gregory the Great, *Moralia on Job*, trans., notes, and indices John Henry Parker and J. Rivington, 1844, chapter 6, para 61.
[25] *Nicomachean Ethics* X, 7, trans. Christopher Rowe, Oxford: Oxford University Press, 2002, 250–252.
[26] One has to say "in itself" for Gregory the Great admits that this side of death there are often circumstances in which the priorities are for the moment reversed, when the contemplative takes second place to extreme urgency of another's need. For the highest work in practice is always that which charity demands.
[27] *Celestial Hierarchy* 10, 273A–273B, in *Complete Works of the Pseudo-Dionysius*, trans. Colm Luibheid, New York, Paulist Press, 1987, pp. 173–174.

Paradiso. Were you to follow Gregory the Great's way of distinguishing the active from the contemplative, *Paradiso* would best be read as telling of a long journey of learning beginning from Beatrice's lecture on the moon's dark patches in *Paradiso* 2 up to the critical point in canto 33 at which the Virgin Mary turns to her Son in response to Bernard of Clairvaux's prayer – "Oh virgin mother, daughter of your son"[28] – and in consequence you would have to say that before that point it is but a journey of preparation, a journey of acquiring the disciplines yet needed before Dante can be admitted to the final, completing vision in Paradise. And though the disciplines called for may not be purgatorial in nature – as we will see, heaven's disciplines are quite different from those of Purgatory – they are not easily acquired. As late as *Paradiso* 22 Dante must still bend to Beatrice's stern insistence that he has more progress to make in learning of heaven's happiness than as, so far, he has achieved. Dante is "[a]stounded, overwhelmed." "I turned to her," he says,

> My constant guide, like any little boy
> Who'll run to where his greatest trust is found.
> And rushing there, as mothers always do,
> with words to help and set once more to right,
> her shocked, pale sobbing son, she said to me:
> "Do you not know you are in Heaven now?"[29]

He is in heaven, but even there Dante sobs. Of course, he, the author of the *Comedy*, is a pilgrim in heaven, a *viator*, not yet at home there. As for this Dante-pilgrim,

---

[28] *Paradiso* 33.   [29] *Paradiso* 22.1–7.

Gregory the Great's account of this pedagogy prevails, for his experience of Heaven thus far occurs not within the final beatific vision itself but only as a last stage of spiritual preparation for it. But were one to stick to the letter of Gregory's distinction between the contemplative and active lives and read *Paradiso* accordingly it will be as if Dante envisaged the whole of *Paradiso* prior to the point with which it closes in that ecstasy of canto 33 as being a journey still within the Earthly Paradise, a proto-heaven, a prolegomenon, and as if a stage of a journey not yet completed; or perhaps you would have to say that what Dante describes therein belongs within that stage of spiritual progress that the Pseudo-Denys called the "illuminative" way, en route to a moment of final union with God,[30] and that it is in that final union alone in canto 33 wherein the formally distinct condition of the blessed in Heaven is at last met.

Though for other reasons than Gregory's, Teodolinda Barolini seems to read *Paradiso* in light of his view that in so far as Dante is described as having anything yet to learn then on that account he cannot yet be in Paradise, or, that if he is there, then it is thus far only as a visitor. This seems, she says, to be implied by the general strategy of Dante's paradisal psychology and epistemology. For underlying that epistemology is a conception of human desire according to which it is "final" only if it is wholly satisfied, and a desire is fully satisfied only when there is no margin of further desire left, and so ceases *as desire*. Thus, it would follow for Barolini that any desires

---

[30] *Celestial Hierarchy*, 3, 165B–168B, in *Complete Works*, trans. Luibheid, pp. 154–155.

remaining unfulfilled leave a person short of happiness, in a condition that is inherently

defective, while the cessation of desire is happiness, beatitude, in a word perfection. Beatitude as spiritual autonomy – as emancipation from the new – is introduced as early as the *Vita Nuova* (xviii.4) where Dante learns to place his *beatitudine* not in Beatrice's greeting, which can be removed (thus causing him to desire, to exist defectively), but in that which cannot fail him ... Since nothing mortal can satisfy these conditions, we either learn from the failure of one object of desire to cease to desire mortal objects altogether, or we move forward along the path of life toward something else, something new.[31]

Thus, to be finally happy in Heaven is to be done with desire as such, the desire fulfilled being that desire's extinction.

It is right, of course, to distinguish between the desires that drive the journey of *Dante-pilgrim* through Paradise that are indeed "mortal," and the desires of those in Paradise who are there eternally rewarded. There is no difficulty in understanding Dante's journey through Paradise as being for him a *paideia*, a journey of learning and discovery: his not being dead, necessarily it is so. And it is a general truth about desire that the desire for *just this* outcome ceases when *just that* outcome is achieved. But it would be a curiously static notion of all desire to suppose that if your desire is satisfied then that is the end of the matter, putting all consequential desire to rest. For it is in the very nature of desire that its capacity is either infinite in that it expands with its satisfactions in a spiral

---

[31] Teodolinda Barolini, *Undivine Comedy: Detheologizing Dante*, Princeton, NJ: Princeton University Press, 1992, p. 26.

of desire and satisfaction without end, or else it contracts and ceases on account of its being met. In fact, it is just here that the distinction has force as defining how Dante's Paradise and Dante's Hell are themselves are distinct, the one a place where desire's infinity, once met, endlessly calls for "the new," the other a place wherein forever it is a frustrated finitude that endlessly imposes only "the same again," finitely satisfying finite desires, eternally ending the matter just there.

Therefore, if we are to understand correctly the nature of Dante's education in the ways of Heaven it will be clear that it must itself be a heavenly education, that is to say, an education by means of the heavenly, and no longer by way of hope's purgatorial disciplines, nor, therefore, by way of faith, but now by way of the "greatest [virtue] of them all, which is charity"[32] by which his will is finally moved. It seems better to say, as better explaining the theological strategy of *Paradiso*, that for Dante there is a distinctly heavenly *paideia* that belongs within an eternity all its own. All of that paradisal pedagogy – it is the general shape of *Paradiso* as a whole – conducted first under the tutorship of Beatrice, then by way of those tests of Dante's faith, hope, and charity under the tutorship of Peter, James, and John in cantos 24–26, and in the climax that is Bernard of Clairvaux's great prayer to the Virgin Mary in canto 33, calling upon her to have her Son bring Dante into the final vision of the Trinity, has the shape of indeed a complex and tough learning curve, a learning that is required not just because Dante is visiting and needs a tour guide, for what he is learning is that learning

---

[32] 1 Corinthians 13:13.

is itself part of what Paradise essentially and eternally is, and not merely a pre-paradisal preparation for a place in which there is, as Barolini puts it, a final "emancipation from the new."

Moreover, in this view of the place of learning within the contemplative life these theologians of the Western theological traditions, among many others, all have a precedent in the theology of the fourth-century Cappadocian, Gregory of Nyssa, though none of these seem to know of his work. This Gregory says that the beatific vision is not to be understood as if its contemplative character consisted in an eternity of timeless blank motionless staring at the divine essence, but as a never-ending, ever-deepening, discovery of the infinite goodness of God as answering to a never-ending, ever-deepening, discovery of the infinite desire for it. Gregory of Nyssa's heaven is a place of endless *learning* how to be truly happy by way of a pedagogy that is itself happiness-led, a wisdom progressively achieved by way of wisdom's own work. "Since, then, those who know what is good by nature desire participation in it, and since this good has no limit, the participant's desire itself necessarily has no stopping place, but stretches out with the limitless."[33]

If Gregory of Nyssa's *theoria* is an act of contemplation it is also an act of responding to that which is forever drawing him "further on and further in." The possession of wisdom in this way is not an ultimate *termination* of desire. This wisdom already possessed opens up

---

[33] See Gregory of Nyssa, *The Life of Moses*, trans., intro., and notes, Abraham J. Malherbe and Everett Ferguson, New York: Paulist Press, 1978, Prologue, n. 7, p. 31.

thereafter upon a never-ending journey, a never-ending desire for more, an infinitely extended pedagogy bearing upon an inherently infinite object of desire that calls upon a subjectively infinite capacity on the side of the desire itself. To sustain such a position on the nature of desire's endless spiral of completion it is necessary not to concede to the position that some claim to inherit from Buddhism, that all desire is inherently defective because all desire is limited by its nature as lack. When my desire was fulfilled upon my first reading Shakespeare's Sonnet 30 it was not as if I had in advance of reading it an unsatisfied Sonnet 30-shaped desire that Sonnet 30 met and extinguished, putting an end to the desire for it. On the contrary, it was the poem itself which elicited the desire it satisfied and, as it were, "read" the desire in endlessly new and unanticipated ways. *I* didn't know of that Sonnet 30-shaped desire of mine until Shakespeare discovered it for me. And in inevitable consequence of it I wanted to read Sonnet 31 and thereafter all 154 of them.

The Demotic Celestial: Smiles

Given that understanding of *Paradiso* as being inherently, and in its own nature, a place of learning, it should be no surprise that the language descriptive of Dante's journey of transformation in Paradise is provided, as all good teaching is, in the most striking way in the language of the earthiest, the most bodily, of human exchanges – by means, as Dante has it, of smiles offered and smiles withheld, by means of music, and by way of music's counterpart, which is silence. These are bodily practices, exchanges by way of earthly images. There is no paradox in this.

There are no other images of the heavenly than the bodily, for there is no other source of them than in the body's meaning. And, as the Pseudo-Denys says, sometimes it is even the very grossness of the discordantly everyday image that is theologically the more appropriate, being less misleading than strenuously high-sounding rhetoric – as he notes, Scripture itself without scruple warrants describing the unaccountable nature of God's providence as seeming sometimes to be like the tetchy behavior of a drunk with a hangover,[34] because that gets the point across perfectly and does so by way of what obviously isn't a literal truth. And, glossing this text of the Pseudo-Denys, Aquinas – who, though no poet himself, has his theological reasons for agreeing – says that high, dignified, exalted, theological language can all too easily seduce you into error by way of a sort of linguistic Pelagianism, imagining that you have grasped the mystery by its means, whereas, by means of the grossly deficient material image, you are, in a manner more apt, epistemically humbled by its obvious impropriety; and so it is by means of the earthly metaphor that in one move both the achievement and the failure of our theological talk are captured.[35]

It is perhaps here in this quite strikingly materialist theological epistemology, and in a corresponding poetics,

---

[34] *Mystical Theology*, 3: 1033B: Though he does not say where in Scripture God is so described.

[35] *ST*, 1a q1 a 9 *corp.* and ad 3. Quite obviously none of these theologians think that any old language about God will do. You can't say "God is evil" is fine because it falls short. It doesn't 'fall short.' It's just false. The apophatic is not the sloppy evasion of the true and the false as if surpassing the distinction. The apophatic failure of speech to reach the whole truth is quite other than the false which contains no truth at all.

that Dante seems closest in spirit to Aquinas. Hence, those smiles of *Paradiso*. "I saw that everywhere | in Paradise there's Heaven, though grace may rain | in varied measure from the Highest Good," says Piccarda Donati, glossing the words of Jesus, who had said that in his father's house there are many dwelling places.[36] Dante, we saw, asks Piccarda how she can be so happy in the lowest place in Heaven when there are so many higher places that she might have occupied – "Have you no wish to gain some higher grade, | to see and be as friends to God still more?"[37] And before she says anything by way of reply, she simply smiles. Her smile wells up from the sheer pleasure of being able to set Dante's mind at rest and learn to smile for himself.

Dante's is the sure touch of the poet. He knows when not to strive, especially, that is, when writing of the beatific vision: Do not, he says, strain to exalt, stay human, earthbound, and the terrestrial will run best. Smiles are what we have and, since all language will fail of the reality, smiles, the earthy human, will "trasumanar," fail to a humanly best effect. Piccarda's smile is the first of many marking the progress of Dante's celestial schooling, a pedagogy that is achieved not by means that point in an external way to something that they do not themselves embody, but rather by means that already contain the end taught: That is the meaning of a paradisal, and therefore mystical, epistemology. Hence the smiles; for they, like music, are at once the most sensuous and at the same time the most immediate acts of communication, at once carnal, lighting

---

[36] John 14:2.   [37] *Paradiso* 3.64–66.

up a face with pleasure and spreading the pleasure to others, and at the same time the most "mystical"; for in a very special way the smile is a "mystical language of unsaying," a language that without a word speaks nonetheless, and says it all.

Smiles don't always accompany an act merely, functioning adverbially so as to denote the pleasure with which an action is done.[38] For unlike merely tactical smiles that hide a devious purpose – for "a man may smile and smile and be a villain"[39] – or those employing deceitful means, as did Judas's kiss of greeting, that in either case subvert as parody the truth they falsely imitate, some smiles *are* the act itself completed, as when in a smile's lips there is no postponement, no promise still unfulfilled. For, as with music so with smiles, they already contain what they express. Such smiles, therefore, are, like good sex, contemplations. It is on your way to the endpoint – as in Purgatory – that you grit your teeth and make a grimace at the effort required, for Purgatory is *all* means to an end, albeit entertained in hope. But Heaven's smiles, like Piccarda's, and even more so those of Beatrice, are like the action of the sacrament. They are not external causes that merely point to something else, themselves being empty of the reality they point to. For the sacraments inaugurate what they signify, in them are contained the means, the vehicle, and the effect, all rolled up into one. And so it is in Heaven that the cause of the pleasure and the pleasure caused are one and the same. In Heaven, the meaning of everything signified is complete in itself.

---

[38] *Nicomachean Ethics* X, 4, 1174a 13ff.   [39] *Hamlet*, Act 1, scene 5.

Such are the smiles that are the means of the paradisal pedagogy. They are not tactics designed to encourage Dante, like a teacher's encouragement at the end of a good essay; they are an education in what heaven *is*. Step by step, smiles teach the heavenly by means of the heavenly, first, in Piccarda's smile in canto 3, then in canto 9 where Folco says "here we don't repent such things. Here we smile";[40] but above all it is Beatrice's smiles that teach him how to be happy there. In canto 10, she says, "In us imagination is too mean | for such great heights," nonetheless "Give thanks," she says

> "Give thanks to Him, the Sun of all the angels.
> In grace He's raised you to this sun of sense."

To which Dante responds

> No mortal heart was ever so well fed
> To give itself devoutly to its God
> So swiftly, with such gratitude and joy,
>   as now, to hear her words ring, I became.
> I set my love so wholly on that Sun
> That He, in oblivion, eclipsed even Beatrice.
>   This did not trouble her. She smiled at it.
> And brightness from the laughter in her eyes
> Shared out to many things my one whole mind.[41]

And then at last in canto 33 there is that gesture of the Virgin Mary herself for whom silently to turn her pleading eyes towards her Son is prayer enough (as it were, "Dante has no wine," her eyes say), and it is by her prayer that Dante begins at last to learn the language

---

[40] *Paradiso* 9.103. [41] Ibid., 10.46–63.

of Paradise, how to speak Celestial. As it turns out in canto 33, this language is the divine Word itself, the Word saying and the Word said, all being in "our *human* form," the inexpressible Word incarnate exhibited in bodily gesture, in smiles and in music. The language of Paradise, Dante says, is the Incarnation, the Word made flesh.

It was by means of the humiliations of *Purgatorio* cantos 29–32 that the stiff and self-assured Dante had learned to drop his moralizing guard, to cease striving to his own ends, and to let a final peace in. But if in Heaven there is no longer any striving, it does not follow that there is no more to be learned. This celestial learning is not hard means to a joy separately defined, for the joy is in the learning itself, and Heaven's work is *all* pedagogy. And just because you can't fail there it doesn't follow that Heaven is no school. In the fullest vision that Dante experiences of the heavenly world to which all the blessed equally belong, all of them sinners forgiven, each person is in their different place in Heaven, each a petal in the concentric, and so nonhierarchical, circles of the mystic rose,[42] each person's reward given in its conjunction with everyone else's – it is as happy together that the individual happiness of each is complete according to their capacity, for there simply isn't anything else that such happiness could be *for*, as if for a good not yet achieved and yet wanting. It is in contemplation of this completeness that Beatrice's culminating smile overwhelms Dante and he can say no more:

[42] Ibid., 30.

> From now on, I'll admit, I'm overwhelmed,
> defeated worse than all before – in comic
> or in tragic genre – by what my theme demands.
>   As sunlight trembles in enfeebled eyes,
> Calling to mind how sweet to me her smile was,
> itself deprives my mind of memory.
>   Not since the day that I, in our first life,
> first saw her face until this living sight,
> has song in me been cut so cleanly short.[43]

Smiles are the speech, the vernacular idiom of the school of bliss, and they elicit smiles in response. For like jokes they create good company; and like the act of creation itself, jokes explode out of nothing, *ex nihilo*, and they fail if before the punchline you can guess where they are going. That is why a joke, also like creation, lights up everywhere it is told with that suddenness that makes you laugh with pleasure at its perfect *convenientia*, at its being both so perfectly surprising, so "out of the blue," and so perfectly *just so*. It is in this way that *Paradiso*'s smiles are to be understood as a celestial pedagogy, not in being causal means whose goal is the achievement of something else, but in that they already contain all the happiness that they signify. In Heaven you are not going anywhere else, for you are already there. And so it is that in Paradise Piccarda smiles unconditionally: My *smiles*, she says, are the answer to Dante's query.

What is more, within that pedagogical frame not only are there smiles exchanged, also there are smiles withheld, since what for Piccarda and Folco is the response

---

[43] Ibid., 30.22–33.

to Heaven's bliss is still for Dante a strategy of Heaven's learning. Even in Heaven, then, Dante is still *homo viator*, journeying, exploring, and it is for this reason that Beatrice in canto 21 of *Paradiso* withholds her smiles from Dante, not, she reassures him, out of displeasure, but because however much Dante longs for her smile Beatrice knows that its beauty unveiled would yet be too much for him, it would burn him to a cinder:

> Now once again my eyes were fixed upon
> my *donna*'s countenance, and drawn away,
> with all my thoughts from any other aim.
> 	She did not smile. But: "If I were to smile"
> so she began, "you would become what once
> Semele was, when she was turned to ash.
> 	For if my beauty (which as you have seen,
> burns yet more brightly as it climbs the stair
> that carries us through this eternal hall)
> 	were not now tempered, it would shine so clear
> that all within your mortal power would be
> a sprig, as this flash struck, shaken by thunder."[44]

And where a smile is withheld from Dante lest it be too much for him, music too is withheld, for what holds for the smiles holds for music's restraint too, namely that as Dante's spiritual condition stands even as far into the sphere of the contemplatives as he has progressed, Heaven's music, like Beatrice's smiles, exceeds his capacity to hear, is still a reality more than his human nature can bear. At any rate, so says that irascibly holy hermit, Peter Damien, when Dante asks him to explain,

[44] Ibid., 21.1–12.

> why the symphony
> of Paradise, which sounds in sweet devotion
> through the other spheres, is muted in this wheel.[45]

To which Peter Damien replies:

> "In hearing, you are mortal, as in sight.
> So, just as Beatrice does not smile,
> likewise," he answered me, "there's no song here."[46]

But in due course the smiles return, and Beatrice tells Dante,

> Open your eyes and look at what I am!
> You have seen things by which you're made so strong,
> you can now bear to look upon my smile.[47]

And the return of smiles is also the return of music,

> Even if all those voices were to sound
> that Polyhymnia and her sister muses
> fed on their sweetest milk so richly once,
>   and aid me, singing of that holy smile
> and how her holy look grew purer still,
> I'd still not reach one thousandth of the truth.[48]

It is no wonder that Dante places smiles and music in so intimate a connection. For by whichever means it is in the poem, music or smiles, both have that immediacy and directness of the contemplative, which loves what it knows for its own sake and not in view of anything else.

---

[45] Ibid., 21.58–60.   [46] Ibid., 21.61–63.   [47] Ibid., 23.46–48.
[48] Ibid., 23.55–60.

In some ways in this role music is more exact than speech, which is why poetry itself calls upon music, its meter, pitch, tempo, harmony, and dissonance, for its own exactness. As Felix Mendelssohn said to the man who proposed to set his *Songs without Words* to verse, as if to supply some missing content, "what the music I love expresses to me are thoughts not too *indefinite* for words, but rather too *definite*."[49]

For it is in music, as in smiles, that one can understand how *theoria, contemplatio* is at the same time a *paideia*: Smiles and music are interactions, relational, and Heaven is well described by Dante as a community in smiles and music, a community of learning by means of both, a true *universitas* embodied. And it is in just such terms that one can understand *Paradiso* as at once *paideia* and *theoria*, learning and contemplation, contemplative learning. For the pedagogy is not merely in the means, as if the end were not already present within the process that moves towards it; or as if from the fact that in Paradise there is endless progression you must conclude that it is not yet Heaven until the progression ceases with the goal attained and desire met. For the best learning is that in which the goal is attained in the process itself, the means being raveled up in the end, as the joy of love is simply in the company of the one loved, and not for the sake of something else. And in so saying one puts an end to the sort of "perfectionism" that would displace the true eschatological finality of Heaven with a notion of Heaven's completeness that would rule out listening to Beethoven's

---

[49] Felix Mendelssohn, quoted in Clemency Burton-Hill, *Year of Wonder*, London: Headline, 2018, p. 218.

C# minor quartet in Heaven because in Heaven you get to listen to the one and only quartet that is absolutely perfect, and so not Beethoven's Opus 131, for all that it is contingently as good as music has got so far; or would have Heaven be a place that has Shakespeare's sonnets on the celestial proscribed list, for they too must give way to the one and only perfect sonnet written by the Holy Spirit. In fact, there is no such thing as the perfect string quartet, no sonnet that God can write so that none could be better. All this seems to get the celestial wrong, not because Heaven is the sort of shabby and second-rate place where you still have to make do with the less than perfect, but because in heaven you will be able ever to see the eternal good somewhere in all of it, and at last be able to put paid to the disheartening disjunctions of the perfectionists. For disjunctions can operate only within the limitations of the finite: God is not – cannot be – set in contrast with anything to its *exclusion*. And in Heaven all exclusions give way at last to the open permissiveness of the infinite, that is to say, to a love wholly inclusive of all creation.

And so, whether by words or by music, love is Heaven's teacher, just as it is the thing taught; and so now the distinction between what Dante as premortem visitor to Paradise can experience and the happiness of those who belong there by right of death, has for the instant of his ecstasy disappeared, as it had done also just for a moment for St. Paul, as he recounts in his second letter to the Corinthians, chapter 12. As for St. Paul, so for Dante, his *paideia* as premortem visitor to Paradise, and the *paideia* intrinsic to Paradise in its very nature, have for that one moment become one single *theoria*, and the work of the *Comedy* done. For the ecstasies of St. Paul and Dante are visions experienced that required their deaths as a condition, and so those ecstasies were for them a momentary death itself in so far as it can be experienced premortem.

Eternal Life

What then are we to say of that eternal life of the blessed, about that moment of mystical silence in which *Paradiso* ends? One asks, because that final silence must be set alongside the preceding thirty-two cantos of many words telling that story of a heavenly *paideia*; and it is not as if canto 33 cancels that story, or as if none of what precedes that final silence truly describes Heaven but only Dante's premortem, and therefore essentially limited, experience of it. Here we have paradox in exactly the right place: In *Paradiso* Dante needs to tell one last impossible story, calling for the affirmation of both propositions about Heaven at once, even if there seem to be no means available to embody both within a single, demonstrably coherent, narrative. It is a story that is also the end of story, though again it is not as if the story's end cancels the narrative that precedes it. For the time-bound sequence and the vision of eternity it leads to relate with one another in the sort of way, and according to the same logic, in which Bonaventure had described the journey of the soul into God, that is, as one in which the end arrived at and the way traveled to get there are raveled up in one another, the *paideia* into the *theoria* and the *theoria* ever active within the *paideia*. And if in the end is the silence, the silence is not some empty apophatic negation, but is rather a fullness of meaning that overflows all the words that have been the necessary means of arriving there. In Heaven's eternity, then, there is silence, a silence not in itself but one not translatable into our human vernacular and is of *our* incomprehension – for within the Heaven of the blest there is conversation so full that we need not just another world but an unimaginably other *understanding* of "world" to enter it. And the only way into that understanding of it is by way of a resurrection to a wholly new life that, by putting an end to time's limitedness, makes way for a share in that eternity which is God's alone.

It is that premortem, and therefore momentary, sharing in God's eternity which alone is possible to a mortal creature that Dante experiences in canto 33 of *Paradiso*. It is a *raptus*, a death within life and is therefore a violent, nonnatural, purely gratuitous moment of death anticipated, a death learned, an *ars moriendi*. But if in that way it is a *raptus*, it is also a free act, for Dante's "will is moved by love," and there is no love where there is no freedom. It is in *Paradiso* 33 that the tension between the narrative of the previous thirty-two cantos and the "eternal now" of its final silence is brought right to the fore; and it seems important to note that because he is not yet dead that tension remains for him unresolved, even there. Before death the resolution of that tension is still beyond his comprehension, for he must affirm both that his was an experience of eternity and that it was given in but a moment of time. Of that paradoxical conjunction he possesses only a "learned ignorance," a *docta ignorantia*, ninety-nine cantos of learning, and just one of the unknowing that, in this life, it leads to.

Even there, these images of the beatific vision in *Paradiso*'s last canto, images at once of the God seen and of the act of seeing, succeed one another throughout its extent like the waves of an ocean that are forever the same though their motion is ceaseless. Strikingly, the first of them is that image of the smile that persists from the beginning of *Paradiso* to its end; for there in the *Comedy*'s very last smile is an image that now tells us just why Dante's education within Heaven has had to be all along by way of them. The last thing he sees is that the very being of the Trinity itself consists in smiles given and returned. And if it is true that even smiles and music fail of the reality of the divine presence in Paradise, as images go, they are the ones that for Dante come closest, for, he says,

> Eternal light you sojourn in yourself alone.
> Alone you know yourself. Known to yourself,
> you, knowing, love and smile on your own being.[50]

That smile reaches into the very core of the Trinitarian life, into God's self-constitution, into the place where God's own being, in the technical language of Trinitarian orthodoxy of his times, is a *relation of persons*, persons who have no independent identities, for they are constituted as persons only by their mutual interactions, and in Dante's metaphor, by the sheer delight that they take in one another. And though those relations supervene upon the divine *essence* as the point of God's inherent identity, it is not for Dante as if the Trinity of Persons in any way displaces that unity, not

---

[50] *Paradiso* 33.124–126.

even as if the Trinity of Persons penetrates in some way more deeply into the divine being than does the unity of essence, as some have said in a theologically obtuse hostility to what in an intellectually lazy term of dismissal gets called "essentialism"; nor is it such that the Persons of the Trinity are more apophatically confounding than any notion of the divine unity of essence, for the oneness of God is every bit as incomprehensible as the Trinity of Persons,[51] but so as to say in resistance to all of those disjunctions that the oneness of essence is not an empty solitude but is realized precisely in that mystery of Persons. And so it is that another image tells of how three circles move towards one another and converge, each being a light shed upon the other, so that all Dante can say in response to this vision is what Bonaventure had said before him: "be amazed"; and, "when you contemplate these things, take care that you do not believe you can understand the incomprehensible."[52] For

> [w]ithin the being – lucid, bright and deep –
> Of that high brilliance, there appeared to me
> Three circling spheres, three-coloured, one in span.
>   And one, it seemed, was mirrored by the next
> Twin rainbows, arc to arc. The third seemed fire,
> And breathed to first and second equally.
>   How short mere speaking falls, how faint against
> My own idea. And this idea, compared
> To what I saw … well, "little" hardly squares.

---

[51] See my *Thomas Aquinas: A Portrait*, New Haven, CT: Yale University Press, 2013, pp. 119–131.
[52] Bonaventure, *Itinerarium*, VI. 3, p. 91, translation mine.

And all of this is contained in the smile that is God's own being.[53] It is a strikingly concrete image in which to express the ultimate mystery, but the concreteness imagined by way of such human gestures of love is not unprecedented. Nearly two centuries before Dante, Bernard of Clairvaux's friend, William of St. Thierry, had said that the soul "in its happiness finds itself standing midway in the Embrace and the Kiss of Father and Son," wherein is the Holy Spirit. For, William says,

> He who is the Love of Father and Son, their Unity, Sweetness, Good, Kiss, Embrace, and whatever else they have in common in that supreme unity of truth and truth of unity, becomes for man in regard to God in the manner appropriate to him what he is for the Son in regard to the Father or for the Father in regard to the Son through the unity of substance.[54]

But it is not in the vision of the Trinitarian life of God that Dante's gaze is finally and undistractedly fixed, for

> when a while my eyes had looked this round,
> deep in itself, it seemed – as painted now,
> in those same hues – to show our human form.
> At which, my sight was set entirely there.

Neither in this further image is Dante alone. William of St.-Thierry's younger contemporary, Alain of Lille, had said that the Incarnation too is a kiss. For

> as in one kiss two lips are pressed together, so in the Incarnation the divine nature is made one with the human ... [so too] is the Holy Spirit's, by whom the Son kisses the Father, by whom

---

[53] *Paradiso* 33.115–123.
[54] William of St.-Thierry, *The Golden Epistle*, II, xvi, trans. Theodore Berkeley, Kalamazoo, MI: Cistercian Publications, 1971, p. 96.

the Father loves the Son, it is he who unites Father and Son, for his is the love of them both, their embrace and their kiss.[55]

For in the end – that is, both in the end of his poem and in the end of all possible theology – the best image of the divine, indeed the only image of the Trinity given *by* God, is the human nature of Christ. It is then, when the Trinity is seen in Christ and Christ in Trinity, that his wings "could not rise to that," and

> All powers of high imagining here failed.
> But now my will and my desire were turned,
> as wheels that move in equilibrium,
> by love that moves the sun and the other stars.

It has taken all three cantiche, each contributing, to get to this final silence whose origin is in the human nature of the Word, Christ. It is a silence like the music of the spheres, each of which plays its own note but when all played together are silent, because too full of sound to be heard. It is like the lark of *Paradiso* 22 that sings only while it is ascending but "when flush with the sweetness of its highest reach" is silent.[56] Just so, the 14,000 lines of *alta fantasia* which made the poem aren't abolished upon arrival at their destination, they don't trip over the limits of meaning into nothing, for it takes Dante all those verses to construct the final silence that they fall into, and that final silence is full of them all. This is what Gerard Manley Hopkins called a silence that, being *elected*, "sings":

---

[55] Alain of Lille, *Elucidatio in Canticum Canticorum in Laude Virginis Mariae*, in Migne, *Patrologia Latina*, vol. 210, 1, 7. For a partial translation, see my *Eros and Allegory: Medieval Exegesis of the Song of Songs*, Kalamazoo, MI: Cistercian Publications, 1995, p. 295.
[56] *Paradiso* 22.73.

> Elected silence, sing to me,
> And beat upon my whorled ear
> Pipe to me pastures still and be
> The music that I care to hear.
>
> Shape nothing, lips; be lovely-dumb:
> It is the shut, the curfew sent
> From there where all surrenders come
> Which only makes you eloquent.[57]

As for Hopkins, so for Dante, not a single verse of the *Comedy* is abolished by this "lovely-dumb" of the lips, for this silence "only makes you eloquent." Within that silence is a house, John Donne says,

> where there shall be no darkness nor dazzling, but one equal light; no noise nor silence, but one equal music; no fears or hopes, but one equal possession; no ends or beginnings, but one equal eternity, in the habitations of thy glory and dominion, world without end.[58]

For Dante, that's enough, and nothing further would be served by any more verses, the number is now exactly right at the *Comedy*'s 100 cantos, for those lines of verse, having arrived at this true silence, are there fulfilled. Not one of them was unnecessary, but all of them together are still insufficient. This silence is where they were always going even though Dante had to pass through the false, sullen, satanic silence of *Inferno* to get there, and then

---

[57] Gerard Manley Hopkins, *Poems and Prose*, Selected with an Introduction and Notes, ed. W. H. Gardner, Harmondsworth: Penguin, 1985, pp. 5–6.
[58] John Donne, *Sermon* CXLVI, Preached at Whitehall, February 29, 1627, in the electronic edition of *The Sermons of John Donne*, vol 8, no. 7, eds. Evelyn Simpson and George Reuben, Brigham Young University Press: Utah, 2004, p. 18.

on through a silence retrieved in poetic aphasia before a ferocious Beatrice at the end of *Purgatorio*. And now, when at last *intelletto, alta fantasia*, Dante-poet himself, having done their work, his desire now liberated and at last moved by nothing but the love that moves the sun and the other stars, only now in that shared silence are poetry, theology, and Dante finally one, and the *Comedy* at an end. And now, but only now, you can read the whole of the *Comedy* from the beginning, for it is only in the light of that end that the truth of the beginning in Hell, ninety-nine cantos earlier, is fully grasped.

The Right Way to Fail

In the end poetry fails Dante. But for Dante in poetry alone is found the right way to fail, failure is where poetry takes you and it is only the poet's failure that is up the demands of theology's inadequacy. But if poetry too fails it is only ultimately that it does so. For in the meantime there is but the poetry *of* the meantime, for it is in that "meantime" that poetry is at home, those 14,000 lines of a truth-making epic verse, gesturing both to what lies beyond and to the impossibility of fully expressing it.

And it is when poetry fails that you know that theology has failed, for theology and poetry meet in the same place, and theology, having available no language of its own is but a borrowed discourse extended from earthly use by means of analogy's infinite stretch. And if theology is in search of a discourse in which appropriately to fail, its demands are severe, even total, it demands that eventually you throw language entirely away, stop talking and let silence come in. Theology ought not settle for halfhearted failure, but only for failure at its best, failure of an ultimate kind when at last achieved. For when you know that even poetry fails then you know you have reached the point at which language as such fails, for all prior failures, philosophical, scientific, historical, are to be expected and have a defined point at which they can go no further, being by dint of their own methodologies self-limited. And it must be said again at the end of this book as I said at its beginning, that too much theology is written by people who seem happy to settle for such finite limitations – these days it is pretty much a requirement of its being allowed to make an appearance in the university that theology conforms to them – by people who appear to know what they are talking about, parading marginal skills in a quaint and untranslatable patois. It is in poetry's failure, and in its failure alone, in its majestic inadequacy, that theology knows its own truth. Theology is at home only when it is thus exiled in a foreign land. For if poetry can't achieve this transcendence nothing else can.

It is in showing how theology fails and when exactly it does so – and especially not prematurely – that theology succeeds as a discipline; not, then, as if in some short-winded apophasis you could buy into a cheap mysticism ahead of the game just by way of an a priori partiality for extravagantly negative-sounding metaphors. That apophatic extremism would abolish Dante's *Comedy* in one *a priori* stroke. It is only as the culmination of a long and taxing peregrination that the *Comedy* fails appropriately, and Dante tells us that it takes that heavy epistemological labor, of that unembarrassed riot of affirmation which is the *Comedy*, requiring as many as 14,000 lines of *terza rima*, to find the right point at which theology's failure is in the end called for. Dante's lesson is that the true apophatic is found in the surplus of affirmation, not in its deficiency.

For which reason, if not too soon, theological failure must not come too late – it must come exactly at the end of the 100th canto, and it is there, Dante tells us, that theology must stop, its failure can be postponed no longer. Anything further would be but idle theological chatter, the discoursing, self-referring patois of the theologically closed shop.

It is in getting that theological interplay of knowing and unknowing right, of word and silence, of knowing where to start and when to end, that the poet's work is done. And Dante tells us that if you do the poet's work aright you may surprise yourself to find that then at last you are *already* doing theology too.

SELECT BIBLIOGRAPHY

Dante's Works

De vulgari eloquentia, ed. and trans. Steven Botterill, Cambridge: Cambridge University Press, 1996.
The Divine Comedy, ed. and trans. Jean Hollander, commentary Robert Hollander, 3 vols, *Inferno*, New York: Anchor Books, 2000.
The Divine Comedy, ed. and trans. Jean Hollander, commentary Robert Hollander, 3 vols, *Paradiso*, New York: Anchor Books, 2007.
The Divine Comedy, ed. and trans. Jean Hollander, commentary Robert Hollander, 3 vols, *Purgatorio*, New York: Anchor Books, 2003.
The Divine Comedy, ed. and trans. Robin Kirkpatrick, 3 vols, *Inferno*, Harmondsworth: Penguin Books, 2006.
The Divine Comedy, ed. and trans. Robin Kirkpatrick, 3 vols, *Paradiso*, Harmondsworth: Penguin Books, 2007.
The Divine Comedy, ed. and trans. Robin Kirkpatrick, 3 vols, *Purgatorio*, Harmondsworth: Penguin Books, 2007.
La vita nuova, ed. and trans. Mark Musa, Bloomington: Indiana University Press, 1973.

Commentaries on Dante

Barolini, Teodolinda, *The Undivine Comedy: Detheologizing Dante*, Princeton, NJ: Princeton University Press, 1992.
Foster, Kenelm, "Dante and Eros," *Downside Review*, 84 (1966), 262–279.
Foster, Kenelm, "St Thomas and Dante," *New Blackfriars*, 55, no. 647 (1974), 148–155.

Select Bibliography

Foster, Kenelm, "The Two Dante's," in *The Two Dante's and Other Studies*, London: Darton, Longman and Todd, 1977.

Frecerro, John, "Allegory and Autobiography," in Rachel Jacoff, ed., *The Cambridge Companion to Dante*, Cambridge: Cambridge University Press, 2007, pp. 161–180.

Frecerro, John, *Dante: The Poetics of Conversion*, ed. and intro. Rachel Jacoff, Cambridge, MA: Harvard University Press, 1986.

Hawkins, Peter S., *Dante: A Brief History*, Oxford: Blackwell, 2006.

Kirkpatrick, Robin, *Dante: The Divine Comedy*, Cambridge: Cambridge University Press, 2004.

Moevs, Christian, *The Metaphysics of Dante's Comedy*, Oxford: Oxford University Press, 2005.

Montemaggi, Vittorio and Treherne, Matthew, eds., *Dante's Commedia: Theology As Poetry*, Notre Dame, IN: University of Notre Dame Press, 2010.

Montemaggi, Vittorio, *Reading Dante's Commedia as Theology*, Oxford: Oxford University Press, 2016.

Oleynick, Griffin, *Dante's Franciscan Way*, New Haven, CT: Yale University Press, 2014.

Purdy Moudarres, Christiana and Chiodo, Carol, eds., *Dante's Volume from Alpha to Omega*, Phoenix: Arizona Center for Medieval and Renaissance Studies, 2021.

Sinclair, John D., *The Divine Comedy of Dante Alighieri*, New York: Oxford University Press, 1961.

Singleton, Charles, "The Irreducible Dove," *Comparative Literature*, 9 (1957), 129–135.

Treherne, Matthew, *Dante's Commedia and the Liturgical Imagination*, Leeds Studies on Dante, London: Peter Lang, 2020.

Other Works Cited

Alain of Lille, *Elucidatio in Canticum Canticorum in Laude Virginis Mariae*, in Migne, ed., *Patrologia Latina*, Vol. 210. [Partial translation in Denys Turner, *Eros and*

Select Bibliography

Allegory: Medieval Exegesis of the Song of Songs, Kalamazoo, MI: Cistercian Publications, 1995.

Anon., "Cloud of Unknowing," in *The Cloud of Unknowing and Other Works*, ed. and trans. A. C. Spearing, Harmondsworth: Penguin Books, 2001.

Aristotle, "Nicomachean Ethics," in *The Complete Works of Aristotle*, Vol. 2, ed. Jonathan Barnes, trans. W. D. Ross, and rev. J. O. Urmson, pp. 1729–1867. Princeton, NJ: Princeton University Press, 1984.

Augustine, *Confessions*, ed. and trans. Henry Chadwick, Oxford: Oxford University Press, 1991.

Bernard of Clairvaux, *Sermons on the Song of Songs*, Vol. 1, trans. Killian Walsh OCSO, Kalamazoo, MI: Cistercian Publications, 1977.

Bonaventure, *The Journey of the Soul into God (Itinerarium mentis in Deum)*, ed. and trans. Philotheus Boehner OFM, New York: Franciscan Institute, 1990.

Chesterton, G. K., *The Everlasting Man*, San Francisco: Ignatius Press, 1993.

Clark, J. P. H., "Time and Eternity in Julian of Norwich," *Downside Review*, 109, no. 377 (1991), 259–276.

Davies, Oliver, *Meister Eckhart: Mystical Theologian*, London: SPCK, 1991.

Eliot, T. S., *Four Quartets*, New York: Harcourt, 1971.

Eliot, T. S., *Murder in the Cathedral*, New York: Harcourt, 1963.

Gilson, Étienne, *Mystical Theology of St Bernard*, Kalamazoo, MI: Cistercian Publications, 1990.

Gregory of Nyssa, *Life of Moses*, ed. and trans. Abraham J. Malherbe and Everett Ferguson, New York: Paulist Press, 1978.

Gregory the Great, *Moralia on Job*, ed. and trans. John Henry Parker and J. Rivington, Oxford: Oxford University Press, 1844.

Hart, David Bentley, *That All Shall Be Saved*, New Haven, CT: Yale University Press, 2019.

Herbert, George, *George Herbert: Complete Poetry*, ed. John Drury and Victoria Moul, Harmondsworth: Penguin, 2015.

Hopkins, Gerard Manley, *A Hopkins Reader*, ed. John Pick, Oxford: Oxford University Press, 1953.
James, William, *The Varieties of Religious Experience*, Harmondsworth: Penguin Classics, 1982.
John of the Cross, *Collected Works of John of the Cross*, trans. Kieran Kavanaugh, Washington, DC: Institute of Carmelite Studies, 1991.
Julian of Norwich, *The Writings of Julian of Norwich*, ed. Nicholas Watson and Jaqueline Jenkins, University Park: Pennsylvania State University Press, 2006.
Kierkegaard, Søren, *Fear and Trembling and the Sickness unto Death*, ed. and trans. Walter Lowrie, intro. Gordon Marino, Princeton, NJ: Princeton University Press, 2013.
Leclerq, Jean, *The Love of Learning and the Desire for God: A Study of Monastic Culture*, trans. Catherine Misrahi, New York: Fordham University Press, 1974.
Lewis, C. S., *The Last Battle*, New York: Collier Books, 1980.
McCabe, Herbert OP, "Eternity," in *Cambridge Companion to the Summa Theologiae*, ed. Philip McCosker and Denys Turner, Cambridge: Cambridge University Press, 2016, pp. 102–116.
Milton, John, *Paradise Lost: An Authoritative Text, Backgrounds and Sources, Criticism*, ed. Scott Elledge, New York: Norton, 1993.
Minnis, Alastair, *Translations of Authority in Medieval English Literature: Valuing the Vernacular*, Cambridge: Cambridge University Press, 2009.
Pseudo-Dionysius, *Complete Works of the Pseudo-Dionysius*, trans. Colm Luibheid, New York, Paulist Press, 1987.
Sartre, Jean-Paul, *Being and Nothingness*, trans. Hazel Barnes, New York: Washington Square Press, 1984.
Sartre, Jean-Paul, *Existentialism is a Humanism*, trans. Carol Macomber, preface Ariette Elkaïm, New Haven, CT: Yale University Press, 2007.
Sartre, Jean-Paul, *Sketch for the Theory of the Emotions*, trans. Philip Mairet, London: Routledge, 2013.
Scotus, John Duns, *Philosophical Writings*, Latin text and English trans. Allan Wolter OFM, Indiana: Hackett Publishing, 1987.

Sells, Michael, *Mystical Languages of Unsaying*, Chicago: University of Chicago Press, 1994.

Shaw, G. B., *Man and Superman*, ed. Dan H. Laurence, Harmondsworth: Penguin Classics, 2004.

Teresa of Avila, *The Collected Works*, trans. Otilio Rodriguez and Kieran Kavanaugh, vol. 2, Washington, DC: ICS Publications, 1980.

Thomas Aquinas, *Commentary on St Paul's Letters to the Corinthians*, in *Saint Thomas Aquinas and Peter of Tarantaise, on the Letters of St Paul to the Corinthians*, Latin text and English trans. F. R. Larcher, B. Mortensen, and D. Keating, ed. J. Mortensen and E. Alarcón, Lander, WY: Aquinas Institute for the Study of Sacred Doctrine, 2012.

Thomas Aquinas, *The Light of Faith* (*Compendium theologiae*) trans. Cyril Vollert SJ, Manchester, NH: Sophia Institute, 1993.

Thomas Aquinas, *De Aeternitate mundi contra murmurantes*, English translation in *Thomas Aquinas: Selected Writings*, ed. and trans. Ralph McInerny, pp. 710–717, Harmondsworth: Penguin Classics, 1998.

Thomas Aquinas, *Disputed Questions on the Virtues*, ed. E. M. Atkins and Thomas Williams, Cambridge Texts in the History of Philosophy, Cambridge: Cambridge University Press, 2005.

Thomas Aquinas, *Saint Thomas Aquinas: Commentary on the Letter of St Paul to the Romans*, Latin text and English trans. F. R. Larcher OP, ed. J. Mortensen and E. Alarcón, Lander, WY: Aquinas Institute for the Study of Sacred Doctrine, 2012.

Thomas Aquinas, *Summa theologiae*, 60 vols., Latin text and English trans., intro., notes, appendices, and glossaries, gen. ed. Thomas Gilby OP, Oxford: Blackfriars, 1964.

William of St. Thierry, *Golden Epistle*, trans. Theodore Berkeley, Kalamazoo, MI: Cistercian Publications, 1971.

Wittgenstein, Ludwig, *Philosophical Investigations*, trans. G. E. M. Anscombe, Peter M. S. Hacker, and Joachim Schulte, Oxford: Blackwell, 2006.

INDEX

Aeneas, 154
akrasia
  (See Moral Weakness)
Alain of Lille, 284–285
Allegory, 10, 32–38, 62, 63, 69,
  128, 138, 180, 181, 192,
  285
amor, 131, 174, 206, 239–240,
  255
anamnesis, 133–160, 188,
  181–187, 193–194
apophasis, 233, 288
Aquinas, St Thomas
  on death and judgment,
    73–74, 78, 104–106
  eternity and time, 252
  freedom of the will, 113–125,
    170
  grace, 79, 196
  on Hell, 63–65, 76, 104–119,
    163
  the natural and the
    supernatural, 175
  on poetry, 17, 26
  sacra doctrina, 16
  on sacraments, 25–30, 204
  on the senses of Scripture,
    33–36
  school theologian, 4, 8, 13
  St Paul's rapture, 237–238
Aristotle, 148, 153, 179, 190,
  252, 263
Augustine, 134–146, 149, 159,
  177, 190, 197, 205, 210,
  214, 226, 248

Balthasar, Von, 72
Barolini, Teodolinda, 265, 268
Barth, Karl, 72
Beatrice Portinari, 18–19, 23,
  27, 41, 50, 52, 83, 120, 128,
  139, 147–151, 159–162,
  166–167, 171–173, 175–182,
  193, 197, 203, 214,
  224, 230, 234, 236, 243,
  256–257, 264, 266–267,
  272–276, 287
Bernard of Clairvaux, 4, 8,
  205–207, 216, 264, 267
Boethius, Manlius, 253, 256
Bonaventure, St, 4, 9–11, 14,
  15, 205, 208–212, 214,
  216–217, 220, 228, 254,
  280, 283

caritas
  See, love
Chaucer, Geoffrey, 56–61, 73,
  81, 83, 162, 232
Chesterton, GK, 135, 160
Church, 16, 26, 30–35, 38, 79,
  118, 174, 182, 205–207, 242
Cloud of Unknowing, 212, 247
contemplation, 262–263, 268,
  272, 274, 278
convenientia, 122, 139, 176, 275
conversion, 1, 16, 18–19, 52,
  75, 78, 118, 127, 129–149,
  153–154, 159–161, 176,
  181, 187, 194, 197, 203,
  223–226, 238, 259–260

convivio, 32
cosmology, 67, 189, 218–221

Damien, St Peter, 276
damnation, 73, 79, 107, 113
De vulgari eloquentia, 21–24, 28, 234, 242
death, 3, 13, 63, 68–69, 71–80, 92, 97, 113, 127, 167, 174, 187, 250, 260, 211, 214, 253–254
demotic, 22–28, 205, 259–269
Denys, Pseudo-, 11, 151, 203, 205–207, 217, 237, 261, 265
Denys the Carthusian, 262–263
desire, 12, 16, 49, 75, 78, 90, 94–96, 100–101, 103–104, 113, 122, 125, 132–138, 141–144, 148, 160, 184, 207, 211, 216, 219, 245, 250, 253–254, 260, 265–269, 278, 285
Donati, Piccarda, 75, 122–125, 271–275
Duns Scotus, 4, 14, 23, 175, 193

Earthly Paradise, 158–159, 165, 195, 197, 222, 226, 234, 237, 244, 259, 265, 269–271
Eckhart, Meister, 13, 24, 152
ecstasy, 201, 239–240, 248, 265, 279
Eden, Garden of, 190, 192, 195, 235
Eliot, TS, 239, 260
eloquentia vulgaris, 21–23, 28, 242
eternity, 42, 66, 69–72, 75, 78, 79, 104, 107, 163, 167, 186, 218–256, 262, 267–268, 280, 286
Eucharist, 26, 29–31, 205

evil, 5, 47, 50, 57–58, 69, 73, 76, 84, 87, 96–111, 125, 131, 153, 168, 189, 190–191, 270

faith, 57, 62, 79, 91, 123, 128, 154, 169, 170–174, 219, 224, 230, 260, 267
Fall, 46–48, 86–88, 187, 189, 192, 234–236
Faustus (Marlowe), 99–102, 132
fiction, 18, 29, 30, 34–38, 70, 81, 84–86, 113–118, 218
Folco, 121, 183–184, 189, 196, 221, 273, 276
fomes peccati
   see sin
forgiveness, 121, 124, 185, 193–196
Francesca da Rimini (and Paolo), 41, 49, 54, 74, 104, 107, 102, 229
Frecerro, John, 32, 127–128, 136, 142
freedom of choice, 87–88, 100–101, 123–126, 174, 180–190, 196–197, 281
Freud, 184

Glossa Ordinaria, 34
grace, 29, 71, 113, 129, 137, 159, 168–175, 194–198, 209, 211–212, 238, 242, 254–255, 261, 271, 273
Gregory of Nyssa, 268
Gregory the Great, 157, 239, 263–265

Hart, DB, 79–81, 83–84
Heaven, 3, 64, 71–75, 120–124, 174, 183, 186–188, 192, 202–204, 215, 218–228, 234, 237, 239, 242, 244, 247–271, 272–282

Hegel, GFW, 140, 241
Hell
  absence of poetry from, 27, 46, 52, 166, 214, 220, 226–230, 234–237, 245, 260, 287
  despair, 55–56, 71, 114, 154–157, 163–165, 183, 214, 231, 249
  no learning in, 94, 166, 215, 224–229, 244, 256, 259, 267
  and memory, 97, 99, 162–164, 183–184, 209, 260
  silence in, 221, 226, 228–230, 236, 239, 256, 287
Herbert, George, 202, 258
Hollander, Robert, xiv, xvii, 41
Hope, 51–52, 56, 65, 70–71, 80, 94–97, 114–119, 142, 155–159, 165, 167–172, 183, 214, 221–224, 228, 233–236, 237, 249, 250, 260, 267, 272, 286
Hopkins, GM, 25, 203, 285

identity, personal, 45, 60, 76, 107–108, 123, 135–139, 161–163, 181–188, 210
immortality of the soul, 252–255
intellect, 16–17, 81–82, 132, 137–144, 151, 209, 216, 240, 243–245, 253, 260, 283

John of the Cross, 203, 258–261, 286
Julian of Norwich, 4–10, 13, 188, 235

Kierkegaard, Søren, 92–93, 100–101, 154, 169, 172
Kirkpatrick, Robin, xvii, 41, 67, 125–126, 158, 170, 256

learning
  celestial, 223, 227, 238, 246, 259, 260, 263, 271, 274
  infernal, 229, 231, 233, 248
  penitential, 51, 244
Lethe, Waters of, 150–151, 162, 180–182, 184, 187, 193, 234, 236
Levi-Strauss, Claude, 87
Lewis, CS, 227
Love, 17, 20, 27, 28, 36, 54, 61, 66–67, 120–122, 126, 158, 182, 188, 193, 206, 207, 210, 217, 220, 221, 236, 240, 278, 279, 281, 284–285, 287
Lucy, Saint, 19, 41, 154, 197

Mandelbaum, Allen, 41
Martha and Mary, 262
Mary, Virgin, 19, 41, 154, 197, 263, 264, 273
Masterson, Patrick, 163
McCabe, Herbert, 49, 65, 240, 254
memory
  forgetting See *anamnesis* in Hell, 12, 20, 42, 49, 97, 102, 160, 164, 167, 197, 226
  and hope, 65, 157, 249
  and narrative, 97, 133, 182–184, 192, 210, 216
  and personal identity, 48, 107
  in purgatory, 158, 165, 182, 189, 216, 272
  and time, 52, 164, 217
Mendelssohn, Felix, 278
Metaphor, 14, 32, 33, 37, 157, 163, 182, 209, 212–213, 214, 222, 270, 282
Milton, John, 63, 84, 94–96, 242
Moevs, Christian, 217

297

Montemaggi, Vittorio, 1, 113, 117, 118, 218
moral weakness, 142, 145
music, 24, 185, 251, 269–274, 276–282, 285–286
mystical, 4, 152, 201–208, 212–214, 221–224, 228, 233, 237, 257–261, 271, 280

narrative
  anti-narratives, 86
  fiction, 18, 29–30, 34–38, 70, 81, 84–86, 113–118, 218
  faction, 30, 114, 117, 134
Nietzsche, Friedrich, 89, 97, 251, 254

Oleynick, Griffin, 9, 10

paideia, 201, 225–227, 259, 262, 266–267, 278–280
Palmbush, Courtney, 12, 229
Paradiso
  paradisal learning, 216, 237, 244, 248, 259, 265–268, 273, 276, 278–281
  and the mystical, 5, 24, 43, 125–127, 207, 235–250, 257–272
  and poetry, 20–21, 52, 166, 216, 226, 229, 234–237, 241, 243, 246, 249, 258–262
Plato, 11, 19, 79, 88, 101, 129–138, 142–143, 160, 188, 217
poetry
  and the mystical, 201, 203, 214, 221, 228, 233, 257, 261, 280, 288
  in Purgatory, 233–244
  and theology, 14, 15, 18–21, 30, 36, 52, 74, 181, 246

and truth, 3, 28, 140
politics, 49, 67, 191–192, 216, 221–222
power, 47, 66, 84, 89–91, 103, 171, 176, 182, 196
  will-power, 148–149, 168
providence, 128–131, 245, 270
Purgatory
  Aquinas on, 64, 155–157, 168–171
  Dante a purgatorial writer, 18–20, 44–53, 117, 187
  distinction from Hell, 52–53, 70, 83, 119, 215
  and happiness, 122, 150, 153, 168, 174, 186, 202
  and time, 2–3, 193, 197
  See Earthly Paradise
  See Hope

Sartre, J-P, 55–62, 85, 93, 124, 163, 229
Satan, 65–68, 83, 94–101, 106, 114, 161, 221, 223–230, 257, 286
self-knowledge, 137, 140–141, 162
  God's, 261
  in Hell, 55, 62
  the Pardoner's, 67
  self-deception, 123, 183
Shakespeare, William, 129, 258, 269, 279
Shaw, George Bernard, 186, 250–255
silence
  in Heaven, 226, 239–242, 256–257, 261, 270, 279–281
  in Hell, 161, 215, 221, 228–230, 236, 256
  in Purgatory, 216, 228–236, 256

sin
　Adam's sin, 46
　fomes peccati, 168, 180–186, 189, 194
　languor naturae, 48
　mortal and venial, 119
　original, 87, 166, 186, 190, 191
　and personal identity, 117
　sin's regime, 45, 46, 55–57, 62–63, 67–70, 74, 77–80, 97, 103–106
Singleton, Charles, 29, 30, 36, 84
smiles, 183, 234
Stump, Eleonore, 168, 174
Synderesis, 110, 125, 235

Teresa of Avila, 152
Theology, 1–4, 14–20, 74, 180
　end of, 266–267, 287
　mystical, 207–208, 212
　and poetry, 21–22, 181, 237, 287
　and sin, 181, 186
　and truth, 79
　vernacular, *See* demotic
Trajan, 113, 120

Treherne, Matthew, 22, 190
Trinity, 20, 23, 209, 227–253, 261, 267, 282–285

Ugolino, 49, 55, 96, 214–215, 229
Ulysses, 27–28, 81–83, 147, 215, 229

vernacularity
　See *eloquentia vulgaris*
Virgil, 41–42, 45–47, 50, 52, 65, 66, 67, 69, 81, 98, 125, 126, 147, 150, 154, 166, 167, 171, 177
Vita nuova, 20, 140, 146–147, 153, 166, 179, 237, 239, 242

Will, 144, 209, 242
　conversion, of, 144
　freedom of, 125, 174, 190, 191
　strength and weakness of *see* moral weakness
William of St-Thierry, 239
Wittgenstein, Ludwig, 14, 156

For EU product safety concerns, contact us at Calle de José Abascal, 56–1°, 28003 Madrid, Spain or eugpsr@cambridge.org.

www.ingramcontent.com/pod-product-compliance
Ingram Content Group UK Ltd.
Pitfield, Milton Keynes, MK11 3LW, UK
UKHW010725160725
460850UK00012B/107